The Illustrated Guide to Great Art in Europe

for Amateur Artists

Frederic Taubes

The Illustrated Guide to Great Art in Europe

for Amateur Artists

Travel
History
Criticism

 Reinhold Publishing Corporation / New York

Acknowledgments

Grateful acknowledgment is given to the following government travel information offices for their permission to reproduce many of the photographs appearing in the book: Austrian State Tourist Department, Belgian Government Information Center, The British Travel Association, Casa de Portugal, Danish National Travel Office, French Embassy Press and Information Division, French Government Tourist Office, German Tourist Information Office, Greek National Tourist Organization, Italian State Tourist Office, Spanish National Tourist Office, Swiss National Tourist Office.

Other Books by Frederic Taubes

Taubes' Guide to Oil Painting—*Reinhold Publishing Corporation*

The Technique of Oil Painting, You Don't Know What You Like, The Amateur Painter's Handbook, Anatomy of Genius, Pictorial Composition and the Art of Drawing, Taubes' Paintings and Essays of Art, The Art and Technique of Portait Painting, New Techniques in Painting, Abracadabra and Modern Art—*Dodd, Mead & Company.*

Painting Techniques, Ancient and Modern, The Quickest Way To Paint Well, The Quickest Way To Draw Well, Better Frames for Your Pictures, The Mastery of Oil Painting, Pictorial Anatomy of the Human Body—*Viking Press, Inc.*

Studio Secrets, Oil Painting for the Beginner, The Painter's Question and Answer Book, New Essays on Art, Oil Painting and Tempera, Pen and Ink Drawing (Vols. I-II), Modern Art Sweet and Sour, The Art and Technique of Landscape Painting—*Watson-Guptill Publications.*

© 1966 Reinhold Publishing Corporation
All rights reserved
Printed in the United States of America
Library of Congress Catalog Card Number 66-12167

Designed, printed, and bound by Port City Press, Inc.
Reinhold Publishing Corporation
430 Park Avenue, New York, N. Y.

CONTENTS

Foreword

A complete guide to the art treasures of Europe would fill a large-size library, and to view and to register even a fraction of the accumulation would go far beyond the capacity of even the most retentive mind. Moreover, not all treasures designated as such deserve this qualification, so much art repeats itself in many closely related examples that a thorough and most carefully considered selection of the characteristic items must be made.

Since frequent references to "masterpieces" will be found, they will have to be qualified, for too often indeed do we hear unwarranted claims as to the "greatness" of a work of art, especially today, when time-tested standards of value in art have been cast aside. Although our guide is not a treatise on esthetics and is a description rather than an analysis of works of art, the writer feels the obligation to state the reasons for assigning a stellar position to this or that work of art or, as the case may be, for minimizing its supposed merits.

No mention will be made of 20th-century art. Since modern art is represented more widely in this country than abroad, seeking out contemporary work in Europe would be a waste of time and energy.

The author found it advisable to divide the text into two parts, the first dealing with historic and critical aspects of art, country by country and city by city, and the second with technicalities and practicalities of travel throughout the European continent.

In the discussions of the cities, it might seem arbitrary that we sometimes begin with museums, sometimes with edifices. However, the order is dictated by the relative importance of the sites or, as the case may be, by the layout of the particular city.

It also appeared practical to describe the tours in this book in geographic order as they unfold themselves along our routes, starting from northeast to southwest. Only the Scandinavian part is an exception—it is placed at the end, after Greece. The reason for such an arrangement is simple: When traveling in search of art and antiquities it is more practical to include Scandinavia on the homeward journey.

Under "art" we understand man-made objects such as paintings and statuary. The collective term "edifices" refers to architecture and its ornaments, generally thought of as belonging to the realm of "applied" art. To separate architecture and in many instances objects that are mere artifacts, from art, is dogmatic and often arbitrary, for they all possess artistic qualities of varying kind and degree. Customarily a great work of art is supposed to inspire us; in what category then shall we place some of the great edifices from the past? Is the term "inspired" not applicable to works that are not framed and hung on the wall or those not standing on pedestals?

To consider art with a capital "A" once more: There is good art and bad art. The question now arises: Should bad work fall into the collective term "art"? Are not many of the great museums burdened with bad, mediocre, or merely indifferent art? From the esthetic point of view, how does a resplendent ancient edifice compare with a hack work of the same period done on canvas or in the round? When subjecting oneself to visual experiences, such considerations must be taken into account.

On these pages the reader will be confronted with the problems of "style." In the compound of art, style has played a much stronger part than is generally assumed. Art and style have always been coextensive and coexisting, and to understand works of art one encounters on a European voyage, a familiarity with the difference in styles is indispensable. Hence a brief discussion of the subject will follow.

PART I

Section 1 / In Matters of Style

THE ILLUSTRATED GUIDE TO GREAT ART IN EUROPE

Without differentiation between the various art styles throughout history, the comprehension and accompanying enjoyment of a
work of art must remain incomplete. There can be little doubt
that an intelligent attitude toward any and every art form can be
developed only when one becomes familiar with the style that
rules its configurations. Style is a manner or a quality in which
a certain period expresses itself in giving form to its trappings,
its edifices, its paintings and statuary.

In this treatise we are concerned with the styles of the Western
world beginning with the Minoan (about 2000 B.C.), which is the
earliest that can be qualified as a "style." We shall make a brief
reference to it also because a visit to the Aegean Islands is un-
thinkable without putting ashore at the island of Crete. In the
discussion of the Greek style we shall deal with the Archaic
(8th–5th century B.C.), the Periclean (5th century B.C.), and the
Hellenistic (after Alexander the Great—4th–2nd century B.C.).

The following styles will next be discussed: Roman (2nd
century B.C.–4th century A.D.), Byzantine (5th–12th century),
Romanesque (11th–12th century), Gothic (12th–16th century),
Renaissance (15th–16th century), Baroque (16th–18th century),
Rococo (late 18th century), and, finally, the neo-Classic style
(early 19th century). This will bring us to the doorstep
of the machine age and the end of all the historic styles
with which we will be concerned in this guide. It must be stated,
however, that some of the dates assigned to these various periods
are not applicable in every country. Styles tend to overlap
and—to take one example—although the Gothic configurations

1

may have disappeared entirely in the south of Europe by the end of the 15th century, they will still be found very much in use in the north, two centuries later.

BEHOLDING ART

Once more it should be emphasized that the customary distinctions between "applied" and "fine" art are tenuous more often than not. Art, we can assume with a degree of certainty, came into being when man started to adorn first himself, then his tools and the walls of his cave. Hence art is basically decoration— whether it expresses man's desire for the ornate, the festive, his religous feelings, or his poetic moods and "sublimations of his soul." As soon as all of this objectifies itself in images, figurative or ornamental, it can be referred to as art. The primitive patterns of the aborigines, the most complex designs of Gothic architecture, the work of a modest practitioner of the art of painting or sculpture, the work of Michelangelo, a Doric temple or St. Mark's in Venice—all possess artistic moments. It is the nature and degree of these moments that put the particular example of art on a higher or lower plane.

One category in which the dubiousness of classification becomes particularly evident is the art of sculpture. Here the distinction between objects of art and what are commonly referred to as artifacts is quite often unjustified. In churches and palaces when examining countless images in wood, stone, and bronze done by anonymous craftsmen, one will experience that much of it stands on a higher esthetic plane than the works of many of the illustrious name sculptors who are celebrated as "artists." Any skilled worker can cast in bronze, hence duplicate, the work of a "genius" or carve an exact facsimile in marble. This is not as easily done with paintings, however, where the artistic elements range over a much wider area (think of the painting technique, color, lighting, treatment in depth, and last but not least, involvement of subject matter, all of which are matters of great complexity). In painting the artistic position, as it were, of a "masterpiece" is much more clearly defined. Thus the works of a genius and a mediocrity will be much farther apart and the difference between them will be recognized at once. At the same time it must be remembered that even great artists did not always produce great works. Regrettably, humanity has become victim to the tyranny of clichés, so that every scrap of canvas signed by a "big name" (the name may even be Rembrandt) becomes automatically a "masterpiece."

Now as to "ornaments," consider the capital of a Greek column (of whatever order) and that of a Byzantine, Romanesque, or Gothic column. The former, because it is not the product of the stonemason's creative imagination—that is, because it follows a preordained pattern the carrying out of which requires mere skill—possesses fewer artistic moments than the latter. It is obvious that whoever created these medieval capitals had to summon up one of art's most precious ingredients: poetic imagination.

Thus, reader, beware of clichés; shake off the conventions that may have put your perception into a straightjacket and when you face the wonders of man's struggle to arrest the flux of time by creating works of art, keep your eyes open and, above all, keep your sensibilities alert.

STYLES IN ART, A SUMMARY

Styles of Prehistory and the Aegean Culture. Prehistory refers to times before the invention of writing—that is, earlier than 3000 B.C. in Egypt and Sumer, somewhat later in China, and as late as a few centuries B.C. on the European continent. Prehistoric art objects in Europe date from the Auregnatian period (Paleolithic age, 60,000–40,000 B.C.), but of interest to us are the highly artistic cave paintings from the Magdalenian age (22,000–17,000 B.C.) found mainly in northern Spain and southern France. The most outstanding of these paintings are in Altamira (northern Spain) and Lascaux (southern France), representing accomplished realistic conceptions. (Because of the deterioration of these works only facsimiles placed in a different cave in Lascaux are now accessible to the public.)

From the Cycladic or Island culture (a chain of islands in the

Cycladic Sculpture

Bull Figurine, Minoan terra cotta, 1300 B.C.

Model of a Doric Temple

Aegean Sea called the Cyclades) dating from 7000 to 2000 B.C. (the Predynastic period in Egypt), a quantity of highly stylized sculptures are preserved in the National Museum in Athens. All these, because of their abstract quality, have a strangely "modern" look. The Creto-Minoan culture (early Bronze Age) dates from 2000 to 1500 B.C. Art objects from that period show a high degree of perfection and sophistication and their style points to Egyptian and Asiatic influences. The Mycenaean age (1500–1000 B.C.) received its artistic inheritance from Crete, but its configurations do not have the refinement of the former.

Greek Sculpture. The period of 1000–600 B.C. is referred to as the Age of Tyrants, the Dorian and Ionian Greeks, and the earliest work comes to us from the 9th–8th century in the form of pottery. These carry geometric patterns, and the style period is referred to as Geometric. *The art of sculpture* began to develop during the 7th century B.C. and the statues of that period called Archaic show frontal views, rigid postures, formalized anatomy, and stereotyped features with "enigmatic" smiles. Egyptian and Asiatic influence is marked in these works.

The 5th century, referred to as Periclean, or the Golden Age,

a. Amphora, 8th Century   b. Amphora, 6th Century   c. Amphora, 5th Century

Archaic Kore, 6th Century   Greek Style, 5th Century

brought Greek sculpture to its greatest glory. In fact the precepts built into this art proved to be more enduring and generally more acceptable to Western man than those of any other style preceding or following it. The characteristics of Greek sculpture of this period are an avoidance of violent body movements and strong animation; a harmonious relationship in the distribution of masses and clarity in their disposition; the absence of exaggeration in the proportions of the human body—stress on the "ideal," rather than the realistic. This implies that a conceptual rather than a perceptual approach to art prevailed. The heads of the figures lack particularization; they are treated schematically and hardly vary in their vacuous facial expression, a characteristic which cannot be considered a failing but is rather a result of emphasis on formal values in representation of the human body.

During the 4th and 3rd centuries, the style of statuary became increasingly realistic, the workmanship more refined; greater attention was given to particular details, and dramatic action was often stressed. From here on (after the time of Alexander the Great), Greek style is referred to as Hellenistic because it embraces not only work of the mainland but from the overseas colonies as well. With the attainment of greater facility in handling marble, a closer imitation of natural appearance was sought, which often resulted in the deterioration of a once-noble style to mere illusionistic art—imitation of nature. This, however, did not prevent some excellent works coming to us even after

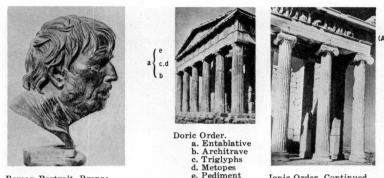

(A)

Doric Order.
a. Entablative
b. Architrave
c. Triglyphs
d. Metopes
e. Pediment

Roman Portrait, Bronze,
2nd Century

Ionic Order. Continued
Frieze

the Roman takeover. We know from well-documented reports that easel as well as mural painting was widely practiced in ancient Greece but except for painting done on pottery, none of it survived.

Greek Architecture. Three Greek styles are noted: Archaic, Transitional, Florid (or Alexandrian), and these are characterized by the following orders: Doric, Ionic, Corinthian. The 8th-century stone buildings that first replaced earlier wood structures were of a rather clumsy Doric order, but in time higher, slenderer columns were used and the execution of details, especially of metopes, showed greater finesse. The Ionic order with its continued frieze gave sculptors an opportunity for developing integrated figural compositions, and the columns supported by a base, their capitals adorned with scrolls, made the structures more elegant and graceful. The Corinthian order is a direct outgrowth of the Ionic, its only innovations being the bell-shaped capital formed by carved acanthus leaf designs. However, when we think of the "Corinthian style," it is its opulence and splendor, the richness of its decorative details, that impress us as its outstanding feature. In Hellenistic architecture this décor is rarely present but we find it employed to its fullest extent in Roman buildings.

Roman Painting. If not for excavations in Pompeii and Herculaneum (begun in 1709), the achievement of Roman mural painting (also mosaics) would have remained largely unknown to us. These murals ranging from flat decorative designs to compositions in depth and using both impressionistic and naturalistic means, often possess a high degree of refinement and sophistication. The Pompeian style was much copied during the *Directoire* and the *Empire* (1795–1815) without ever achieving the vitality of the originals. From examples found in Egypt, chiefly from the

2nd century A.D., we know that portraiture was also practiced in ancient Rome. These portraits were executed in encaustic, a technique employing colored pigments suspended in wax.

Roman Sculpture. One is accustomed to hear that Roman sculpture is inferior because it copies Greek sources. This assumption is incorrect, for successful "copying" at a time when a genuine style ideology exists is not the same as copying in a styleless age. Some of the Roman statuary, done in the so-called neo-Attic style, though not "original" is as fine as the best Greek work and the Roman sculptural portraiture produced over a period of four centuries remains unequaled. We may also add that Etruscan tomb effigies, dating from pre-Roman time (before the 3rd century B.C.), have a very special quality about them, quite different from the realism of the Romans. Often referred to as "crude" and "barbaric," they possess an aura of surrealism, a dreamlike quality which is far more expressive than that seen on Egyptian funeral effigies.

Roman Architecture. Whatever Classic architecture remains from the time of the Renaissance is totally dependent on Roman inventions. Although the Etruscans were the first in Europe to employ vaults in their buildings, the ingenuity and technical prowess of the Romans in constructing majestic arches, vaults, and domes in various combinations has never been equaled. They retained the Greek orders—Doric, Ionic, and Corinthian—but these were endowed with luxuriant surface ornamentation, giving

Pompeian Wall Painting   Etruscan Figure, 4th Century B. C.

them a splendor that formed the basis of all Renaissance palatial architecture.

Byzantine Style. With the decline of Rome and the transfer of the capital of the Roman Empire to Constantinople in the 4th century, there came into being an art, part Oriental, part Roman, but in its essence different from either—the art of the early Christian Church. This art, because of its antirealistic figurations, its stylization, and distortions, evokes a strong response in the predilections of our own time. But these are not the characteristics of the style that first come to mind with the term "Byzantine"; it calls forth images of brilliance, splendor of color, and sumptuous décor. In fact, no age of the Western world has ever indulged in such a proliferation of costly ornaments as witnessed in Byzantine interiors. However, Central European art from the 7th-11th century, as seen chiefly in illuminated manuscripts, cannot always be identified as "Byzantine."

Byzantine Painting. All Byzantine art is ecclesiastic. What remains of illuminated manuscripts (the earliest dating from the 6th century), shows Hellenistic and Oriental influence, but the style is rather crude. Characteristic work, done on panels, the so-called icons, are plentiful. These devotional pictures, generally small in size, are also patterned after Roman and Oriental styles. The earliest panels (also from the 6th century) were painted in encaustic while later a heavily varnished tempera was used. Their production continued for many centuries in Greek-Orthodox countries such as Greece, the Balkans, and Russia. Hence the original Byzantine style in painting went through many modifications, but always retained the mannered, archaic, linear character which is still evident in 18th-century icons.

The glory of Byzantine art, however, expressed itself in mosaics. The art of mosaics—the use of tesserae (small colored squares of glass or stone)—was well understood by the Greeks and Ro-

Roman Ruins, 1st Century B. C.

Byzantine Church

Byzantine Church Interior

Byzantine Mosaic

mans but their mosaics were predominantly monochromatic. In Byzantium the Oriental taste for brilliant color and sumptuous decoration covering large surfaces dictated the use of multicolored tesserae. These were made of tinted glass and gold foil incorporated into the semiliquid glass surface. Like mirrors, the little squares reflect the light in dim churches, and the varying angles of their surface produces incomparable effects of light and texture. Moreover, the art of ivory carving and enameling used in conjunction with gold and silversmithing reached a high level of perfection before the year 1000 A.D.

Byzantine Sculpture. The earliest examples of figural and ornamental representations came off the sarcophagi; probably carved in Asia Minor, they show Greco-Roman traits, but the ornamentation is distinctly Oriental, especially in the proliferation of vine designs, which are of Mesopotamian origin. Various objects and devotional figurines from the 7th through the 9th centuries in ivory, silver, or bronze, came to us from Egypt and Syria as well as from Europe. All these show a characteristic linear rather than a sculptural bias.

Byzantine Architecture. From Rome came the basilica form of building—the vaults, and the dome; the typical feature of this architecture is the use of pendentives on which the dome rests. The earlier domes had at their base small windows, the only source of light in the building. To support the main vaults, internal abutments were used. These architectural features accounted for the bare and inconspicuous appearance of the exterior. From Rome also came the preference for polished monolithic columns and multicolored marble panels used for wall incrustations. The marble blocks were often split in two and then rejoined, thus forming striations of symmetrical zig-zag patterns. In contrast to the plain look of Byzantine church exteriors (St. Mark's in Venice is an exception), the interiors are extraordinarily rich and ornate.

Romanesque Painting and Sculpture. The art of painting in the 11th and through the 13th centuries limited itself to stained-glass windows, illuminated manuscripts, enamels, and occasionally murals. In contrast to the high artistic merit of the stained glass (the earliest were made in the 11th century), painting of that period either continued in the Byzantine tradition or, whenever it made an attempt at verisimilitude, fell into crudeness. But sculpture, always a part of church architecture, entered its most fertile era during the 13th century. What are, then, the outstanding qualities of this sculpture? Fantasy, audacity, inventiveness. Together these qualities created a wealth of images —monsters, goblins, angels, and devils, grotesques of all kinds— and all these appear very real for the iconography of the medieval man was not a literary whimsy but a way of spiritual life. Unhampered by obligations to realistic representation, the freedom that the anonymous stone carvers dared to exercise has charged his (in many instances diagramed) images with a furious vitality and authenticity rarely achieved in all of history. Mention should also be made of ivory carvings much used for covers of liturgical books. These are of exquisite workmanship and great refinement in sculptural as well as ornamental detail.

Romanesque Architecture. The chief characteristics by which these predominantly monastic structures can be identified are heavily built walls with external buttressing, hence flat and plain interiors; small windows; and rounded arches. The western façades are often arranged in graceful gabled porches, arches with clustered piers, and jamb shafts with heavy carved moldings. In many instances the façades are adorned with elegant blind arcades, colonettes, and pilasters. A charming detail of Romanesque décor is columns resting on the backs of fierce-looking animals—lions and monsters. Sights of endless delight, they are found in the doorways and the pulpits. The ceilings of the churches are sometimes barrel-vaulted, often constructed of ribbed groin vaults. Elaborately carved leaf, geometric, and

Romanesque Painting

Romanesque Capital

Romanesque Church

grotesque ornaments were used extensively on the capitals of the columns, in the doorways, corbels, and moldings. Splendid figures grace the walls, niches, portals, and tympanums of the churches. Until the beginning of the 12th century the bell towers, square or octagonal with little adornments (such as gabled porches on top of the shafts), were separated from the body of the church.

Gothic Style. The term "Gothic" appeared for the first time in Italy during the Renaissance, when it was erroneously assumed that the buildings of the Middle Ages were the works of Goths who overthrew the Roman Empire. Because of this association, Gothic was a rather derogative term and meant "barbaric." In France, where it first appeared, the style was referred to as *Opus Francigenum*, but it spread rapidly throughout Europe and, depending on its geographic location, lasted from about 1150 to 1550. Often, Gothic coexisted with a much later style such as Baroque, and when the latter, for example, was at its height in Vienna, the Tyrol was still deeply steeped in the medieval mode. In fact, we could say that in England the Gothic style (or its equivalents) never entirely went out of existence.

Because of its long duration, definite variants of the style can be noted, and these are referred to as *Early, Middle,* and *Late* or *Flamboyant* Gothic. A more specific term would be "Ogival," for this form more than anything else characterizes the system which developed logically and organically from the preceding Romanesque style.

Gothic Painting is an outgrowth of the Byzantine art of the icon. In Italy this influence persisted almost to the advent of the Renaissance—that is, late into the 14th century. But it is in the north where the Gothic style, lasting well into the 16th century, developed its most pure and perfect form. As usual, when traditional forms are abandoned, a newly acquired expression will show deficiencies. At first northern painting and that influenced by the northern school was characterized by a certain stiffness and crudeness, although the naïveté of some of these works is not without charm, and its craftsmanship is always admirable. Around 1400 a high degree of realism was achieved, but the characteristic rectilinearity in the treatment of folds—a very important element in figure painting that does not consider the nude body—was retained during the later development of the style. Hence, the term *"Harter Stil"* (the hard style) is used in Germany in referring to late Gothic art. The greatest perfection in the development of the style took place in Flanders. At the beginning of the 15th century an extreme realism appeared, and minute details, regardless of their position in space, were treated with great precision. All objects seem isolated by an

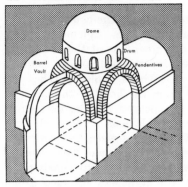

Construction of a Byzantine Dome.
Raised on Drum supported by Pendentives

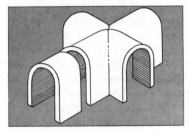

Groined Vault formed by intersection
of Barrel Vaults

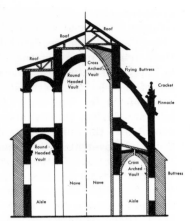

Romanesque and Gothic Comparative
Structure

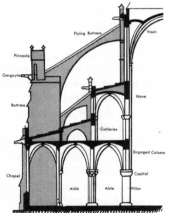

Half-cross section of a Gothic Cathedral

Gothic Orders. 1) Clerestory,
2) Triforium, 3) Main Arch,
4) Engaged Columns, 5) Pillar

Sexpartite Vaulting

Gothic Painting. Giotto

outline, which forms self-contained units, in other words, the entire composition—the foreground as well as the background—is an assembly of mutually independent parts. Yet this hard-focused conception made a concession to aerial perspective by reducing the intensity of colors with spatial recession.

Another feature of Gothic painting is the bird's-eye view which the painter assumed in depicting scenes from above, in effect a cartographer, mapping out wide vistas and placing the horizon high on the picture plane. But the most striking quality of all of Gothic painting is the consummate craftsmanship—the jewel-like appearance of the colors, their brilliance and clarity, the technical perfection of their execution; these have never been equaled in the entire history of art.

Gothic Sculpture attained at once a very high level of accomplishment, not only in France but in other countries as well. It is hardly an exaggeration to say that Western civilization produced two great classes of sculpture: the Greek and the Gothic. In regard to depth of expression and range of imagination, nothing has since been created to equal Gothic sculpture.

Gothic Architecture. What did Gothic builders borrow from Romanesque architecture? The rib vault. What did they invent? The flying buttress. This appears like an oversimplification, but the entire development of the style depended on this innovation. For it changed a solid enclosed space to one that may best be called "skeletal."

By introducing flying buttresses (these resisted the outward thrust of the vaulting), a suppression of walls became possible, and thus unlimited window space could be created. The ogive became the hallmark of the style. It was applied to the pier arches, the doorways, and the windows made of stained glass and becoming ever larger in size, requiring more complex tracery.

Gothic Sculpture

To dramatize the upward surge of space, the engaged columns of the piers often reached to the vaulted ceilings, now an important part of the decoration. The ceiling consisted of independent ribs, which met at a center point called a "boss," often an elaborately carved ornament, which adds splendor to the interior.

The *Early Gothic* period, because of the architects' preoccupation with structural problems, is distinguished by simple and vigorous design, narrow windows, and scarce ornamentation. In England this period is known as *Early Pointed.* The Italians did not especially favor the Gothic mode, regarding it as a foreign importation; they preferred small windows in their churches, and the large wall space gained thereby usually served for fresco decorations. However, because of the absence of architectural subdivisions and the large size of the constituent parts, these churches look barren when not decorated by murals, and their vaults are also less interesting, for they lack the subdivision of even minor ribs.

In the *Middle Period,* with the appearance of the flying buttress, the windows grew larger, the structures higher, the bar tracery more delicate, and the proportions more slender. In England this period is referred to as *Early Decorated, Mid-Gothic,* or *Geometric.* In the last stage, which is called *Flamboyant* or *Florid,* structure was gradually overwhelmed by extravagance of décor. This late development, in England called *Perpendicular,* is

Gothic Sculpture   Gothic Church   Gothic Church Interior

distinguished by vertical window bars with horizontal transoms and four-centered arches. The ceilings are arranged in extraordinary fan vaulting, a remarkable feature of these structures, which in their later phases are sometimes called "Tudor." In Germany, at the termination of the Gothic style, "branch" tracery used for adornment of stained-glass windows became a national feature.

Like Romanesque buildings, Gothic edifices teem with statuary; allegoric and symbolic images adorn the deep doorways, archivolts, pier arches, niches, parapets. Grotesque beasts, monsters, gargoyles, devils, saints, and angels bear witness to the exuberant imagination, the creative energy of the generally anonymous craftsmen, who usually were superb artists in their own right.

Renaissance Style. The Gothic style had as little effect on the Italians in painting as it did in architecture. Because antique monuments were always present, they remained an ever-active influence; one can say that in Italy Classic antiquity remained alive to a certain degree throughout the ages.

Renaissance art dates from the beginning of the 15th century and can be divided into three periods: *Early, High,* and *Late Renaissance* (referred to as *Mannerism*). However, such divisions usually suffer from oversimplification, for even the Early Renaissance was not all of a kind. Within it a purely Classic style appeared—in Masaccio, Piero della Francesca—and some of their contemporaries—Carpaccio, Uccello, the early Bellini—retained much of the archaic in their work.

What is the characteristic of the Early Renaissance style? Simplicity of form elements and solemnity of attitude, both analogous to the Classic style of the Periclean age. The High Renaissance, on the other hand, developed forms much more complex, with stress on rich surface ornamentation not unlike that of ancient Rome. The style had currency from about 1475 to 1525. Mannerism appeared during the post-Leonardo period, about the middle of the 16th century. With it the Renaissance entered a period of decline.

Renaissance Painting. In the 15th century Renaissance painting experienced a phase which we may call "ideal realism." Pictorial treatment underwent certain radical changes. Compositions were constructed along frontal planes and stratified in depth on horizontal and vertical axes. Outlines of objects lost some of their rigidity, thus no longer isolating the objects completely from their surroundings. Polychromy (the mainstay of Gothic painting) was no longer sought after, and emphasis on tonal values rather than on stridency of color, asserted itself. (A comparison between the early and the late work of Bellini best

Early Italian Renaissance. Pollaiuolo   High Renaissance Painting. Titian

illustrates these two different approaches.) Another innovation that distinguishes 15th-century painting from that of earlier epochs is the use of light-shade relationships—that is, one source of light, the so-called chiaroscuro. Employed at first with a certain restraint, the dramatic possibilities of chiaroscuro were consciously exploited in the High Renaissance (around 1500), and Leonardo da Vinci became the first and the most prominent exponent of this system.

In art, style developments always take their organic course from simplicity to complexity. And complexity, as a rule, does not place art on a higher plane; it merely adds décor and luxury. However, Mannerism, the last phase of Renaissance art, was characterized not by added decorativeness but rather by a decline, a deterioration of those qualities that had distinguished the earlier style. It would seem that after Leonardo all the mines were worked out, and artists, in a frantic search for the new, steeped themselves in all manner of exaggeration and affectation. Mannerism is essentially a hysterical expression.

Renaissance Sculpture was in a measure patterned after classic Greek style, inasmuch as it sought "ideal" rather than realistic expression. Yet these ideal aspects were different from those of 5th-century Greek art, for the Renaissance sculptors' concern was with the representation of humanized attitudes rather than with formal values. Thus stricter observation of natural appearances, modified by idealistic features and heroic overtones, is characteristic of 15th-century sculpture. As in painting, this sculpture stressed the frontal view; it favored the wall and

Mannerist Painting.
Bronzino

Renaissance
Sculpture.
Donatello

Early
Renaissance
Facade

Renaissance
Ceiling

did not quite free itself from it—it remained a part of architecture. In consequence, it must be seen largely by its outlines, that is, by contours, for we are dealing here with isolated, "closed" forms. In contrast, Baroque forms are "open," because their contours are unstable.

Renaissance Architecture gave the Western world a style that endured into the 20th century. The source of inspiration for the builders of the 15th and 16th centuries was Roman architecture, whose principles, however, were not imitated but rather developed and most ingeniously utilized. Renaissance style was not ideal for church architecture (although the lantern-crowned dome placed on a high drum has become one of the most impressive features of cathedrals); it favored palaces, villas, and municipal buildings. As in painting, we may divide the style of architecture into three phases: from 1400 to 1450, from 1450 to 1500, and from 1500 to 1550 (these dates are, of course, approximations). Early Renaissance is recognizable by the simplicity and often austerity of façade design; all its ornaments are close to the wall—none of them appear to extend beyond the surface of the building. The proportions of the structure's stringcourses, its fenestration—in other words, the composition of the façade—is such that only a frontal view gives us a clue to its probity. (The opposite is true in Baroque buildings.) Gradually the simplicity of the early style gave way to luxuriance; Roman ornamental details were increasingly copied; fanciful moldings and pilasters covered with arabesque patterns appeared. Interiors were adorned by marble inlays, terra cotta and stucco work, and the ceilings became veritable riots of sculptured and painted decoration.

Baroque Style. The term "Baroque" implies irregularity, contortion, and has often been used as a pejorative to denote clumsy, florid forms. In Italy, the Baroque reached its mature configuration about the middle of the 16th century (about 50 years later in the rest of Europe) and lasted well into the 18th century. In some quarters the style was considered a degeneration of Renaissance art. This is manifestly false, for it rests on diametrically opposite premises. On the whole (if we exclude the few men of genius working within the ideology of the Baroque), it gave a more powerful expression to architecture and sculpture than to painting.

Baroque Painting and Sculpture. As stated, the guiding principles of Renaissance art are clarity of exposition, observance of empirical perspective, and the use of firmly drawn contours. In Baroque art none of this applies; instead, ambiguity and concealment prevail, and vaguely defined contours are the rule. The Baroque, its swirling movements changing the horizontal and vertical into diagonals and the planimetric into the recessive, blows, as it were, drift and turbulence into the static form, thus preventing the objects from becoming solidified within definite silhouettes. Its overcharged compositions change tranquillity into restlessness, reticence into theatrical magniloquence. The use of chiaroscuro also becomes intensified and its application distorted, for no longer does light and shade serve to clarify the form but, by obscuring it, injects ambiguity into the scene. This pictorial system is present in its most dramatic manifestation in the work of Tintoretto and El Greco.

As for sculpture, the same principles rule its configurations, even in matters of chiaroscuro. This sculpture partakes of tone rather than of line, for its contours have been depreciated and its solidification within the given boundaries impaired. By pulling the forms apart, recessions and protrusions have been created; these catch light, receive or cast shadows, thus depriving the figure of its substantiality and making it pictorial rather than sculptural. Sculpture is no longer static, but in flux.

Baroque Painting. Tintoretto

Baroque Sculpture. Bernini

Baroque Architecture. In older books on architecture we find references to Baroque style that read "lawless and tasteless," "debasement of the classical architectural taste," "pretentious sham," all of which point to the lack of recognition of the principles that make the Baroque a style that does not share the precepts of the orthodox Classic esthetic. Hence, pejorative verdicts such as "broken and contorted pediments," "huge scrolls," "heavy moldings," "sculptures in exaggerated attitudes," do not constitute a negative assessment. Indeed, liberated from the flatness of façade, porches and loggias sprang up on buildings, rustication became confined to basements and corner quoins, once-engaged columns and pilasters detached themselves from the walls, adding more recessional depth and giving greater variety to the effects of light and shade; pediments and exquisite enframements began to appear over doors and windows. The interiors, too, were enriched by convoluted columns with stuccoed capitals, wood was painted to resemble marble, moldings and cornices of exquisite design were elaborately decorated; sculptural lunettes and ceilings of incredible sumptuousness were constructed; niches were filled with statuary and interior courts were graced with columnar arcades.

No matter from which angle one views these edifices, the pictorial quality expressed in the variety and irregularity of the total effect becomes fully revealed—and this variety and irregularity is the very core of the style. It should also be understood that the major decorative elements in the Baroque are not extrinsically attached embellishments but are in essence intrinsic parts, or subdivisions, of the larger architectural scheme.

Baroque Church

Baroque Altar

Rococo Interior   Rococo Figurine

Rococo Painting, Sculpture, and Architecture. Essentially a style of the court and the affluent society, it is characterized by over-ornateness, chiefly in interiors. It flourished late in the 18th century. In painting, it is the art of the salons concerned with the depiction of scenes of life in the elegant world; in it the style of Baroque painting was devitalized; in sculpture, it was, in fact, debased. Conventional portraiture, porcelain figurines, faïence, and bric-à-brac, these are the chief products of Rococo sculptors. Although architecturally Rococo style did not produce any innovations, it deprived the Baroque of its ponderousness and massiveness and reduced its ornaments to an extrinsic, frilly décor, exquisitely delicate and precious.

Directoire and Empire Style, or the Classic Revival. With the end of the reign of Louix XVI, the Rococo became defunct, and the reappearance of a classicistic mode followed. Hence the art of the Napoleonic period can be referred to as neo-Classic. In architecture, simple forms based on Classic precepts prevailed, and although these never attained the beauty of the original models, they nevertheless remained within the boundaries of good taste.

Neo-Classic Painting

In art, however, the neo-Classic produced hard-edged paintings tinted with brittle, glassy colors and compositions full of specious rhetoric—the heroic effort to resuscitate the grand manner of a Raphael proved to be futile. With few exceptions, the neo-Classic style was more successful where the spirit of incipient Romanticism made itself felt, but in sculpture it must be looked upon as a failure—the climate of the Napoleonic era had nothing in common either with the Periclean age or the age of Donatello.

We have considered the salient aspects of styles as they appeared in Western civilization from its beginnings to the advent of the machine age, that is, up to the second quarter of the 19th century. In making the reader conscious of the diverse style configurations, his more complete understanding and commensurably greater enjoyment of the art of the past can be hoped for.

Section 2 / England

INTRODUCTION TO THE ART OF ENGLAND

Mention was made in the Introduction that arbitrary and illogical distinctions have often been made between "fine" and "applied" art. At certain times such classifications are valid; but when esthetic ideologies are the property, the woof and warp as it were, of a community of people, these distinctions are pointless. Alas, it would seem that in art more than in any other field of human activity, conventions have replaced criticism and unwarranted claims have assumed legislative power. Thus anything in a frame or on a pedestal is considered art (whatever its quality), whereas reticulated or foliated tracery that seems a poem in stone, psalter illuminations, stained glass, or recumbent statues, are relegated to "crafts." Why do I refer to recumbent sculpture? Simply because such medieval tomb effigies, found in England, have not yet been put on an equal footing with upright statuary although the quality of the former may be vastly superior. True, England produced neither a Pisano nor a di Cambio, nor can its Gothic statuary match the best of the French or the German. In England we do not find a Cimabue or a Giotto, but then only Italy can boast of such giants. In all, we can say that the art of 13th- and 14th-century England—as with all Gothic art—stood consistently on a high level. In fact, the Gothic style established itself as a truly English national style to such a degree it largely excluded the Renaissance influence which left its mark on practically every Continental nation. Thus no native Renaissance artist appeared on the English scene, despite a climate that favored art in all its manifestations. Foreign artists were therefore highly prized and found employment at the courts of the kings; Holbein, for example, was the court painter of Henry VIII, and Van Dyck became attached to the court of Charles I. Besides these great artists, many German, Dutch, Flemish, and Italian painters of lesser renown were employed in England and produced pictures of every kind. Strangely, English painting succeeded in asserting itself only with the appearance of Hogarth. This brings us to the middle of the 18th century and the beginning of a truly native art that expressed itself first in portraiture, with Reynolds, Gainsborough, Romney, Raeburn, Hoppner, and some lesser academicians and second in landscape, with Wilson, Crome, Constable, and finally Turner, who died in 1851. These were the outstanding names in a century of English painting, and the quality of their art is generally much higher than that of France during the same period.

As regards English Gothic architecture, the commonly held opinion is that it is merely a provincial variety, a derivation from the French style. Granted, the French have "priority" when it comes to creating the style, but this fact is of historic, not of esthetic importance. Stylistically, English Gothic in no way competes with the French, for its salient features are thoroughly original and distinctly national. To take one important instance, English fan vaulting and its bosses: the beauty, audacity, and inventiveness of their configuration, whether structural or merely decorative, has never been equaled in any European country. In comparison, French vaultings are soberly uniform. English interiors are also much more ornate than the French. The highly decorated triforium, the multiplicity of moldings in pier arches, the great east windows, and the minute paneling so characteristic of the Perpendicular style make the English churches and chapels appear the more graceful and ornate of the two. However, they usually lack one important element of décor: statuary.

Indeed, anyone who has ever seen one of these magnificent cathedrals must be thoroughly baffled at statements made by some of the most enlightened men. Aldous Huxley writes, for example: "And then, suddenly, the 17th century gave birth to two English architects of genius. It produced Inigo Jones, and a little later, Wren." Evidently he has committed the building geniuses of the 13th, 14th, and 15th centuries to oblivion. In fact, we could go further back in time, for the great building period in England started after William the Conqueror won the Battle of Hastings (1066), and Norman style (corresponding to the Romanesque) established itself in that country. But the English never developed a taste for the Romanesque, as the Germans did (retaining its crude features in the so-called *Baukastenstil* for centuries). In England it was the Gothic mode that was eagerly adopted and translated into a peculiarly native idiom that endured—though in an impure form—well into the 19th century. Following are the dates of style developments: Norman, late 11th and 12th centuries; Early Pointed, 1175–1260; Decorated or Mid-Gothic, 1260–1350; Perpendicular, after 1360. All these phases correspond approximately to the development of comparable styles on the Continent.

Lastly it must be mentioned that in England, perhaps more than in other European countries, neglect and the catastrophic demolition of the Reformation and the Enlightenment, as well as calamitous restorations carried out by well-meaning but misinformed experts in the 18th and 19th centuries, have depleted a vast store of treasures of the Middle Ages.

In the 16th century, during the reign of Henry VII and Henry VIII, Gothic metamorphosed into what is known today as *Tudor,* a kind of English Renaissance that never lost its Gothic patrimony and was employed chiefly in the erection of patrician country mansions. During the next phase, referred to as Elizabethan, the heavy Tudor battlements and obligatory pointed arches were replaced by orders of Classic origin. This trend continued during the Jacobean period (the reign of James I), but with the advent of Inigo Jones (first half of the 17th century), the monumental style of the Italian Classic masters, such as that of Andrea Palladio, came into full use. The results were often unfortunate, for the Palladian and the English climate had nothing in common. With Christopher Wren, known principally as the architect of St. Paul's, the Classic style reached its apogee. Wren died in 1723 and with him the great building period—unless one accepts the Classic and neo-Gothic revivals that followed, as authentic style expressions.

Museums in London

National Gallery. The reader concerned with the great European museums will be confronted with repetitious classifications, such as "the greatest museum," "the richest collection." Which really is the greatest? I don't think that it is possible to make such an assessment. After leaving the National Gallery in London, we could say with full conviction that nothing had impressed us more, even if we had just visited the Louvre or the Uffizi. It is astonishing indeed to learn that this public institution was established only in 1824, however, its wealth can be explained by the fact that the British, more than any other nation in Europe, developed a taste for art collecting as early as the 17th century. Hence England had an immense accumulation of art treasures among its affluent and much-traveled citizenry which the gallery could draw upon.

The Rokeby Venus. Velázquez

St. Sebastian. Pollaiuolo

The Battle of San Romano. Uccello

Woman Bathing. Rembrandt

Baptism of Christ. Piero della Francesca

But the personal taste of the collector was often poor and interfered with the acquisition of important works of art. In 1836 Sir Robert Peck, a gallery trustee, justified his opposition to the purchase of Italian paintings prior to the cinquecento saying, "We do not collect curiosities." And Horace Walpole averred that, "All qualities of perfect painting were never met but by Raphael, Guido Reni and Annibale Carracci." The leading esthetician of the Victorian age, John Ruskin, is quoted: "Guido Reni is ten times greater than Leonardo." Thus Raphael was put in the company of Baroque hacks, and Leonardo suffered an even greater indignity. Indeed, a history of taste is full of absurdities; Ruskin, whose esthetic pronouncements were almost always false, contributed largely toward the revival of neo-Gothic—an execrable corruption of good taste—and inadvertently fostered the appreciation of true Gothic.

It is interesting to consider how taste arbiters influenced the art market. Before Gothic was in fashion, Van Eyck was not thought much of; in 1842 one of the most valuable paintings of the gallery, The Marriage of Arnolfini, sold for only $2,000. At the same time, for reasons difficult to understand, the proposed purchase of Titian's Rape of Europa (now in the Gardner Collection in Boston) for $1,200 was rejected. But paintings then in fashion were sold at high figures. In 1884 the gallery paid $70,000 for a Van Dyck. And some 40 years later an American collector paid $300,000 for a minor painting by that master. In 1963 this same painting was sold at auction for $30,000.

To further illuminate the incongruities of "informed" taste, it should be remembered that during the 19th century most of the old masters' paintings in England acquired a deep brown color, commonly referred to as "gallery tone," as they were not cleaned but repeatedly coated with inappropriate varnishes. In fact, this brown color was considered the hallmark of authenticity. Thus a patron of the gallery and a leading collector, Sir George Beaumont, made this memorable remark: "A good picture like an old fiddle, should be brown." Only after World War II was a general cleaning of the gallery paintings initiated, and even then certain circles voiced strong opposition to changing the look of the beloved, grimy, colorless canvases. Today practically all of them appear almost as they did when they left the easel.

The direction one takes when entering a museum, is often of consequence for the first impression establishes the mood of the viewer. When entering the first large hall in the National Gallery which starts, oddly enough, with 18th-century paintings, among them some of the finest Canalettos and Tiepolos, it is a good idea to turn left to face a roomful of Crivellis, and nowhere else are so many of his panels assembled in one place. Carlo Crivelli's reputation seems to suffer from the usual bias toward medieval works, in which artistry is thought to reside solely in the décor, considered a minor art. He is looked upon as retrograde in his technique, a provincial—working away from the main stream of Renaissance art. Indeed, he shares with many of his predecessors of equal skill a passion for exacting elaborations of minutiae, but his passion is not for mechanical craftsmanship; his hard-edged, deeply etched emblems possess an unearthly beauty—here "technique" becomes the vortex of the medievalist's *Weltanschauung*.

Luckily, Pisanello (*Madonna and Child with Two Saints*) and Paolo Uccello (*The Battle of San Romano*) had not quite abandoned the medievalist's world. Both stubbornly clung to old precepts, allowing the new spirit to raise its voice ever so faintly. It is not difficult to guess that Pisanello began as a medalist, for his prowess lies in his phenomenal handling of contours. Because the convolutes of lines can best be exploited on flat surfaces, the early Italian painters favored representation in profile. Uccello went in a different direction; his was a passion for the problems of perspective, aiming at achieving recessional depth, with the curious result that his perspective is always utterly unrealistic as are all the personages in his paintings. It must be understood that an artist's ostensible or professed aims and the results as they materialize in his works stand, more often than not, at cross purpose. Uccello must be judged on a different level, perhaps as a "naïve" artist and, of course, as one who functioned within the framework of medieval tradition.

Two other artists, Andrea Mantegna and his brother-in-law Giovanni Bellini, are represented with identical subject matter—each with *Agony in the Garden,* painted in 1460. Yet they have no medievalism in them; on the contrary, the Classic appears in its purest form and in all its beauty and grandeur. Although still archaic in nature, this style has not as yet achieved the illusionistic effects that mark the high Renaissance. Moreover, there is a quality in the compositions of these masters that has gone out of paintings produced at the height of the Renaissance—namely, the creative incident in the use of the then newly discovered laws of empirical perspective. Perspective is one of the phenomena inherent in the composition of pictures, which is itself an organization of objects in space. At no time before or after has space been energized to such a degree and with as much originality as in the earlier works of Mantegna and Bellini. This, of course, basically implies that their system of pictorial composition was in some respects at variance with Renaissance style.

Another great painting of the same epoch is Jan van Eyck's

Marriage of Arnolfini, perhaps his most popular work. When facing it we are compelled to admit that it could have been produced only within the Gothic ideology; in other words, only when a style united and controlled all spheres of artistic, intellectual, and social life, when man belonged to one great community of creed and thought, could an ordinary genre have assumed such transcendental scope. Among other Flemish works of great significance are Jan Mabuse's *Adoration of the Kings* and Mateo di Giovanni's *Madonna of the Girdle.*

Of the Italians, Antonio Pollaiuolo's *St. Sebastian,* a tour de force of fierce body movements, was painted at a time when the study of anatomy was still a creative pursuit and hence has great impact. Piero di Cosimo's *Death of Procris* has, like some other works of this strange, insufficiently appreciated master, almost surrealistic overtones; the same can be said of his *Fight between the Lapiths and Centaurs.* Further, Sandro Botticelli in *Mars and Venus* and *Adoration of the Magi* and Fra Filippo Lippi in *Annunciation* expressed, each in his own way, the vernal mood of the age.

When facing works universally acclaimed to be among the highest artistic attainments, we could confine ourselves to categorizing them with one simple epithet: "the greatest." But without scrutinizing the elements that account for greatness, our understanding, and consequently our enjoyment of a work of art is impaired. This accurate and just statement could easily be contradicted when we are confronted with a work that defies all efforts of scrutiny and when a fair analysis is unable to sufficiently account for its greatness. Thus, whenever we face a Piero della Francesca, the unfathomable becomes at once the significant. To suggest, as some scholars do, that his representations are "symbolic," is not satisfactory, for a symbol—that is, an abstract meaning given to a concrete form—must be generally understood to function as a symbol. But the hidden meaning that is so strongly felt in Piero's images is *not* understood; in fact, such an understanding would not enhance our enjoyment of the *Baptising of Christ* or the *Nativity,* his most important works to be seen outside of Italy. Technically there is nothing remarkable about Piero's paintings; not only does he shun the entrapment of decorative exposition but he even avoids the slightest show of animation. His is an impassive world of majestic monuments, steeped in utter solemnity. Can marble be instinct with a soul? In Piero's works one finds the answer to this paradox.

The 16th century appears with an array of masterpieces, among them Titian's *Bacchus and Ariadne* (1520), representing the culmination of Renaissance style. This does not imply that after

1520 this style took a downward trend, but by and large, the post-Leonardo period in Italy showed marked signs of fatigue. In the portraits of Hans Holbein, however (the *French Ambassadors* and *Christina of Denmark*, both painted in the 1530's), there is a consistent appearance of confidence and vigor. The deliberate unemotional approach and impeccable craftsmanship obviously relies on Flemish patrimony. Mention should be made of the so-called Leonardo, the *Virgin of the Rocks*, painted some 20 years after the original version, now in the Louvre. All one can say concerning its authenticity is that compared with the Louvre paintings, it is inferior; nonetheless, it is possible that a painter, no matter how great his genius, may not succeed in copying his own work. However, the landscape motif is so miserable that it could only be an overpainting by inept hands executed at a later date.

The tenor of the following century did not weaken in countries such as Holland, Flanders, and Spain. The 17th and 18th centuries are dominated by the Baroque, although this style had its full impact much earlier in Italy. But the Baroque, so well defined in architecture, cannot always be identified in the work of painters of the same period. Diego Velázquez cannot be labeled a Baroque painter; nor can Rembrandt. Velázquez's *Philip the IV*, painted in 1636, the so-called *Silver Philip* because of its prevailing color, is totally impressionistic in the handling of its brush strokes. Not so the *Rokeby Venus*, painted some 15 years later, which is, strangely, much more conservative in style. Rembrandt can be termed a Romantic (there is a full room of these), and El Greco, represented only with three of his smaller works, among them the *Agony in the Garden*, could be numbered among the present-day Expressionists for he distorts both form and color with great freedom. Of the great names of that century, only Peter Paul Rubens shows configurations typical of the Baroque. Here he appears in one of his rare, great landscapes, the *Château de Steen*, which served him as a summer seat, also one of his best single-figure paintings, the *Chapeau de Paille*, a bravura piece in *alla prima* technique of enormous charm. Of no lesser quality is Van Dyck's portrait of Charles I on horseback.

Other great late 17-century landscape painters hail from Holland and are quite numerous; among them Meinert Hobbema's the *Avenue Middelharnis* has the rare distinction of being a universally admired picture and a real masterpiece at the same time. The secret of its success can be explained only by the compelling composition and the undefinable "mood" that pervades the scene; this mood can largely be attributed to the quality and function of light. We find similar qualities of light in many Dutch landscapes of the period, amply represented in the gallery by works of Ruisdael, Van Goyen, and others. When examining landscape painting in the Low Countries, it is interesting to note how the level of the horizon, at first high in the picture's plane, assumes a progressively lower position to yield its dominance to the area of the sky.

How different is Claude Lorrain, a great favorite with the British; ten of his synthetic, romantic landscapes, reminiscent of theatrical backdrops, are in the gallery, and all suffer from an artificially "poetic" illumination and vapid sentimentality. The Italian Guardi, on the other hand, equally popular in England and represented in even larger numbers is convincing in spite of his ostensible exploitation of the effects of declining light. A painter of great gifts, the sensitivity of his staccato brushstrokes is inimitable.

In the field of portraiture Thomas Gainsborough and Sir Joshua Reynolds by far outrank their contemporaries of other countries. The portrait of *Lord Heathfield* by the latter is perhaps his best, and the sketch of Gainsborough's daughters makes us feel that in most of the commissioned portraits he had to make some concessions to his patrons.

Finally, there is in the gallery, a limited selection of Goya's work and, of course, an almost full contingent of 19th-century miscellany.

British Museum. This museum offers us a picture of the enormous complexity of man's artistic and intellectual history from its earliest beginnings; therefore, when visiting it we should keep in mind that our capacity to absorb—or even to visualize—is limited. Moreover, this guide is concerned primarily with the artistic attainments of Western civilization; hence the Greek, Medieval, and Renaissance departments will occupy our attention. If more than one visit to the museum is planned, the illuminated

Mausoleum of Halicarnassus

The Fates. Elgin Marbles

Dionysus, from the Pediment of the
Parthenon

Fragment from the Pediment of the
Parthenon

manuscripts (there are a few rooms of these), the art of Sumer,
Egypt, Africa, the Near and Far East might be studied.

The museum is a veritable labyrinth and finding one's way
through the halls and rooms is a formidable task, even with a
printed floor plan; hence it is best to ask the attendants for directions. In fact, in this museum one is tempted to pass from hall to
hall just to immerse one's mind in foreign and distant climes.

Of greatest interest to us, however, is the collection of Greek
statuary named collectively the "Elgin Marbles," after Lord Elgin,
who in 1801 acquired the treasures from the Turks, at that time
the rulers of Greece. They are unique, insofar as works of such
importance of the Periclean period (middle of the 5th century)
cannot be seen elsewhere. Following are the monuments from
the east pediment of the Parthenon. The head of the horse—the
most ideal of all artistic representations of horses—aroused
Goethe's highest admiration (he had a plaster cast of the marble
sent to him in 1820). However, he criticized the schematic arrangement of the horse's mane. (Incidentally, it is almost impossible to judge marble works from plaster casts, for the refraction
of light on such a material falsifies the object's true mass.) It is
assumed that Phidias, who was in charge of building the Parthenon, carved some of the statues or at least designed them.
The fact remains that these are among the few objects connected
with his name that have survived. Among them is the group of
so-called *Fates;* rightly considered one of the greatest achievements in sculpture. Its rhythm has the inevitability of an ocean
wave—its rise and flow, its descent and ebb. Of equal excellence
is the statute of *Dionysus;* simply to praise its counterpoise of
limb and torso, stress and relaxation—in short, its perfect representation of man in harmony, external and internal—does not adequately explain the secret of its perfection. All we can say is that
these sculptures represent the epitome of Classic art, which in the
words of Bernard Berenson "is the standard art toward which

the Europeans in the course of history have always turned back after no matter what occulations, aberrations, declines, and rebellions."

Another work from the Parthenon is a frieze, over three feet high, which originally ran around the wall of the cella. Also thought to be the work of Phidias, it is now assembled around the walls of the Elgin Hall and shows great finesse in design and execution. Intended to be viewed from the edge of the platform and from a short distance, the entire frieze tilts inward toward the beholder, thus preventing a distortion of the perspective. The metopes of the Parthenon, at least those that found their final resting place in this museum, do not come up to the level of the other sculptures and were evidently executed by Phidias' assistants. One of the caryatids from the Erechtheum (replaced at the temple itself by a copy), despite its ostensible beauty, does not, separated from her companions, evoke in us the same feelings we harbor when encountering the solemn maidens on the Acropolis.

Of almost equal artistic merit are the sculptures from the Mausoleum of Halicarnassus in Asia Minor, which came from the tomb of the Persian satrap Mausolus. Built during the tyrant's lifetime, in the middle of the 4th century, it was looked upon in antiquity as one of the Seven Wonders of the World. According to Pliny (1st century A.D.), it was Scopas who carved the frieze, but whoever its creator, his were gifts of the highest order. The designs of the Halicarnassus frieze differ radically from those of the Parthenon, chiefly in the rather violent animation of its actors. The colossal statue of the Mausoleum's chief occupant, Mausolus, reconstructed from 60 fragments, is of lesser artistry.

Victoria and Albert Museum. Like the British Museum, this is also a labyrinth seemingly filled with any and every ethnological curiosity, artifact, art. When only one visit is planned, the traveler, unless it is of interest to him, might omit the second floor which contains armor, jewelry, metalwork, glass, ceramics, and porcelain. First on the ground floor is a small but exquisite collection of medieval statuary and relics and a large hall hung with Gothic tapestry from the schools of Tournai, Brussels, and Germany. Also of highest quality is the collection of Renaissance statuary. Raphael's designs for the Vatican tapestries, as well as Renaissance paintings, can also be seen here.

Surprising as it may sound, the two halls containing copies of medieval and Renaissance statues and architectural components are of great importance to the student. For these polychromed facsimiles are hardly to be distinguished from the originals. The fact is that much statuary cannot be properly viewed in its original

Hall of Casts

setting. Here we can study the details on the Giotto tower far better than in Florence, for example. The copy of Ghiberti's Baptistry door can also be seen in this museum more advantageously than in the original and the same can be said of many other sculptural and architectural objects.

The **Wallace Collection** is housed in a mansion (the former residence of the marquesses of Hertford) that loudly proclaims: Money was no object. Here, in great profusion, among most elaborate furnishings are amassed faïence, majolica, silver, glass, medals, ivory, armor (enough to outfit a regiment), small bronzes, bric-à-brac, and a great many paintings. The poor taste of the

Sculpture Fragment. Donatello

Renaissance Statuary

furnishings, even at the time they were produced, should have been recognized by their owners. These Boulle, marquetry-type concoctions with their mounts of bronze, chased and gilt—the Sun God's (Louis XIV) favorites—are perfect examples of parvenue taste. How well the paintings of that period—the Bouchers, Fragonards, Lancrets, Greuzes, and even the Watteaus—fit into the fatuous setting. This, indeed, is a spurious art made expressly to please the penchants of the pompous snob.

There are other paintings in this collection: febrile Guardis, crisp Canalettos (there can be beauty even in sobriety), and the never-disappointing Dutch masters of the unpretentious genre. But the real surprise awaits the visitor in the large exhibition hall upstairs, where some paintings of primary importance are hung, among them Rembrandt's *Titus* and *Centurion Cornelius*, Veláz-quez' *Don Baltasar Carlos*, and the portrait of his daughter, *The Lady with the Fan*. And when it comes to "official" portraiture, let us not forget Romney. In his simplicity and economy of means he achieved an artistry worthy of the highest praise. Here also is Frans Hals' most popular painting, the *Laughing Cavalier*. It may be of interest to know that early in the 19th century it was bought by Lord Hertford for $200 at an auction in Paris. Possessor of many paintings by Frans Hals, he again put it up for auction, bidding the price up to $2,000, and then bought it back. Thus he established a new "official" market price for this painter's work; a trick practiced ever since by manipulators of the art market.

The **Courtauld Institute** houses the Lee, Courtauld, and Roger

Lady with a Fan. Velázquez   The Laughing Cavalier. Frans Hals

Bar aux Folies Bergère. Manet

La Loge. Renoir

Fry collections. The first is made up of a small contingent of anonymous works from the 13th to the 15th century, informed by a style that has never gone "wrong." A great deal of mediocrity is displayed in elegant 18th-century interiors. Of the Impressionists' paintings the following can be studied with profit: Edouard Manet's *Bar aux Folies Bergère,* Auguste Renoir's *La Loge,* Vincent van Gogh's *Self-portrait,* and a Toulouse-Lautrec. The Roger Fry wing is quite dismal. The leading art critic of his time proves to have been a very poor judge of contemporary paintings.

The *Tate Gallery* has a specialized collection of English art from the 18th century to the present. Those interested in the works of Hogarth, the portraits of the elegant world, William Blake, Turner, Constable, the Pre-Raphaelites, Whistler, Sargeant, the English Impressionists, as well as the contemporaries will find a comprehensive array of paintings.

London and the Cathedrals

As does every modern metropolis, London poses a problem for the traveler in search of beauty, and I am referring not to the accretion of works of art in hallowed repositories, but to the relics one expects to find in a city whose history reaches back to Roman times. In this respect London will prove disappointing. In 1666, the year of the Great Fire, four-fifths of the dwellings and 86 of the churches perished. Fifty-one of the latter were rebuilt by Sir Christopher Wren. But apart from the churches, judging from contemporary sources, there was not much of architectural interest even before the holocaust. Then came the blitz of World War II, inflicting further great damage to the city.

Before Christopher Wren appeared on the scene, Inigo Jones'

(whose chief surviving work is the *Banqueting House,* Whitehall) adaptation of Palladian architecture started the Classic period, which culminated in Christopher Wren's St. Paul's Cathedral. Obviously inspired by Michelangelo's St. Peter's, it is the most impressive domical edifice in England and replaced the earlier Gothic church destroyed in the Great Fire. This author, however, is not enthusiastic about Wren's rebuilt churches except for their steeples (among them *Mary-le-Bow* and *Christ Church*), which are comparatively sober, lacking the exuberance and *élan* of Italian, German, or Austrian designs.

Of the older structures, **St. Bartholomew the Great** and its gatehouse in Holburn date from the beginning of the 12th century; *Lambeth Palace,* a medieval structure, looks like a 19th-century imitation; the classicistic *Kensington Palace* was the residence of English kings before they moved to Buckingham Palace; the grim complex of the *Tower of London,* built by William the Conqueror as a fortress, is the best-preserved Norman structure in the country, though it somehow does not appear authentic. It is of interest to those who enjoy looking at armor or at the crown jewels housed in the White Tower, or who might relish the guide's gruesome tales of its past history. But there nestles at a corner of the Tower, the *Queens House,* a charming half-timbered Tudor structure. *Fulham Palace* is a noble, part 16th-century Jacobean building, the residence of the Bishop of London. Strange, how unpretentious these dwellings appear compared with the palaces of high nobility on the Continent. The greatest of the ancient edifices is, of course, Westminster Abbey.

(Although the number of sites I mentioned is modest, finding them—and some of the "quaint" spots—in a sprawling city built helter-skelter, is another matter.) Of course London also boasts Georgian structures from the beginning of the 18th through the beginning of the 19th century. Patterned after Classic designs, characteristic buildings are Cumberland Terrace, Chester Terrace, Park Crescent, and other elegant but dull and architecturally uninteresting edifices. Oddly, when we think of Georgian style, we do not mean the showplaces but the unassuming middle-class dwelling (Queen Ann's Gate being one of the finest among them) of red or gray brick, three or four stories high, generally three windows wide, and erected along streets or around the sides of squares so familiar to every New Yorker. These buildings always present satisfying relationships between wall and window space; a simple, civilized, native architecture that owes no debt to foreign modes. Edifices constructed during the latter part of the 19th century—the Parliament (in which original Norman and Gothic features exist in comparative obscurity), the big metropolitan squares, the Tower Bridge—we may rightly term "tourist" sights.

Except for *St. Paul's* and *Westminster Abbey*, churches will not be in our London repertoire. The first ranks with the finest European domical cathedrals; it is the work for which Sir Christopher Wren justly earned his pre-eminence as an architect and engineer. Built in late Italian Renaissance style, it was begun in 1675 and completed during Wren's lifetime, 35 years later. Externally, it is composed of two stories of Corinthian order, the upper designed to screen the clerestory and to give greater height and mass to its overlong exterior. The most successful feature of the structure is the dome, whose graceful lantern rises 360 feet. It springs from a high drum over the central area and is surrounded by an exquisite colonnade and flanked by two bell towers, part of the west façade. Wren succeeded in creating an edifice of just scale and proportion, harmonious withal, possessing great nobility and grandeur. Like all Renaissance palatial edifices, the interior of the church has a nonecclesiastic look. It is worldly, aloof, unimpressive in detail, and its chapels are lined mainly with 19th-century tomb statuary, disconcerting in their marble whiteness.

Westminster Abbey was rebuilt between 1245 and 1269, for coronation purposes. Modeled after its prototype, the Cathedral of Rheims, it was built largely over old foundations, between a Norman nave and the Lady chapel. The latter was reconstructed early in the 16th century and is now know as the *Chapel of Henry VIII*. Although structurally the present church is Early Pointed, later additions, restoration, and Victorian ornamentation

The Tower of London   Westminster Abbey

Westminster Abbey, Henry VIII Chapel

Fan Vaulting, Henry VIII Chapel

—above all the accumulation of tombs and memorials—have virtually ruined the interior. It seems that everybody who was anybody in England during a period of many centuries made an (successful) effort to have himself (or herself) buried in the church. The result, regardless of the merit of the individual monuments, is difficult to assess because of the prodigious accumulation of trivia and gives an impression of disorder and confusion. Hence it is best to repair oneself directly to the Chapel of Henry VIII, internally and externally the most resplendent example of the

St. Paul's Cathedral

St. Paul's Cathedral Interior

Perpendicular style. Its fan vaulting and hanging pendents are the finest in the country. The chapel is also (in the niches of the triforium) rich in statuary, choir stall carvings, and other ornaments.

The Country

To say that the English countryside is particularly attractive is a truism. We know that it is entirely different from what we are accustomed to seeing in America, but it is not under any better cultivation than the best-kept land on the Continent, where trees, shrubs, fields, meadows, and hillsides have been tended, pruned, and reshaped for centuries. In other words, in Europe, what we refer to as "landscape architecture" has been consistently and purposefully carried out through the ages, creating art out of nature. In England, paradoxically, nature follows art— art, as it were, bending, amending, and reforming nature's propensities for making "pictures." But these pictures are no longer ubiquitous. And as for the quaint thatched, half-timbered cottages so familiar from the paintings of George Morland, these are few and very far between. In short, much of the countryside is being rapidly bedecked with what is referred to as "low-cost, middle-income" housing projects, dismal, mass-produced, deprived of even modest nicety, at least this is so along principal roads.

CANTERBURY: *Christ-Church Cathedral.* Of all the cathedrals in England, this one combines all the superlatives: It is the grandest, noblest, the most picturesque and renowned; it is also the most closely associated with the history of the country. Since the end of the 6th century, Canterbury has been the seat of the Primate

Canterbury Cathedral

Becket Shrine (Canterbury Cathedral)

Choir (Canterbury Cathedral)

Christ Church Gate (Canterbury)

of England. The early church was destroyed by fire and the present structure was begun at the end of the 11th century. The subsequent phases of building have gone through many vicissitudes, finally combining Romanesque with Gothic features. In the early stage, stones for the building were shipped from Normandy, and the chief architect was French, Master William of Sens, who is responsible for some of the French designs of the edifice. After the murder of Thomas à Becket, Archbishop of Canterbury, by Henry II in 1170, the cathedral became the most famous pilgrimage center in the country. Becket's chapel, or "Becket's Crown," a circular structure added behind the choir by William the Englishman, the successor to Sens, is one of the purest examples of the Early Pointed style. Like the ambulatory, it also has remnants of the finest stained glass of the 13th and 14th centuries, said to have come from France.

Late in the 14th century, the nave and transept were rebuilt on the Romanesque foundation, and the central tower, called the Angel Steeple, was finished a century later. Of the square, massive, typically English towers, the one in Canterbury is considered the most perfect. Internally it forms a lantern over the crossing, and the multiplicity of lierne ribs in the fan vaulting creates an incredibly complex design.

The choir screen, the first important work of its kind, was added at the same time. Comprised of six portrait statues of English kings, each about seven feet high, it shows greater artistry than any other sculpture hitherto done in England, though not of the quality found in the great contemporary cathedrals in France.

There are some particularly beautiful tombs in the cathedral—the one of the Earl of Lancaster (late 13th century), the Black Prince (14th century), Henry IV and his wife, Joan of Navarre —and many other Late Gothic monuments. The unusual features of the church are its ascending levels, with the main altar on the top level. Also of great interest is the large chapter house built in the 11th century; its present appearance dates from the 14th century, when it was roofed with a vast barrel vault, superbly carved in Irish bog oak.

The entire complex of the cathedral—the unusually long nave; its two transepts (the second, a rudimentary one); the two rectangular chapels, each of them set slightly at an angle; the rectangular treasury and the great cloister on the north side; the chapter house and library room set within the "close" of the monastery and surrounded by trees and shrubs—offers an unforgettable picture. It is quite in contrast to the churches on the Continent, which, with some exceptions, are hugged, as it were, on all sides by a dense mass of small dwellings.

WINDSOR. This largest and oldest inhabited fortress, encircled by a castellated, turreted wall, has been the residence of English kings for eight centuries. William the Conqueror began *Windsor Castle* at the end of the 11th century, and its Great Round Tower, made of granite, was erected during the 12th century. Since then the large enclosed area received many additions, ranging from Early Gothic to 18th- and 19th-century versions of neo-Gothic style, and inevitably, extensive restorations were made in recent times. The royal apartments are located in the newest part. The most interesting structure on the compound is the *St. George Chapel;* it is built in finest Perpendicular style with an extravagantly intricate fan vaulting and has side chapels filled with fine old tombs—as well, alas, as some of the modern cemetery variety. Particularly beautiful are the Gothic choir stalls carved in black oak.

The art collection housed in the royal apartments contains works of the highest quality, among them paintings by Holbein, Van Dyck, Memling. But the most famous is the Windsor collection of drawings; assembled here is a unique group of graphic works by Leonardo, Holbein, and Raphael.

HAMPTON COURT. Cardinal Wolsey started this modestly planned building in red brick at the beginning of the 16th century in Tudor style. It was then quickly confiscated by Henry VIII, who considerably enlarged and enriched the original structure. The ornamented chimneys give the building its principle decorative touch, but compared to French chimney design (just think of the Château de Chambord) these, indeed, are quite modest. The in-

Windsor Castle   Hampton Court

terior of the state apartments is impressive, especially the Great Hall with its open-timbered ceiling and ingenious roof trusses. In the orangerie nine cartoons (designs) by Mantegna are displayed; these were woven in Flanders into tapestries now hanging in the King's Gallery. The palace garden was built by Sir Christopher Wren for William and Mary, and their Italian Classic appearance stands in strong contrast with the Tudor complex. Although incongruous styles can frequently harmonize when combined, this is not the case in the Wren addition.

OXFORD. There is always something isolated, even parochial, in the general aspect of university towns, and this condition impresses us at once when in Oxford. Its first fully instituted college, *Merton,* was founded in 1264, and *New College,* in 1379. The former has the oldest quadrangle court (common to monasteries, almshouses, and manors); called the **Mob Quod,** and its chapel tower, built in the middle of the 15th century, is the noblest in the city. New College also has a beautiful chapel (much restored during the 19th century), and gardens bordered by the old city

Magdalen College, Oxford

Christ Church Cathedral, Oxford

Divinity School, Oxford

Christ Church, Oxford

wall from Saxon (pre-Norman) times. The chapel has two interesting features, the sculptured altar, reaching to the wooden roof, and the roof itself. The latter is of typically English construction in which master craftsmen of the time excelled. They invented and developed a variety of forms of roof trusses, employing in the process a highly decorative treatment of the surfaces between the trusses as well as those of moldings and arcading.

The finest structures, perhaps are *Magdalen College* (its interior is a 19th-century restoration), and *Magdalen Tower*, standing at the eastern end of Oxford's main street. Another interesting building is **Christ Church** (the cathedral). Founded by Cardinal Wolsey in 1525, it is in Tudor style with fan vaulting in the choir and an open-timbered ceiling in the Church Hall. Exquisite also is the fan vaulting in the *Divinity School*, the chapel of the *All Souls College*, and the *Bodleian Library*, founded in 1602 and one of the greatest repositories of manuscripts in the world. These are but a few of the ancient buildings, and all have a typically English Gothic look; it is not a cheerful one, for it should be noted that secular buildings in this style appear rather gloomy.

In Oxford, too, is the oldest public art collection, the **Ashmolean Museum.** I have often stressed the importance of a proper presentation of works of art, and here, these are superbly displayed, the elegant surroundings are just the kind to give the paintings and statuary their right foil. The Ashmolean possesses a great variety of objects: Roman statuary and pottery, finds from Asia Minor, Egypt, Crete (collected by Sir Evans, the discoverer of the Palace of Knossos), old master's paintings and drawings, and small bronzes. Incidentally, why do the museum people always give the bronze statuettes a high wax polish? There seems to be no awareness among them that the natural patina is the soul of ancient bronze. The same mistake is sometimes made in the restoration of ancient paintings and statuary. Cer-

Screen Altar, New College   Paradise. Piero di Cosimo (Ashmolean Museum)

tainly not all broken noses and missing limbs enhance ancient objects, and not all paintings are improved when made to look brand-new. There is, for example, a Uccello in the museum. I saw it some years before, covered with the patina of age, and more recently again, minus the patina. There can be no question about it: This Uccello should never have been scrubbed clean. His *Hunting Scene* has lost almost all of its former charm.

GLOUCESTER. An important building in the history of English architecture, ***Gloucester Cathedral*** was founded in the 7th century as a nunnery and reconstructed in Norman-Romanesque style in the 11th century. In the 14th century the building assumed a fully realized Late Gothic appearance, although much of its Romanesque design remains in evidence. Many new and original features bear witness to the genius of the builders, whose creation was to influence Gothic edifices in England for centuries. The east wall of the choir, for example, which replaced the Romanesque wall, was built of glass, 72 feet high and 38 feet wide. Here, as well as in the Lady chapel with its exquisite lierne vault (east of the choir), the essence of Perpendicular style was realized

Gloucester Cathedral   Fan Vaulting, Cloisters   The East Window

for the first time. Other remarkable features are the entrance to the northern wing, remodeled in Gothic style and with pendent fans reminiscent of Moorish ceilings; the buttress carried through the wall of the south side; the lierne vault of the presbytery with its sculptured roof bosses; the tomb of Edward II and its complex tiered canopy studded with pinnacles; and finally, the cloister's extraordinary fan vaulting, constructed in the middle of the 14th century and later, generally adopted in England until well into the 17th century.

BATH. One of the few cities planned entirely in Georgian style as a luxury resort, the first rule of architectural probity impresses itself on us here: unity and coherence of well-proportioned components. But at the same time, it must be said that the architecture is deficient in creativity. Robert Adam (also well known as a furniture designer) and John Wood, a follower of Jones' and Wren's doctrines, are responsible for its chief edifices: the *Royal Crescent* ("crescent" refers to semicircular buildings); *Putteney Bridge,* flanked by shops à la Ponte Vecchio (although it has little resemblance to its prototype); *Queen Square* and the *Circus* (in England "circus" refers to a circle from which streets radiate); and the neo-Classic *Assembly Rooms,* completely burned out by incendiary bombs in 1942, but now restored.

Bath's history as a health resort began in Roman times, and many of its ancient installations are preserved adjacent to the pump room, which supplies radioactive water from the hot springs to the baths and the fountains. Of all the Roman remains in England, these are the most complete.

Bath Abbey, the last great church to be built in Late Per-

The Roman Baths

The Abbey (Bath)

pendicular style, was begun in 1499 on the ruins of a Norman structure. From the north and from the south, it is nearly all window which gives it the appearance of a lantern. In fact, it is referred to as the "lantern church." There is superb fan vaulting, similar to that in the Henry VIII chapel in Westminster in the north aisle, and rows of pendents with painted heraldic shields along the central line of the aisle vaults. One of the charming decorations on the face of the west turrets is stone ladders, reaching to their top, with angels climbing serenely up and down. Unfortunately, these are but recent copies; the original figures have deteriorated beyond recognition. A particularly elegant room is Prior Bird's chantry. With its crested transom, thickly foliated spandrels, and delicate tracery, it is an outstanding example of 16th-century Gothic art.

WELLS: *St. Andrew's Cathedral.* Personal preferences are not always valued judgments; even when they are, they can be many-faceted. The author's approach to the visual is that of a painter; hence it will not necessarily conform to the orthodoxies of an architect. It will seek out the picturesque quality and originality of an object, always remembering that the picturesque may be superficial and that mere originality may possess little or no esthetic value. In the *Cathedral of Wells*, the picturesque and original elements are present in the highest degree.

The bishopric was founded in Wells in 909; in 1191 the church was begun, and 50 years later its salient features were established, although work actually continued into the 15th century. Its ground plan, viewed from the east, contains the Lady chapel, the retrochoir (the part behind the choir), the chapter house to the north, and the Chain Gate and double row of small houses, known as the Vicar's Close, behind it. To the south, in line with the façade and extending 180 feet, stands the enormous cloister; next to it is the bishop's palace.

The screen facade with its massive square towers, of unique design, is more richly adorned with fine Gothic statuary than any other church in England; some 350 figures are set in niches in a constantly recurring rhythm. The builders of the cathedral were fortunate in being able to secure expert stonemasons, for the sculptured details in this edifice are numerous and particularly well carved, though badly weathered. Interesting are the capitals in its interior, the corbels with their humorous heads, the episodic grotesques of the misericords (hinged seats), and the tombs. Especially remarkable is the tomb of Bishop Beckington; for he appears as a corpse, decaying in shrouds beneath the effigy on the upper platform, where he lies in pomp. Though not infrequent in English tombs, such gruesome reresentations originally came

Wells Cathedral

Cathedral Interior

Toothache, South Transept Capital

from France. A large choir screen with statues of kings (on the order of that in Canterbury) which once graced the interior, has wholly vanished; nonetheless the cathedral is one of the very few in England to escape wholesale looting and devastation, especially during the time of Henry VIII and the Commonwealth (1649–1653).

The nave with its heavy, 24-shaft piers and inverted buttress arches of the crossing, which form a figure eight in a bold, imperious sweep, stands alone in the entire history of church building. Whoever conceived this design must have been gifted with the keenest imagination—a man of genius, and I am not given to using this epithet lightly. The same can be said of the builder of the chapter house. In its polygonal hall stands a "palm tree" pier supporting the main vault and unfolding one of the most beautiful arrays of ribs. The vault ribs radiate from the central column to the sides and angles of the polygon, forming a heavenly umbrella; the same construction can be seen in the Lady chapel, where the multiple palm vaulting was applied to a more complex space with effects of great elegance and finesse. This type of vaulting, in which architectural forms almost assume the function of organic growth, was first introduced in this cathedral.

SALISBURY: *St. Mary's Cathedral.* Like the one in Wells, it is a typically English structure, and the "typical" expresses itself in the length and narrowness of the nave, its moderate height (the English did not build for height), a square east termination (a French apse is always round), and the presence of two transepts. Flying buttresses, in general use in France at the beginning of the 13th century, were not greatly favored in England. Erected between 1220 and 1258, *Salisbury Cathedral* is all in Early Pointed style, but much restoration went into its interior and much damage was done, first during Cromwell's Protectorate and later when a "purist" restorer of the 18th century had many of the Romanesque and Gothic tomb effigies and their splendid canopies destroyed.

The outstanding features of this edifice are the 404-foot tower, built only for luxury and beauty (it has no bells), and the nave. The side aisles, the clustered piers, and the piers of the side arches are surrounded by pipe-like shafts of black marble; all of these elements are organized into an exquisite ensemble. The greatest attraction of the nave is the bridge buttressing of the crossing— on the order of those in Wells, with one cardinal difference: Here the stress is on the decorative and ornate; in Wells it is all structure and the emphasis is on dynamic design. Charming also are the interiors of the Lady chapel and of the octagonal chapter house, with its single slender palm tree pillar supporting the fan vault. The west façade, built as a screen, is picturesque, and its most interesting feature, formed on its fourth course, is a quatre-

Salisbury Cathedral

The Crossing

foil frieze that continues around the corners of the south and north towers. Adjoining the church to the south is the enormous cloister. Much interest is added to the entire complex by the landscaping of the grounds and the houses around the close, some of which date back to the 14th century.

WINCHESTER: *Cathedral of the Holy Trinity.* Here Egbert was crowned the first King of England in 827, and Edward the Confessor in 1043. The building of **The Cathedral,** however, was started at the end of the 11th century and was continued over a period of more than 300 years. Today the original Romanesque part remains only in the transept and the crypt with its two aisles. The utter austerity of the old structures, unadorned as they are but supremely well composed, stands in stark contrast to the portions in Decorated style. The sculptured arcade at the back of the choir entrance with its complex ogival lines of the arches, the gables with their elaborate crockets and finials, and the nave, whose Norman shell was transformed in the new Perpendicular style. These contrasts well exemplify the late acceptance of the new style, and with it the accent on verticality in interior design, here expressed in the multiple vertical lines of the window with its four-centered Tudor arch. Because of the adoption of shallow fan vaulting, the arch had to fit under the depressed apex of the vault, thus providing a logical basis for this late Gothic development. In all, the interior design—the arcading, the triforium, and vaulting all highly decorated, molded pier arches, colored columns clustered around the core of the main pillars, and enormous east window—gives these English churches an atmosphere quite different from the French. Of the tombs, that of Cardinal Beaufort is crowned by a forest of niches and pinnacles—ornamental redundancies that never fail to enchant our senses.

Thus we have completed our circuit of the most important

Winchester Cathedral

Vaults, Winchester Cathedral

ecclesiastic edifices nearest London. Other great cathedrals—among them those in Ely, Peterborough, Norwich, Lincoln, York, Durham—are with the exception of the first two more distant. All are Norman structures that have in the course of time received Gothic additions and without exception are magnificent in the fullest meaning of the word.

IRELAND

Because of its proximity to England, Ireland deserves mention. However, if traveling mainly in quest of art, it is pointless to visit the island. Dublin, the capital, very much resembles London, minus the metropolitan aspect but because it is so small the Georgian architecture is more apparent and this softens the rather dreary picture of the provincial city. Of the ancient relics, two Gothic churches, *St. Patrick's* and *Christ Church*, retain their basic structure—Pointed English in its cruder form—but a thorough 19th-century restoration has almost made a travesty of their original appearance.

There are two public collections in the city, the **National Gallery** and the **National Museum.** The first contains paintings of most of the European schools from the 15th to the 20th century. Although there are a few fine examples amid the large accumulation of mediocre works, the traveler who has visited London or the Continent will hardly be impressed by the collection. The same can be said of the National Museum, which contains archeological finds and miscellany in the categories of utilitarian and decorative art.

As for the Irish countryside (the southern part of the island, easily accessible from Shannon or Dublin), it is as "green" and "lush" as the travel pamphlets say it is, but without exceptional allure. The lowlands and hilly country are of the common variety; the heather-covered highlands and the lake region are very "scenic," but the tasteless architecture everywhere is quite depressing. Indeed, small dwellings as well as larger structures are devoid of charm. The country churches, no matter how ancient, are in bogus Gothic style and their interiors are often equipped with atrocious plaster of Paris casts. The monasteries are in ruins, as are most of the castles. Some of the latter, however, like the famous *Blarney Castle,* overgrown with lush vegetation, are highly picturesque. On rare occasions one does find a few of the vaunted, thatched-roof, half-timbered cottages (the most interesting are in the village of Adare, in the vicinity of Cork), but quaint as they are, one could hardly consider them of esthetic significance.

Section 3 / The Low Countries

INTRODUCTION TO THE ART OF BELGIUM AND HOLLAND

First, it should be said that the reference to "Flanders" whenever the art of present-day Belgium is discussed is convenient, but not correct. It would be more accurate to refer to the Southern Netherlands (present-day Belgium) and the Northern Netherlands (present-day Holland), rather than to Flanders. But in the 15th century there was not much distinction made between these two countries. Not until the 16th century and the wars of liberation from Spanish domination did a clear division take place; when Holland became Protestant and Belgium remained Catholic. At that time iconoclasm in Holland did away with most of the ecclesiastic art of the preceding century that filled the churches and monasteries.

During the 15th century it was Bruges that first led the art of the North, but its men of genius—Jan van Eyck, Master of the Flémalle, Rogier van der Weyden and Petrus Christus, came from Germanic and North Netherland areas. Later it was Antwerp, the most prosperous city in Europe, that developed the greatest export of paintings, surpassing even that of Florence. Antwerp attracted painters from all over the Netherlands, and to try to distinguish which is Dutch and which Flemish would be quite futile.

I qualified the four painters above as geniuses, but the list can be vastly expanded with artists all living before the middle of the 16th century: Hans Memling, Hugo van der Goes, Hieronymus Bosch, Geertgen tot Sint Jans, Gerard David, Quentin Massys, Joachim Patinir, Lucas van Leyden, and Pieter Brueghel. This is only a partial listing. The names of many of the great painters of this era are not known and they are referred to as "Master of the Life of Mary," or "Master" of this or that altar, and so on.

51

Yet it becomes apparent that at no time, and in no other country, did so many great artists appear within so few years. At this juncture the forces that so gloriously sustained and furthered Gothic configurations seem to have worked themselves out. Painters looked increasingly to Italy for inspiration, which resulted in the adoption of an alien mannerism. Scorel, Heemskerck, Peter Aertsen, were the representatives of the new direction. Their models, the simple peasants, began to affect elegant and heroic attitudes—in short, a fatuous estheticism crept into the work of the painters, vitiating whatever delights their superb craftsmanship could offer. But contemporary with these lived a genius of the highest order, a man outstanding in the history of art—Pieter Brueghel. He died in 1569; eight years later Rubens was born and then Van Dyke, his pupil, and a host of minor artists.

What is there in Flemish art that is so different from that of the Italians? It is the simplicity and piety of the northern spirit; if we may say so, the "non-arty" approach of these masters makes us feel that the idiomatic in nature appears in their work with clearer resonance.

Now we have reached the 17th century, and it is all Holland's. After 200 years of great art, one might expect the creative force to abate, but Holland, having entered its most prosperous period after shaking off the Spanish yoke, was still to produce artists of great magnitude: Rembrandt, Frans Hals, Vermeer. These are the stellar names, but next in line appeared Gerard Dou, Pieter de Hooch, Gerard Terborch, Ruisdael, Hobbema. I have mentioned just a few of the more popular painters; to list them all would fill many pages. At a time when pompous hack work was the currency of the day in Italy, in the north literally countless Kleine Meesters (little masters) produced a plenitude of genre paintings of such excellence—landscapes, cityscapes, interiors, still lifes, seascapes—as will probably never appear again. Conscientious craftsmanship, mastery of pictorial means wedded to refined taste produced gems by unassuming, almost self-effacing painters whose social status and living standards were hardly higher than that of a common laborer. With the passing of the 18th century the era of good genre painting came to a close.

BELGIUM

In some countries our attention will be centered on churches and other edifices and on ecclesiastic sculpture, but in Belgium as well as in Holland, our main interest will be the paintings. Not that the cathedrals in these countries are of no consequence: They are Gothic, and the Gothic master builders, as I have frequently stated, have never gone wrong. Moreover, in Belgium they were conceived after French examples and retain some of their sculptural décor, although it is not as rich as that found in Latin countries. In Holland the influence was German, which was not to the best advantage of the architecture. Furthermore, the interiors are whitewashed—the Reformation eliminated all images that once graced the churches and they now appear barren and cold. However, the most noteworthy edifices in the Low Countries are the town halls and the guild halls; their unique style is found only in the north of Europe.

It is remarkable to what degree much of the Belgian countryside remained unchanged through the ages. In the direction of Bruges, the landscape appears very much like that depicted in early Flemish paintings; it is flat and undramatic yet it has great charm. This is no longer true in regions (near Antwerp, for example) where industrial installations have nearly destroyed the beauty of the land. Nor is most of the Dutch landscape any longer that of Ruisdael, Hobbema, or Van der Neer.

Brussels

Strangely, its capital does not possess the greatest paintings in the country, but in spite of its nondescript character it has charm and is altogether hospitable.

In the **Museum of Ancient Art** (Musée d'art ancien), run-of-the-mill Flemish art prevails; yet this art, it must be quickly added, stands on a high artistic level. Although contemporary with Italian Early Renaissance, it remained Gothic in stylistic allegiance and even in its pedestrian manifestations is not without merit. This was not the opinion of Italian connoisseurs of the Renaissance, who condemned the northern style as "barbaric." The mistake of looking upon any alien or unfashionable style as inferior has been made perpetually by the arbiters of every era. Even if we consider only the poetry and imagination with which northern painters handled enormously complex artistic problems, these alone should enable us to place their work in its proper place in the value scale. Moreover, for the beauty of its technique, the jewel-like quality of Flemish 15th-century painting remains unmatched.

Among the foremost works in the Museum are the following: Gerard David's *Adoration of the Magi;* Jan Gossaert's (known as Mabuse) *Portrait of the Donors;* Pieter Brueghel's *Landscape with*

Portrait of Guillaume Moreel.
Hans Memling

Veneration of the Magi. Gerard David

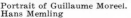

the Fall of Icarus and *Census in Bethlehem.* These are the outstanding examples, but noteworthy minor works are plentiful in
this collection.

The **Cathedral St. Michele** (which is also known as St. Gudule),
built in Gothic style during the 13th to 16th centuries, has a clean,
austere look and shows a strong French influence. As in all northern churches, its interior is quite light, but 'it does not filter
through the original stained glass windows; these have all been
replaced. Only a few Gothic statues are in evidence, but on each
of the columns, Baroque figures stand on ornate consoles, and they
seem to deflect the column's upward thrust, giving them a strange
sideways movement. The **Church du Sablon** is another Gothic
edifice of interest.

The pride of Brussels is its **Grande Place,** dominated by the

Portrait of the Donors.
Jan Gossaert

Redemption of St. Anthony. Bosch

The Town Hall (Brussels)

St. Michael's Cathedral, St. Gudule

The Pulpit, St. Michael's Cathedral

15th-century *Town Hall* and surrounded by sumptuously decorated guild houses and dwellings of the merchants. The façades are of northern Baroque design (although some structures are older), and all of them possess the characteristic gabled dormers and rows of mullioned, horizontally aligned windows, forming a fenestration suggestive of keys on a gigantic piano. At night, under illumination, the Grande Place is a fairytale sight—this is no modern shopping center! However, as a composition, as a balanced grouping of masses arranged to form a harmonious whole, it does not evidence ultimate perfection.

Ghent

In the 14th century the old city was at the very height of its prosperity and power. This power was vested in the citizenry—hence the splendor of the civic edifices: the *Town Hall* (part-

St. Bavon Cathedral   Adoration of the Lamb. Van Eyck

Gothic, part-Renaissance) ; *The Belfry,* erected at the beginning
of the 14th century; the various guild halls and the houses of merchants and traders—all are characterized by stepped gables, high
dormers, and graceful volutes flanking each diminishing stage of
their design. The exquisitely ornamented, elegant façades organized along horizontal divisions of the stories (the so-called stringcourses) and the verticals of the mullioned windows lend distinction to the appearance of street architecture.

Because it houses Van Eyck's famous *Adoration of the Lamb,*
the *St. Bavon Cathedral* is the most famous place in Ghent. The
tryptich, which serves as the decoration of a chapel at the right
of the ambulatory, is—like all highly prized museum possessions—

Adoration of the Lamb. Van Eyck (Detail)   Adoration of the Lamb. Van Eyck
                                              (Detail)

The Castle of the Count

Study. Jacob Jordaens

roped off, and thus does not allow for the close examination that should be given to works of that particular school in order to savor the wizardry of its craftsmanship. When facing the central panel, we must shake off the tyranny of the experts and admit that the painting shows a deficiency in composition. The absolute symmetry of design robs it of interest; the repetitious proportions (arrangement of the masses in the foreground, middle, and background) do not offer variety to the eye. In fact, it is difficult to associate this work of large dimension with the genius of the Van Eycks, which to all intents and purposes expresses itself best in the miniaturistic. (Incidentally, the left wing of the tryptich is a modern replica.) But there are also large paintings like the *Adoration* in the Groeninge Museum in Bruges, which miraculously succeed in creating miniature on a monumental scale.

As for the cathedral, its construction lasted from the 13th to the 16th century. The exterior is unimaginative, and its plain appearance contrasts strongly with the grace and elegance of the

St. Jerome. Hieronymus Bosch

Flemish School, 15th Century

17th- and 18th-century interior, in which black and white marble wainscoting has been used effectively. Many of the side chapels also deserve closer attention.

Other edifices on our tour are the *Castle of the Count*, a ruined, forbiddingly gloomy medieval fortress, not worthy of inspection; *St. Michael's Church*, which is Late Gothic and has fine statuary and glass windows; and of course, the noble guild halls one meets on one's way.

Flemish paintings are displayed in the **Fine Arts Museum** (Museum voor Schone Kunsten). A few masters are represented with excellent examples—Hieronymus Bosch, Anthony van Dyck, Lucas Cranach, and, among the minor luminaries, Nicholas Maes, Thomas de Keyser. It is interesting to find here a brilliant small head study by Jordaens which makes us realize how dismally even a great talent can fail when it becomes the victim of poor taste, as did Jordaens when he ventured to depict ambitious narratives à la Rubens. Many of the examples by unknown 16th-century painters also serve to demonstrate that a good prevailing style can help "simple craftsmen" in the creation of superb works of art.

Bruges

Once in a while commonly held acceptances have validity— Bruges is indeed the most enchanting town in northern Europe. It is studded with gems as is no other place of its size and has the rare distinction of being entirely free of eyesores. Unity and consonance of all parts prevails here, and one's equilibrium is not jolted by the ugly incongruities encountered nowadays in almost every city. The tiny dwellings as well as the pretentious merchant houses burdened with florid Flemish Baroque design have a probity and grace about them that forever enchants us.

Two splendid collections should be visited in Bruges. One is the **Memling Museum,** which occupies a 13th-century room of the St.

The Mystic Marriage of
St. Catherine. Memling

Madonna with the
Apple. Memling

Van Nieuvenhoven.
Memling

Veneration of the Child. Van Eyck   Baptism. Gerard David

John Hospital and where several great pictures by that master
can be seen as well as lesser known 15th-century work and Gothic
statuary. The other is the **Groeninge Museum,** and small as it is,
it possesses some priceless paintings. Nowhere else is the work
of Jan van Eyck and Gerard David better represented, with
examples of superior quality. Van Eyck's *Adoration* is in point
of execution and detail a painting beyond compare; here the
miniaturistic and the monumental are combined in a manner that
defies description. There are other excellent Flemish works, and
a sprinkling of Italian, which, as is usual in Flemish museums,
do not cut a wide swath.

The most conspicuous edifice is **The Belfry,** an image of medieval severity; it was begun in the 13th century, finished in the
15th, and restored in the 17th. For those interested in statistics,
its carillon has 47 bells and weighs 27 tons. The church of **Notre
Dame** boasts of a great rarity—an early work by Michelangelo,
the *Madonna and Child.* It is a fine Renaissance work, but by no

The Belfry   An Altar, Church of Notre Dame   The Cathedral (Bruges)
(Bruges)

Virgin and Child.   Tomb of Mary of Burgundy. P. de Beckere
Michelangelo

means does it reveal Michelangelo's genius. It could be argued
that the statue of Mary, wrought in gilded brass in the *Mausoleum
of Mary of Burgundy,* and of *Charles the Bold,* are more impressive, although the name of the sculptor is barely remembered. ***The
Cathedral*** (begun in the 10th century) is Romanesque-Gothic and
of massive, simple contours. The many changes and restorations
do not make it interesting, but the black and gold organ, with the
black and white marble portal and the gilded bronze door (17th
century) beneath it, together form a beautiful ensemble.

The row of buildings on the *Burg Place* is most remarkable.
From left to right, they are the *Court of Justice* (16th century);
the ***Old Recorder's House*** in an elegant Flemish Baroque (18th
century); and the ***Town Hall,*** a Gothic building finished in the
15th century. The latter is perhaps the finest of all the public
edifices in the Low Countries. Its façade forms a lace curtain of
ogive windows with rich traceries divided by a single mullion
into two narrow, long rectangles, and between them on corbels
under spiral canopies are figures of saints. (At this writing
most of them have been taken down for repairs.) A particularly
beautiful feature of the building is its proud roof flanked by six
slender turrets and elaborately designed chimneys. Next to this
building is the ***Basilica of the Holy Blood.*** The Romanesque crypt

Old Recorder's House, Town Hall, and
Basilica of the Holy Blood (Bruges)

is 12th-century, and its construction is like that of a bomb shelter. Why did medieval man have to give even his chapels six-foot-thick stone walls? Its interior is dungeon-like and the statuary is of a much later date.

Antwerp

During the 15th century the city was the foremost shipping and commercial metropolis in Europe, and as an art center only Florence could challenge its pre-eminence. When Dürer visited it in 1521, he marveled at the prosperity of its artists. No wonder, for besides the flourishing domestic market, the export of paintings from Flanders covered all of Europe. At that time, according to contemporary statistics, more painters than butchers were registered with the local guild. Some 60 years later, however, after the war with Spain and the siege of Antwerp by Alexander of Parma (in 1585), its population was reduced from 125,000 to 55,000. Gradually the silting of the river Scheldt cut off its access to the sea and Antwerp's fortunes faded away. A bustling, prosperous industrial metropolis today—and correspondingly unsightly—it has few relics left.

The **Royal Museum of Fine Arts** is the foremost in all of Belgium. Here one finds paintings by masters whose names are hardly familiar to the layman, designated merely as "Antwerp Master" or "Flemish Master," as well as those well-known: Herri met de Bles, Lucas van Leyden, Gerard David, Quentin Massys, Dirk Bouts, also Hans Memling, Pieter Brueghel, Rubens, Van Dyck, Lucas Cranach, Jean Fouquet—all represented by major works.

Mayer van den Bergh Museum is a former patrician residence which has been donated to the city. It contains an important collection of Late Gothic statuary (much of it in the so-called "hard style" characterized by angular folds of the drapery). The

Angels Playing Musical Instruments.
Memling

The Annunciation.
Simone Martini

Annunciation.
Rogier van der
Weyden

Detail. Rubens   Detail. Quentin Massys

Flemish paintings are not particularly distinguished except for Pieter Brueghel's *The Dulle Griet,* reminiscent of Bosch. But the house itself, although much reconstructed, possesses enough antiquities to be of interest.

The **Rubens House** is also not quite authentic, but it should be visited if only to experience the surroundings of a man of wealth and position in 17th-century Antwerp. That the effects found in the mansion are not necessarily of his inventory should not disturb us. And even if we cannot appreciate the rather heavy-handed Baroque ornateness of the architecture and the massive Flemish furnishings, it has, perhaps because of this emphatic solidity, a strange appeal.

The Studio, Rubens House

View of Antwerp with Cathedral

Cathedral, Elevation of
the Cross. Rubens

Cathedral, Assumption of the Virgin. Rubens

The *Cathedral*, built in the 14th century (its west façade is of
the 15th and 16th centuries, in florid Gothic style), is the biggest
church in Flanders, and its interior is formed by a seven-aisled
nave. But its clerestory windows admit too much light, and the
lack of detail makes it somewhat sober. Remarkable is its graceful
tower; the spire rising over 400 feet is the tallest in the country.
There are two famous paintings by Rubens in the church, one in
the left transept and the other on the main altar, and we can't
help but feel that their florid and sumptuously carnal style does
not go well with the spirit of the New Testament.

I mentioned the cheerless picture of modern Antwerp. But there
is a bit of the old town left, too, and how could its aspect be
anything else but interesting? Besides the few ancient relics here
and there, the solid compound of the *Grote Markt* (the great
marketplace) with its ever-present high dormers and fanciful
stepped gables is the city's greatest attraction.

HOLLAND

The countryside is not the same as that in the pictures of
the 17th-century landscape painters—at least not along the
main route Amsterdam-Haarlem-The Hague-Rotterdam. Where
thatched dwellings and windmills on wide open spaces once stood,
ugly communal houses now appear in profusion. The wide-open
spaces—how much allurement there can be even in the flattest of
flatlands, where the eye searches out with utmost cupidity the
smallest detail and savors it voraciously.

In Holland one need not search out either ecclesiastic or secular
edifices, for with few exceptions they are unrewarding. This is
the land of painters—and very important ones. Because of the
short distances, Haarlem and The Hague can be leisurely visited
in one day.

Amsterdam

As every traveler will have experienced, some cities invite us to linger, some make us feel like moving on after having accomplished what we set out to do. After a visit (or several visits) to the Rijksmuseum there is little to deter us from our desire to leave Amsterdam.

View of the City (Amsterdam)

The *Rijksmuseum,* I was about to mention the trite phrase: is "studded with gems." But the same observation would have to be repeated with every museum in Holland, and the Rijksmuseum is the greatest gem repository of them all. Now before inspecting the paintings, let us walk through the 12 rooms of Romanesque and Gothic sculptures reaching to the 17th century. With endless pleasure we realize that 17th-century sculptors did not have the faintest concern about being considered retrograde: for Gothic style had gone out of fashion in the south of Europe two centuries

La Seinte Parentée. Geertgen tot Sint Jans

Maria Magdalena. Jan van Scorel

Winter Scene. Adrian van der Neer

The Jewish Bride. Rembrandt

earlier. When contemplating these works it is obvious that no group of average Renaissance masters (apart from Riemenschneider the Rijksmuseum boasts of no renowned Gothic sculptors) has attained such a uniformly high level of artistry.

On to the paintings, and, of course, to Rembrandt first. How could one best evaluate his (or any painter's) work? Simply, one shall have to examine the work of his circle, his students and followers—that is, those who have adopted the same or similar pictorial conceptions. Was he above such men as Ferdinand Bol, Carel Fabritius, Nicholas Maes (whose best paintings are hung in the museum)? It is obvious that Rembrandt's work is, in every possible respect, superior. Did he produce any "potboilers?" Of course, he did, and not infrequently. Is his most renowned painting, *The Nightwatch*, a "holy cow" too? No, in this instance the general acclaim given to this painting cannot be refuted. In fact, I am tempted to say that there is not one group portrait combining so many figures that could measure up to this work. To arrange a composition made up of commonplace characters in a manner so complex, in a design so varied, and at the same time so formally unified, to endow these formal members of the composition with a chiaroscuro so poetic and mysterious as to transport

The Windmill. Jacob van Ruisdael

The Night Watch. Rembrandt

the whole to the sphere of the transcendental, this, indeed, is a supreme achievement. And when we consider his technique, none of his followers could challenge his authority—Rembrandt's brush-stroke, his treatment of the contours and texture, evidently could not have been emulated by lesser talents. Other great works by this master are the *Jewish Bride,* the *Syndics of the Cloth Hall,* the *Betrayal of Petrus.* Strangely, the Rijksmuseum is endowed with fewer Rembrandts than The Metropolitan Museum in New York. Next we find Geertgen tot Sint Jans, Jan Mostaert, Jan van Scorel, Maarten van Heemskerck, Joos de Momper, Aert van der Neer, Albert Cuyp—names not very familiar to the non-specialist, yet deserving of highest praise. Of course, there is a roomful of Frans Hals' masterly portraits, but the Rubens and Van Dycks are mediocre. Other highlights are Jacob van Ruisdael, Pieter de Hooch, and Jan Vermeer. Here you see Vermeer's popu-lar and much-reproduced *Kitchenmaid,* the *Letter,* and the *Reading Woman,* but if one has not been cowed by official verdicts, he will find Gerard Terborch's paintings hanging near-by, superior.

Dutch paintings have in common a quality of high excellence that makes description of a collection such as that of the Rijks-museum difficult, for one feels obliged to indulge in constant pane-gyrics, a process which is difficult to maintain over a long period. It appears that with few exceptions there are no inferior works of native art in this ensemble, and when we turn our attention to the Italian paintings, we realize with some dismay that these fall to second rank. But then again, the Renaissance is not well represented in the Rijksmuseum.

One may ask why I didn't mention the **Rembrandt House,** the inevitable pilgrimage of every tourist. It is really a chamber of commerce affair and has no apparent connection with its one-time tenant, although it has many of his etchings and incomparable drawings on display. Being enamored of drawings, I must confess that like letters, I can't very well study them under glass and hung on a wall; I prefer to read them sitting at a desk—even though they be in facsimile.

Haarlem

The **Frans Hals Museum** is felicitously housed in an elegant Baroque palace, and its collection of paintings is, of course, won-derful. There occurs a thought one cannot easily dismiss when in Haarlem: Are there good painters living here now? There were far more than a hundred at the time of Frans Hals—little wonder that the competition was fierce—and a great many of them led a life of privation. That Frans Hals was the foremost among

The Cathedral (Haarlem)

them is obvious. He succeeded in rendering the human form and physiognomy with vitality. For sheer virtuosity—the facility of hand and acuteness of observation—this painter's superiority remains unchallenged to this day. That he cannot contest Rembrandt's supremacy as an artist is due to the limitation of his imagination and the sobriety of his vision. As far as portraiture is concerned, his single figure pieces are in a class by themselves. Not so the many group portraits; although impeccable in technique, they are, as a rule, poorly composed. Blame the artistically illiterate patrons and the pressure under which he was compelled to labor! One of his last group portraits, for example, the *Lady Governors of the Almshouse in Haarlem,* painted when he was 80 years old, is a work of great depth and perceptiveness. Yet it suffers from faulty design—observe the four figures strung diagonally across the canvas at almost identical intervals.

There are other noteworthy painters in the museum: Jan Mandyn, very close to Hieronymus Bosch; Gerard David; Maarten van Heemskerck; Cornelis Cornelisz van Haarlem. In writing these names, I realize that some are not even mentioned in books by such outstanding specialists in the field as Max J. Friedlander, and should I continue to enumerate the Kleine Meesters, it would be a long list and no one would remember the names!

The Hague

The *Mauritshuis,* like the former, is a princely palace and can perhaps be looked upon as the finest small museum in Europe. I cannot think of any other collection of its size that is less burdened with irrelevantia; the eye is rewarded at every turn with the fine and the noble, with the great and the greatest—all in surroundings of rare elegance. Here, in two works, Vermeer justifies the distinction his name conveys, and let us not for a

Girl With Blue Turban.
Jan Vermeer

View of Delft. Jan Vermeer

moment believe that it is the physical charm of the portrait of the *Young Girl* that captivates us—it is the physical charm of the painterly rendition. And how has this charm been achieved in his *View of Delft?* I have often tried to look at this painting with an x-ray eye, yet I cannot accurately pinpoint its allure. After all is said, in a great work of art there always will remain a residuum of the unfathomable.

Rembrandt's *Saul and David,* a sublime performance, and *Suzanna Bathing* are here to marvel at, as is his famous *Anatomy of Dr. Tulp,* painted when he was 26 years old. Showing outstanding technical facility for anyone so young—it is a frigid, rhetorical performance. Another masterpiece is Holbein's *Jane Seymour;* and who remembers the name of Bartolomäus Bruyn? His portrait of a *Young Woman* need not fear comparison with that of Holbein. Of course, everybody has heard of Rogier van der Weyden, Lucas Cranach, Pieter de Hooch, Jacob van Ruisdael, and Gerard Terborch—these are all represented by their best

Susanna. Rembrandt

Saul and David. Rembrandt

Jane Seymour. Holbein

Descent from the Cross. Rogier van der Weyden

works, as are the Kleine Meesters, who painted unpretentious little pictures of street and harbor scenes, church interiors, and the trite and unheroic genre! How exquisite is their technique and understanding of the painter's means: composition, lighting, and the rendering of texture. Why couldn't any of the latter-day genre painters measure up to their level of achievement?

Rotterdam

The *Boymans Museum.* By now the reader must be aware that I have hardly mentioned architectural or sculptural monuments. But these are of no surpassing interest in Holland. As for

St. Christopher.
Hieronymus Bosch

Flat Landscape. Philips Koninck

Maria and
Elizabeth.
Master of the
Life of Maria

Sodom and Gomorrah. Joachim Patinir

Saint Christopher. Herri met de Bles

Rotterdam, largely a new city (rebuilt after World War II), I suggest heading straight for the Boymans Museum. It has a number of great paintings, among them Bosch's *St. Christopher* and the *Prodigal Son;* many panels done by Rubens—without the collaboration of assistants; and some exquisite Gothic statuary.

Section 4 / France

INTRODUCTION TO THE ART OF FRANCE

In the public mind, France is considered the leader in the field of pictorial art. However, this leadership existed only during the latter part of the 19th and the beginning of the 20th century. At the time that Gothic style developed in France (around 1150) and gave it a dominant position in church building and sculpture (interesting murals also date from that epoch), and later, during the 13th and 14th centuries, when such major figures as Duccio, Cimabue, and Giotto were active in Italy, pictorial art in France was of little significance. As exceptions we must consider the art of illuminated manuscripts, stained-glass windows, and tapestries, of highest quality.

The first major figures to appear on the scene were Jean Fouquet (1415–1480) and the Master of Moulins, both of whom worked in the Flemish manner many years after the death of Van Eyck. The French Renaissance in the 16th century saw a rather flimsy Italianized Mannerism represented by the School of Fontainebleau under the patronage of Francis I. The leading painters of that period were the Clouets (Jean, his son of the same name, and his grandson François). In the following century the brothers Le Nain (Antoine, Louis and Mathieu) and Georges de la Tour adopted the realistic manner of Caravaggio but with better results. The best-known names of the 17th century are Philippe de Champaigne, and the much-overrated Nicolas Poussin, and Claude Lorrain.

The sculpture of the glorious Romanesque and Gothic periods is, in the opinion of this author, unparalleled in the entire history of Western art (including that of Greece). The Renaissance, however, can boast of no great names except for that of Jean Goujon

71

(16th century), a skillful Mannerist. French Baroque sculpture is characterized by a vapid pomp. This meager chronicle covering some four hundred years shows that none of the painters of France came up to the level of any one of the many great masters of Flanders, Holland, Italy, or Spain.

After the Baroque had run its course and degenerated into a fussy though charming surface decoration, French art sank to a low level; sculpture became bric-à-brac, and painting hardly managed to advance beyond trite illustration. Among a host of mediocrities, a few men of considerable talent, Chardin and Watteau, succeeded in producing masterpieces in a minor key. But to assign a high position in the hierarchy of art to men like Boucher and Fragonard as do text books on art is sheer folly. It can only be explained by the fact that for some strange reason certain reputations have never been dealt with on a critical level. The jolly time of the Rococo! The artifice, debauche, and frivolities—all were swept away by the Revolution and ended with the reign of Louis XVI in 1792. Reaction set in swiftly and with it the Directoire style, a neo-Classic revival, came into being. With Napoleon I, the Empire style was born and neo-Classic bedecked itself with Pompeian and Egyptian doodads, becoming glittery and very formal. The return of the Classic worked well in architecture inasmuch as it confined itself to simple rectilinear forms unencumbered by extraneous decorative trappings. In sculpture, Classic ideas were enfeebled and devitalized by the preoccupation with the pretty and sentimental. In painting, the following leading names appeared: Prud'hon, David, Gros, Ingres. Heroic scenes from history and mythology were the themes of their paintings, and their technical proficiency seemed merely to emphasize their fatuousness. Alas, Raphael's art could not have been recreated in the climate of the First Empire, and only in portraiture did painters (particularly Ingres) manage to reach a high level. This brings us to the threshold of Romanticism and, following it, Impressionism, the gateway to modern art.

Paris

Accounts of this city always sound as if the authors in elaborating had suffered attacks of euphoria—there seems to be an obligation to panegyric whenever the magic word "Paris" enters into discussion. As for myself, I can only repeat the old stock phrase that Paris is one of the "most beautiful" cities in the world. The beauty of a city is expressed in the type and arrangement of its buildings. As in any visual matter, as soon as a number of members congregate to form a whole, we refer to it as "composition."

The qualities that gratify the eye are unity and coherence; these, in turn, result in an over-all harmony. Paris is harmonious withal. It began with the organization of several of the squares during the 16th and 17th centuries. Later, the Tuileries, the Champs Elysées, and the arcaded Rue du Rivoli, were added. The last of the city planners, Baron Georges Eugène Haussmann (19th century), is responsible for the Place de l'Opéra and various boulevards. It was he also who imprudently "cleaned up" the Ile de la Cité of most of its ancient houses.

It is not only the design of the city itself that is so satisfying; the incorporation of the river and its vistas into the general plan is most felicitous. To understand what a river can mean to urban architecture we need only remember the cheerless aspect of Seville or Vienna. Even the Tiber in Rome and the Thames in London do not seem part of the city. In none of the metropolises of Europe did the builders understand how to give their waterways the eye-appeal of the Seine. Here the river seems ever-present; its vistas, open and ever-changing, glorify the city.

When we examine the general architecture of Paris it is far from exalted—but never offensive, as are many buildings elsewhere in Europe of the latter part of the 19th century, which chiefly produced architectural monstrosities. Renaissance and Baroque structures are found to be few and far between. The Napoleonic era brought about the revival of Classic style, referred to as neo-Classic, which is dull but not without a certain dignity. Even the neo-Baroque of the Second Empire did not come off badly. In certain buildings, such as the opera house constructed in 1857, the total effect is quite resplendent in spite of silly exterior decorations. Even the stylistic folly of the *fin de siècle* (*vide* the Métro entrances), so absurd elsewhere in Europe, impresses us as a forgivable caprice in France. For here it is not a particular building or statue that attracts our attention, but rather the total effect. Thus when walking through the gardens of the Tuileries, for example, our sensibilities are deeply gratified by the probity of the general design, and it would hardly occur to us to take seriously the vacuous pseudo-Classic stance of the garden statuary.

Unlike Italy, we do not seek out particular edifices (with but few exceptions, it must be understood), not because of difficult accessibility (the Métro is fast and affords excellent communications), but because Paris is just not the place for the casual tourist to spend half a day locating a church or a palace. Somehow our mental picture of the buildings here remains vague; they just don't register acutely on the retina.

Surprisingly, in this great metropolis our quest for art objectives will be limited to a few places—the Louvre, Musée de Cluny,

Musée de Jeu de Paume, Notre Dame, Sainte Chapelle. One may ask, "How about the Dome des Invalides?" Its exterior is certainly gorgeous French Baroque (and we shall see it on the conducted tour anyway), but who would care to examine its tasteless interior, including Napoleon's tomb? Other famous sights are the Arc de Triomphe at the end of the Champs Elysées, Tour Eiffel, Sacre Coeur—all 19th-century and all strictly "tourist." We could continue to enumerate ancient and not-so-ancient edifices, such as the *Madeleine*, which changed its style, shape, and purpose several times in one century, only to end up as a travesty of a Greek temple. Through the ages political upheavals brought about so much destruction and alteration that many of the great palaces and churches can hardly be looked upon as authentic. The Place Vendôme column, built by Napoleon's order and replacing an earlier monument, can be considered a symbol of these conditions. The figure we see on top of it today was preceded in less than one hundred years by six different effigies!

The **Louvre.** For the art-conscious traveler this museum is the high point of the trip. In variety and number of art objects in its possession it challenges the Vatican. Once a fortified feudal fortress that changed its size and appearance during the course of a few centuries, it was converted by Francis I in 1546 to an Italian-style palace. The complex of edifices known today as the Louvre endured many alterations until the middle of the 19th century, when, during the reign of Napoleon III, Haussmann joined the formerly disconnected structures to form the grand design it possesses today.

The part of the complex that faces east (toward the Rue du Louvre) and turning the corner at the Rue du Rivoli is, if not the oldest, at least the most harmonious architecturally; it dates from the middle of the 17th century. However, for a casual tourist to become involved with the Louvre's architecture or its décor (the best done by the sculptor Jean Goujon) would be foolhardy; to cope with what is to be seen and studied inside will require all the attention we can muster.

The pavilions of the Louvre were occupied only intermittently by the court and its offices. Eventually abandoned by Louis XIV, who moved to Versailles, it remained without royal occupants until the advent of Napoleon I. As for the art collection, it started on a modest scale with Francis I, who developed a love for art and upon whose invitation the aged Leonardo da Vinci came to France for the remainder of his life.

In the 17th century, the *Cabinet du Roi* (the king's picture collection) numbered 200 paintings; under Louis XIV the count was 2,500, and today the catalogue lists over 200,000 items. It may be of interest to recount that Napoleon, in his conquest of Europe, looted an enormous number of works of art. These had to be returned in 1815 after his defeat, but the commission dealing with restitutions did not bother to order the return of paintings then considered of no value; among them were works by Giotto, Gaddi, Cimabue, Gozzoli, Mantegna, to name but a few. Curious are the ways of connoisseurship in art!

The first public exhibition of the pictures in the King's Picture Collection was given in 1679; however, the idea of a museum open to the public was not conceived until Louis XVI. His death on the guillotine prevented carrying out the project. After the Revolution the painter David, then director of the collection, ·arranged the first public showing. These scant data hardly indicate the vicissitudes suffered by this stupendous repository of man's achievements in the realm of art. Suffice it to recall that once, on the Court du Carousel (facing the main entrance), stood a very busy guillotine.

Should one join one of the guided tours to visit the collection? As I shall repeatedly state in this book, enjoyment of a work of art is greatly impaired by the presence of a guide, for as a rule he demands greater attention than the exhibit. Moreover, experience teaches us that when taking stock of our accumulated knowledge after the lectures, we find that very little remains in our memory.

When in the Louvre, it is important to familiarize oneself with the layout so as not to become lost in the maze of corridors, halls, and rooms. Our visit will start at the *Porte Denon*, the main entrance (on the Court du Carousel), leading to the ground floor. Ahead of us to the left and right are Greek and Roman antiquities assembled in 19 halls. Continuing from the entrance to the far left, we find Egyptian and Oriental collections occupying just as many halls (these can be more easily reached from the *Porte Egyptienne* on the Rue du Louvre). To the far right of the entrance are sculptures from the Middle Ages through the 18th century, displayed in 11 halls. There is a direct entrance to this department from *Porte Trémoille* on the Quai des Tuileries (along the Seine).

Back to the Porte Denon and continuing for about 100 feet to the left, we face the *Winged Victory* standing high on the landing of the staircase. Now we ascend the stairs to the first floor. It is here that the main body of paintings from the 13th to the 19th century is assembled. Also on this floor is a vast accumulation of furnishings and decorative art of all descriptions from France, ancient Egypt, the Orient, and Greece. Here man's endless labors, his ingenuity, and quest for beauty find their incarnation. Con-

Winged Victory

trasted with his pitiful perishability these prove so overwhelming, they depress rather than elate us. Such, at least, is my reaction to a vessel of porphyry, shaped and hollowed—by what unknown implement?

On the second floor are 18th-century paintings. Not all is froth and foam that spills off the Rococo: Remember Goya, Guardi, Gainsborough, Tiepolo; and one can enjoy the work of such minor figures as Magnasco and Longhi. Here, too, are the glorifiers of the elegant world—Boucher and Fragonard.

With this map in one's mind, one can plan a sensible visit to the museum according to one's predilections. We shall start by discussing the paintings, then proceed to the sculpture.

The Collection. The finest paintings in the world, one is tempted to assume, are assembled in the Louvre. This is true. But we could, with equal justification, say the same of other European museums, for after having surveyed the art of Europe, as I have done on many occasions, we must arrive at the conclusion that the "finest" paintings have been produced—at certain times—in profusion and great variety.

As a rule, in every museum we begin with the earliest paintings, which invariably are accorded the highest encomium. Before the passing of the 16th century, our enthusiasm starts to abate (except for an occasional resurgence), but when we reach the 19th, our dejection becomes firmly entrenched. (Always remember, Goya is not a 19th-century painter, even though the date of his death is 1828.) In the Louvre, because of its particular shape—there is an immense hall called La Grande Galerie, with other halls and rooms branching off at either end—and because one is not obliged to start at the entrance—Gothic art confronts us first and 19-century art is near the exit—we may as well start in the middle with the *Mona Lisa.*

Is this really the "greatest" picture? It certainly is the most

Le Concert Champêtre. Giorgione

The Avignon Pietà

The Virgin of the Rocks. Da Vinci

La Belle Jardinière. Raphael

The Disciples of Emmaus. Rembrandt

Madonna of the Quarries.
Mantegna

The Lace Maker. Vermeer

Princess d'Este. Pisanello

Self Portrait. Dürer

Joan of Aragon. Raphael

popular, and as far as the portrait genre is concerned, it has never been surpassed—but the same can be said of other contemporary portraits hanging near-by: Raphael's *Joan of Aragon* and *Balthasar Castiglione,* Titian's *Francis I,* and so on.

Let us begin by quoting from an unknown source: "Each generation has to rewrite history." This certainly is applicable to art history. How much havoc has Leonardo's *Mona Lisa* played with connoisseurs of former generations? Berenson, for example, did not like her; he thought her "watchful, sly, secure, self-

Parthenon Frieze Fragment, 5th Century B. C.   Venus de Milo

Metope from Olympia   Angel, 15th Century

Annunciation, 14th Century   St. Magdalen, 15th Century

Romanesque Column

Roman, 3rd Century

Diana, 16th Century

Slaves, Michelangelo

satisfied, and above all supercilious;" the eminent scholar R. Langdon Douglas said of Leonardo's *St. John* (hanging near-by): "This picture represents no holy personage, but some creature of dubious sex, some minister of vice. . . .," but today when beholding works of art we consider it entirely wrong to allow the human representation to intrude upon our judgment; neither title nor subject matter is really of importance in comprehending paintings. Therefore should we be concerned about the meaning of Leonardo's most outstanding work, *St. Anne, Mary and Child,* for example, our esthetic enjoyment would be seriously impaired. Why did I refer to the former, and not to *The Madonna of the Rocks* as Leonardo's "best"? Because the latter has darkened too much, hence its full artistic significance cannot very well be assessed; and also because as a composition the former is more complex, shows greater ingenuity, and posed more difficult problems for the painter. Indeed, the Louvre owns Leonardo's most important works.

In the Grande Galerie (to the left of the center) hangs Giorgione's *Concert Champêtre;* this is another painting of elusive qualities so difficult to define! Along the same route we also find Uccello's large battle scene, Cosimo Tura's *Pietà,* Mantegna's *St. Sebastian.* Next Antonello da Messina, Bellini, Perugino, Botticelli, Fra Filipo Lippi, Daddi, Giotto, and Pisanello are all represented by major works. There is also Raphael's *La Belle Jardinière,* the embodiment of sweetness, charm, and grace. Did he have the license for such sentimentalization? Indeed he had. But just think of how the same subject matter imbued with similar sentiments would have impressed us in a 19th-century version!

And in the Salle des Etats, Paolo Veronese's colossal *Marriage at Cana* simply staggers the imagination when we consider the titanic effort that went into the making of this canvas. Other Veronese paintings in which unsurpassed virtuosity is displayed can be seen here, as well as Titian's late *Entombment* and *Christ Crowned with Thorns.*

In the Salle Van Dyck, Rubens appears with excellent smaller work, however, in the next room his *Marie de Medici* series is Baroque hack work, though highly competent. Van Dyck, always elegant and in the best of taste, has never put his faculties to better use than in his portrait of *King Charles I* of England.

Back in the Grande Galerie we meet Velázquez, El Greco, Caravaggio, and La Nain, looking very much like a close relative of Manet; then Georges de la Tour, the tenebrist who learned from Caravaggio and far surpassed his precursor. Of course, no museum would be complete without Poussin, whose compositions are always faulty and who when at his best (in some of his landscapes) faintly echoes Giorgione's lyricism. In this part of the gallery, there are only a few good paintings, among them Antonio Canaletto's *View of Sta. Maria della Salute,* one of his finest works by virtue of its extraordinarily ingenious composition, or rather, perspective. Inevitably, the 19th century now appears before our weary eyes, with examples of atrocious taste displayed by so many artists whose reputations rank high in art history books.

We now enter the smaller rooms, which are, in part, "studded with gems." First there is the *Pietà of Avignon,* an anonymous work recently attributed—in my opinion without valid reason—to the Portuguese Nuño Gonçalvez. It is a painting of strong emotional impact, a composition worthy of a great master. But it is a 14th-century work, and "could have happened" to even an anonymous "craftsman" at a time when Gothic style shaped the world of artists. Other paintings in the rooms are small in size but of great artistic significance. Foremost is Jan van Eyck's *Rollin Madonna,* which represents the Flemish-Gothic and the Renaissance as well, for it combines sharp-focus vision throughout the entire pictorial space and observance of minutiae regardless of their plastic significance. Every inch of the panel forms a separate unit—in fact, the entire painting is but an assembly of a great many independent parts—but, characteristic of the Renaissance, the principles of linear perspective have been scrupulously observed. The little panel by Mantegna, *Madonna of the Rocks,* belongs to almost the same category, a typically Italian work faintly influenced by the Flemish. Massys, Patinir, Mabuse, Holbein, Bosch, Dürer, Rembrandt, and so many others are also represented here with works on an intimate scale—a relief after the assault on our vision by gargantuan pictorializations.

The Sculpture. Two departments parted by a long walk are under one roof in the Louvre: antique sculptures and those from the 13th to the 17th century. A sign leading to the antique department reads: "Venus de Milo," and it should have been complemented (for the sake of consistency) by another one upstairs: "To the *Mona Lisa.*" In other words, the glamorization technique is at work here and is not without danger, for the technique is often one of deception. The great Venus standing apart and aloof, as behooves its fame, is, after all, just another Greek statue, and I can think of dozens and dozens of other works that equal or outrank it in esthetic appeal. At any rate, this appeal will become highly gratified in the department of medieval antiques, and the gratification will—or I should say "should"—reach its peak in the section close to the *Porte Trémoille.* Not only the finest examples of sculpture from the Middle Ages but also great works of the Renaissance are preserved in this area.

Musée de Cluny. After the collection of medieval statuary in the Louvre, a visit to the Cluny Museum, one might think, would fade into insignificance. But if one is anxious to see more marvels of the Middle Ages, this museum offers the opportunity to assuage this desire most satisfyingly. On this occasion we again realize that statuary can be studied with much greater thoroughness and enjoyment in a museum than in its original habitat, for in an architectural context sculpture is seen not in detail but merely in its broad contours.

In this partly crumbling, partly restored and modernized Gothic edifice, once the residence of the Bishop of Cluny, a great variety of small objects of ivory and bronze, precious reliquaries, enamels, faïence, and glass of the 12th to the 15th century are assembled—as well as sculpture. But the *pièces de résistance* are the 15th-century tapestries, especially the *Unicorn* series, the finest of their kind and comparable to those at the Cloisters in New York.

Musée de Jeu de Paume is the last one on our schedule. It houses works from the late 19th century, chiefly those of the Impressionists, and demonstrates again that unless represented by their best paintings, the great names of that era do not seem to deserve their reputations. Because of the avalanche of trivia that fills the rooms here, we shall limit ourselves to pointing out the very few highlights: paintings by Van Gogh, the most original of all the Impressionists; a large, fantastic Henri Rousseau; Manet's most ambitious works in the tradition of the early Velázquez; Degas, who never failed in composition, though here he is represented with minor works; and finally, Toulouse-Lautrec, who, within the confines of his art that stresses social comment, always reached the absolute heights.

Notre Dame. The cathedral is located in the oldest part of Paris, the Ile de la Cité, an island between the two arms of the Seine. Walking to the site, you can take one of four bridges: The *Pont Neuf* is the first one to connect the Cité with the main canal; it is also the oldest and widest of all the bridges, and the most famous. From its completion in 1604, it was the gathering place of traders, craftsmen, quack doctors, jugglers, money-changers, and hangers-on. Even today strange characters populate it. The other bridges connecting the Cité are the *Pont au Change*

Notre Dame

Notre Dame Interior

(leading directly to the Sainte Chapelle), *Pont Notre Dame,* and *Pont d'Arcole,* the nearest to the cathedral.

First a Roman settlement and later the seat of the Merovingian kings, the island served as a bastion in which people from the surrounding countryside sought refuge during foreign invasions. This small area was crowded with ten parishes, two hospitals, a marketplace, and many houses clustered around the cathedral. Many of the buildings disappeared with the passage of time, and the remaining antiquities were razed by the famous city planner, Baron Haussmann, when he went on his modernization binge during the middle of the 19th century. Today only a few of the old houses can be seen, most of them on the Ile St. Louis, separated from the Cité by a small bridge.

The cathedral, the pride of Paris, now solitary and aloof in the empty square, is one of the earliest Gothic structures and in point of simplicity and harmony of design—if not picturesqueness— one of the finest. It served as an example for church builders in France as well as in Spain. The name of its architect is un- known. Founded by the Bishop of Paris, Maurice de Sully, in 1163 on the site of a Romanesque church (which in turn had been preceded by a Christian basilica and a Roman temple), the two short towers are its characteristic features; evidently these were never finished, for the original plan called for steeples. This, how- ever, does not diminish their beauty, for the large, arched openings provide lightness and give them a unity with the tripartite ar- rangement of the lower orders of the façade. It is recommended to ascend these towers for the view of the city (the entrance is along the Rue du Cloître Notre Dame). At the termination of the ascent is the Grande Galerie, in Rayonnant style ("radiant" style of the middle-Gothic period), which binds the towers with a delicate ribbon of open arches. Underneath, in the second di- vision, the rose stained-glass window, 31 feet in diameter, glorifies the façade as it did 700 years ago; its construction is so perfect that it has never required restoration. Below this window is a horizontal arrangement of 28 statues of the kings of Judah and Israel. These form the Galerie des Rois, a decorative subdivision adopted by the finest cathedrals of France, among them Chartres, Rheims, and Amiens. Alas, all the statues are reproductions, for the originals were destroyed by the Revolutionary mob in 1793. The greatest aggregate of sculptures is contained in the three main portals, and the best are to be found in the tympanum and the archivolts of the left portal. It has been said that these sculptures served as an example for all decorative statuary in the Middle Ages. On the two upper lintels of the tympanum the right portal carries the oldest sculptures, still in Romanesque style, dating from 1170. The largest portal is in the center and it suffered severely from the ravages of time. Most of the sculptural works in the cathedral have been heavily restored, and some, such as those on the splays (lower part of the door entrance) and the gargoyles and monsters (at the angles of the buttresses), are copies. In fact, the only work actually dating from the 13th century, miraculously preserved intact, is the statue of the Virgin on the pier of the transept portal (facing Rue du Cloître Notre Dame), but the Christ Child in her arms is largely destroyed. The restorations of this, as well as of many Gothic churches and edifices, were carried out during the reign of Louis Philippe and Napoleon III by Viollet-le-Duc, considered at one time to have been the leading expert in the field.

After admiring the façade and before entering the cathedral, I suggest a walk around the exterior; it will prove just as thrilling, but in a different, and most dramatic way. Here we encounter a forest of flying buttresses; these start right behind the towers that terminate at one side of the portal of the transept (the one facing Rue du Cloître Notre Dame is called *Cloister Portal* and the one on the opposite side, *St. Etienne*). Beyond, in an exquisite bursting coronet, the buttresses encircle the apse with a span of 50 feet. These are the boldest medieval structures of their kind. The portals of the transepts are masterpieces of Rayonnant Gothic design, and date from the middle of the 13th century; their rose windows, however, are much restored, as are most of the stained-glass windows of the cathedral.

Thus we have surveyed the exterior and on entering the edifice find its simplicity and cool aloofness surprising; its austerity arises from the fact that Romanesque structural ideas are alive in it, such as the internal galleries which serve as a support for the buttresses of the nave. This construction was in use before the invention of flying buttresses, which were quickly adopted by the builders of the cathedral while work was in progress; however, to preserve the unity of the interior the gallery system was maintained. A French invention, clusters of pillars rise triumphantly, straight to the vaulted ceiling; uninterrupted by terminating capitals they create the effect of soaring height. The east end of the interior is the most impressive. Here the apsidal choir is surrounded by an ambulatory that extrudes chapels all around. These continue between the internal buttresses throughout the building, an innovation first seen in this church. In front of the choir, at the pier of the left transept, stands a statue of the Virgin and Child called *Notre Dame de Paris*, a 14th-century creation typical in its curvilinear stance and late Gothic elegance.

Sainte Chapelle. A short distance from the cathedral, the small church stands within the compound of what is now a hodgepodge of offices dominated by the *Palais de Justice* (Law Court). Once the site of the Roman prefect's palace and later that of the early French kings, the Palais was rebuilt many times. Radically altered in the 18th century during the reign of Louis XVI, it was finally botched up beyond recognition in the 19th century. Hence our interest will be centered on the Court Chapel, built in Rayonnant style 100 years after Notre Dame. Its past was stormy; neglect and vandalism especially during the Revolution have defaced it. To understand how little reverence was at one time given the relics of the past, it suffices to know that it was occupied by shops and legal archives; only in 1837 was restoration begun, and continued for 26 years. It is also of interest to know that the actual building of the entire edifice did not take much more than as many months. Erected by Louis IX (who was later canonized as St. Louis) as a sanctuary for the Crown of Thorns and a fragment of the Cross that Louis bought for a fabulous sum from Baudoin, Emperor of Constantinople, when he went on a Crusade to the Holy Land.

The chapel once stood alone in the middle of the courtyard, but an unfortunate 18th-century addition put it at a disadvantage. Today it is cramped between incongruous buildings that obstruct our view. The chapel is divided into two superposed sanctuaries; the upper story served as the king's private chapel; it can be reached by a winding staircase on either side of the lower floor which was used by the servants. Two small side aisles with flying buttresses support the pillars of the central vault—an ingenious construction that allowed the upper story to be raised on an in-

Sainte Chapelle

Sainte Chapelle Interior

credibly delicate framework of stone pillars and tracery, making the walls appear to be entirely of stained glass. We gain this impression when standing in the vitreous enclosure, where, on a sunny day, incandescent light envelops us with waves of ever-changing color. We can even forget that much of the glass is not original, that the statues of saints standing against the pillars are, with but few exceptions, copies, and that the building is actually over-restored, which becomes only too apparent on examining the details more closely.

Cathedrals in the Country

CHARTRES. At the beginning of this guide I stated that to divorce the art of painting and sculpture from the art of architecture, and to categorize the former as fine and the latter as applied art is arbitrary. The assumption that what serves utilitarian and decorative purposes is of a lower order than that which is produced in the spirit of *l'art pour l'art,* does not always hold. Is not a devotional painting or a statue that is part of a façade utilitarian? How much art is there in a portal of the **Cathedral of Chartres,** as compared to the sum total of this ingredient in the work of a contemporary "genius"? I wonder, if these data were fed into a computer, what answer it would come up with. In just what way does the reaction of our psyche differ when facing a work on canvas and when facing a cathedral, for

Chartres Cathedral

Chartres Cathedral, Porte Royale
(Detail)

Christ in Glory,
Porte Royale

Chartres Cathedral, North Portal

example. Which of the two arts is capable of transporting us more effectively into the realm of the sublime? And, speaking of the sublime, the cathedral of Chartres certainly is!

The site served as a place of worship during the pre-Christian era. The preceding buildings, the last one Romanesque, disappeared, and what presents itself today is a Gothic structure into which a fragment of the Romanesque church became incorporated. The cathedral was finished in 1210 after a building period of only 25 years; some 20 years later the porches of both transept arms were added. The façade with its towers lacks unity; the older north tower is entirely of Romanesque design; but in the 16th century it received an ornate Late Gothic spire. Originally, this tower stood separate from the (now nonexistent) earlier church; the second tower was erected at its side and the façade finally built to join them. These towers form an odd juxtaposition—utter simplicity face-to-face with a decorative debauche. Which one is more acceptable esthetically? Each is perfect in its own way. The designs of their horizontal subdivisions are also dissimilar, a circumstance arising from the fact that a great deal of improvisation went into building Romanesque and Gothic edifices.

Is this lack of conformity a fault? Not necessarily; we may say that such absolute symmetry as that of the façade of Notre Dame, in forcing the imagination to travel along preordained lines, may dull rather than sharpen our sensibilities.

Another "fault" of the façade is the size of its rose window—it is too large to harmonize with the rest—but its design is, in my opinion, more intriguing than any other I can think of. Curiously, its concentrically radiating colonettes are repeated in the flying buttresses raised against the thrust of the clerestory. Its stained glass, as well as the glass throughout the cathedral (with the exception of the rose window in the south arm of the transept),

is exceptionally beautiful and has not been changed from its
original condition when it was delivered from the shops of St.
Denis and Notre Dame, 700 years ago.

In contrast to the royal (west) portal, which is Late Romanesque, the north and south portals with their deeply recessed
porches are Gothic at its best. Their archivolts, tympanums,
doorways, jambs, and piers are filled with statuary, as are the open
galleries above the porticos of the south transept and the *Galerie
des Rois;* all—including the twisted columns, fantastic capitals,
canopies, and other heavenly décor—are authentic, in a relatively
good state of preservation, and of breathtaking beauty.

To some, conditioned by dogma and conventional acceptance,
this may prove to be an odious confrontation: Are these monuments less satisfying esthetically than Greek masterpieces of the
Periclean Age? I do not think so; I am even disposed to believe
that the best of Gothic art possesses moments more imaginative
and of higher spiritual and emotional voltage than the art of any
other time.

When we enter the cathedral, whose nave is wider than that of
any other French church, we are met by the magic blue light—
the Chartres blue, so characteristic of its vitreous surfaces. It
issues from the clerestory, now having become much larger
with the introduction of the narrow arcading of the triforium.
This innovation was first introduced in Chartres and later was
adopted in almost every Gothic cathedral. The interior has the
noble beauty found in all French edifices of this age. Observe the
screen around the chancel, a Renaissance work from the 15th to
the 17th century, and the Virgin of the Pillar, a 14th-century
wood statue in the ambulatory at the north arm of the transept.

Last—or perhaps I should have said—first, there is the majestic
silhouette of the complex; viewed from afar it rises high above
the rustic flatlands, dominating the entire countryside.

SAINT DENIS. *The Abbey* is of historic value to the French.
Suger, later to become the famous abbot and minister to Louis VI
and Louis VII, was brought up in the abbey, which at that time
was the richest and most important in the country. In 1136 he
built a basilica, the first large edifice in Gothic style and the prototype of all Early Gothic churches in France. In the 13th century
the structure was enlarged and greatly embellished. In its crypt
(the largest exclusively royal cemetery) are the tombs of the
French kings. Gradually the church fell into neglect and in time
suffered unbelievable depredation. During the Revolution all the
sarcophagi were opened and the remains thrown in ditches; even
the lead roof was stolen, leaving the edifice nearly ruined. In
1847 Viollet-le-Duc began a restoration which took 20 years. It is

interesting to realize how the place was venerated, for during the building, stones were carried to the site on carts drawn by the faithful from a quarry 12 miles away.

SENLIS. We so often find that architectural gems, and even paintings and sculpture, lose much of their appeal in inferior or inappropriate surroundings. *Senlis Cathedral* is not only most picturesque, but is set amid ancient dwellings lining narrow streets, where the antique past reveals itself in fragments of Roman stonework, in the ruins of a 7th-century castle, or in the former city ramparts. Senlis has a history 2000 years old; it antedates Paris as the capital of the country. Today, it has fewer than 10,000 people. The cathedral is one of the oldest Gothic structures; built over a long period of time, it combines Romanesque as well as Flamboyant Gothic features. Its tower is particularly graceful, and the façade, simple and austere, was much imitated by the builders of Early Gothic churches. The 12th-century statues in the tympanum and the jambs are of high quality, but all the heads are 19th-century replacements of the originals destroyed during the Revolution.

I suggest you climb to the exquisite galleries above the side aisles for a better look at the interior, and from there to the top of the tower for an enchanting view of the town and surrounding countryside.

BEAUVAIS. The **Cathedral of St. Etienne** represents the Gothic idea of church building at its most exalted and audacious and the Rayonnant style in its greatest splendor. It would seem that the citizens of Beauvais in the year 1247 decided to erect a Tower of Babel, for the soaring spire rose 500 feet—it must have been the tallest in the world at the time. But the tower at the crossing of the transept had insufficient support; it exerted too much

St. Amion. The Spire of Senlis

St. Pierre Cathedral (Beauvais)

pressure on the structure, preponderantly of open stonework over solid masonry, and it collapsed, destroying the vaults.

Standing inside looking up, one feels the precipitous height of the building which equals that of the Arc de Triomphe in Paris; with its roof the edifice reaches the height of the Notre Dame towers. After the vaults collapsed, additional piers were erected and the buttresses strengthened, but the church was never completed and to this day lacks a nave.

Bombing by the Germans in 1940 wiped out the center of the town and badly damaged the cathedral. The glass and window tracery are even now in the process of restoration.

RHEIMS. This provincial town is considered the national shrine of France, its Parthenon. Here in 496 the Merovingian founder of the French Empire, Clovis, was baptized; the present **Cathedral,** built in 1210 and finished 100 years later, stands on the same site as the original church. Here, for centuries, the French kings were annointed, among them Charles VII, in the presence of Jeanne d'Arc, after she had taken the town from the English. But it is not only its history that makes the monument memorable; its corporeal magnificence alone sets it among the world's greatest masterpieces. Because of its close connection with the rulers of the country, it boasts elaborate decoration, and the quality of the sculpture has nowhere been surpassed. Strangely, many of the Gothic images have a characteristic Roman (not Romanesque) look, and all of them—a prodigious number—appear to have come off the chisels of great masters who seemingly worked in complete anonymity. Alas, many of these are in a poor state of preservation. Shelling by the Germans in 1914–1918 and the burning of the scaffolding also inflicted scars.

Before entering the cathedral, it is good to circle the edifice— to stalk it, as it were, for we fear that it is unreal and may dis-

Rheims Cathedral

Statues from the
Main Porch

The Rose Window

appear like a mirage. There is the front, turned toward the west, and the first impression of this marvel is that in spite of its fecundity of detail, the underlying structure is never smothered. From the stays and the five gables of the porches (the tympana of which are replaced by windows over the doorways) to the top of the towers, the unity of the façade design is carried out to perfection. The same can be said of the south side with its row of heavenly decorated buttresses and, proceeding toward the apse, we face its arcaded screens above the extruding chapels and the aggressively imperious thrusts of the flying buttresses. The north transept, the oldest, with its porches and tympana, its celestial winged creatures—saints, birds, and beasts—its window traceries —they all are blessed with a celestial beauty.

AMIENS. The construction of its **Cathedral** began in 1220. It is larger than any other Gothic edifice, and since our vocabulary of encomiums has been thoroughly depleted, all we can say is that it is even more elegant than Chartres and Rheims. We may add, soberly, that more fortunate than both the former, its statuary was not vandalized by the Revolutionary mob, because the burghers rallied to its protection.

AUTUN (Burgundy). The **St. Lazarus Cathedral,** started in 1120, is not impressive on the outside perhaps because much of its original design has been altered. The architecture of the interior is austere, Romanesque-Gothic; the nave, transept, and choir have pointed barrel vaulting, and the aisles, groin vaulting, both with transverse ribs. But when we consider the décor, we can justly say that no other church can boast of ornaments so unified in style and sculpture so distinguished in originality. The edifice

Amiens Cathedral

View of Autun

contains, in fact, the only one-man show of Romanesque work extant, and its creator is one of the few whose name has come down to posterity. He signed his work "Gislebertus," and it can be found carved in the tympanum of the main entrance; the sculptor must have been well thought of to have had such an honor bestowed upon him.

To realize how boundless was his imagination, consider the capitals of the 60 columns in the cathedral—they are all different and tell different stories in a most fantastic idiom. Whether in the round or in relief, the freedom of expression is such as only a nonrealistic style informed by Romanesque iconography and unhampered by convention would allow.

COLMAR (Alsace). For those interested in painting, the pilgrimage to this city should be of great importance, for its museum houses a unique work of art. The old city looks almost as it must have five centuries ago when Martin Schongauer worked there. The great **St. Martin Cathedral** (Romanesque-Gothic and very beautiful), which dates from the 13th century, contains his masterpiece, the *Madonna of the Roses*. However, our reason for traveling here is the *Isenheim Altar* by Matthias Grünewald. It was commissioned by the Antonite monks who maintained a lepers' hospital in the village of Isenheim, some 11 miles away from Colmar. During the French Revolution the cloister was destroyed, but fortunately the polyptych was removed for safekeeping and is now displayed in the museum.

It consists of four hinged panels. When closed, the two outer

St. Martin's Church (Colmar)

Virgin of the Rose Bush. Martin Shongauer

Isenheim Altar. Grünewald (Detail)   Isenheim Altar. Grünewald (Detail)

panels reveal the *Crucifixion* flanked by two stationary panels, *St. Anthony* and *St. Sebastian*. When open, the two wings fold over the stationary panels, revealing the *Nativity* (two center panels) flanked by the *Annunciation* and the *Resurrection* (on the reverse side of the top panels). When the secondary panels are folded, the retable with carved figures and Gothic ornamentation appears, flanked, in turn, by *St. Anthony in the Wilderness* and *St. Anthony's Temptation,* both painted on the reverse side of the second set of panels. There is also a predella on which the *Entombment* is represented. This was how the altar appeared originally in Isenheim; today the panels have been separated to allow the work to be viewed in its entirety.

Without reservation we can say that in the history of art there is hardly a painting capable of exerting a greater impact on the beholder, since no one could have rendered human suffering with more compassion. In the *Crucifixion* suffering has been glorified and transfigured and agony intensified to the limit of endurance. The panel of the *Nativity* is no less compelling; here the artist invokes everything that is loveliness, tenderness, and not of this realm—one almost hears the music replete with the promise of unearthly fulfillment played by a host of angels. The six subsidiary panels are just as overwhelming in their poetic imagery; the painter seems to have metamorphosed his own personal history in this work: his loneliness in the *Meditations of the Saints,* set in a landscape only a German master could invent; his love for music almost audible in the ethereal chant of the descending cherubs celebrating the *Nativity;* his obsessions, in the terrible nightmare of *St. Anthony's Temptation.* And finally, there is the panel of the *Resurrection*—Johann Sebastian Bach never expressed it with greater celestial brightness—this scene is flooded with an incandescent aura of pink, gold, and violet; the draperies ascend in ripples on the radiating light into billowing space, and in swirling motion the folds envelop Christ resurrected, like petals of exotic flowers. On the ground below is darkness; here chaos and infernal storm rip the jagged, tortured forms.

In these images the medieval spirit addresses us, and its language is that of Bosch and Brueghel. Here the echoes of Gothic and Renaissance ideas coalesce, but German mysticism does not allow the Classic and rational to bring the images down to a human level.

I mentioned the originality and poetry of this master's paintings; but they do not show the polished technique characteristic of Dürer's work. Was it this circumstance, or perhaps the quality of Grünewald's imagination, that stood in the way of his popularity? Even an enlightened spirit like Melanchthon did not recognize his greatness, for he mentioned him in his writings with respect, but without enthusiasm. It remained for those familiar with Modern Expressionism to fully understand and evaluate his sublime art.

One might argue that the expressionistic, the emotion laden, and the emotions arising from the enjoyment of purely formal esthetic values are at cross purposes; indeed, the human element in a work of art can interfere with the enjoyment of its esthetics proper. But in a conception such as Grünewald's, where the medieval spirit is still alive, the human element is the mainstay; in fact, it potentiates and enhances our esthetic enjoyment of the work. In our time, this can happen only in surrealistic conceptions.

It is quite understandable that an artist commissioned to paint the Sistine Chapel or the Ducal Palace should summon all his faculties to produce his best work; but here, miraculously, an obscure village hospital received the greatest, most sublime artistic achievement of German painting.

It is recommended that the traveler stay overnight in Colmar— if possible in the Grand Hôtel du Centre, on the ancient marketplace facing the cathedral—just to allow his experience to last for a while.

Palaces in the Country

VERSAILLES. The seat of the French kings from 1682 until the Revolution and built in what is referred to as French Classic

Versailles   Hall of Mirrors, Versailles

style, it served as a model for many courts in Europe and was much imitated, though on a smaller scale (*vide* Schönbrunn in Vienna and Sans Souci in Potsdam). Versailles is the greatest, most luxurious, pretentious palace ever built in Europe. But it is also coldly aloof. How could it be otherwise? Its façade, extending for 2,200 feet, is noble—and uniformly monotonous. The part of the interior open to the public is gorgeous beyond description, with the result that after viewing a number of rooms one remembers nothing. The simple truth is that its gorgeousness is simply tasteless. The original furnishings were looted during the Revolution, but we cannot regret its absence, for Louis XIV, the Sun God, had a taste too rich for common mortals. The present furniture was installed at Napoleon's order, and even this is too opulent for "normal" appetites.

The château's formal gardens cover 250 acres; they are arranged in perfect geometric patterns of mathematical precision. Originally there were 1,000 fountains, countless statues, colonnades, an opera house, and so on. Louis XIV started it all, and the building continued for over 50 years. At times nearly 40,000 men were employed at the construction of the palace; it was populated by 1,000 nobles and 4,000 servants—all these figures merely serve to demonstrate on what a gigantic scale the realm was planned.

But this is not all. The king and the kings after him (Louis XV, Louis XVI) felt the need for a more "private" abode. Hence they established on the adjacent 250 acres a conglomeration of small and still smaller châteaux—the Grand and the Petite Trianon with their obligatory parks and requisite amenities: grottos, pavilions, lakes, rustic cabins, temples—in short, all the trappings worthy of the rulers of the mightiest kingdom of the age.

An urgent thought insinuates itself into the mind: How can we cope with it all? We cannot very well; hence we shall have to submit to the standard—and limited—guided tour and try not to concentrate on anything in particular, but to take in this gigantic monument, the triumph of a debauche in luxury, with equanimity.

FONTAINEBLEAU. The château and the park are next on our list. In the 12th century the château was a small hunting lodge of the kings of France, as well as a retreat for their mistresses, and remained so through the ages. In 1527 Francis I enlarged it to a palace for his mistress and summoned for its decoration Italian masters (among them Primaticcio and Rossi) and the leading decorators of France. The artists working on the project thus established the famous School of Fontainebleau, distinguished by an elegant Mannerism that suited the court and its frolics. Henri II redecorated the château for his mistress, the famous Diane de Poitiers, and Henri IV, true to form, for Gabrielle d'Estrées. Louis XV and Louis XVI enlarged and changed it again. Eventually the complex, together with its gardens, grew to enormous proportions. Came the Revolution and it was emptied of all its furnishings—to be refurnished by Napoleon I.

The forest of Fontainebleau, adjoining the château, is picturesque with its heath and rocks. There is a 23-mile circular route through its park in addition to 37 miles of other roads. The 19th-century artists who worked there are known as the School of Barbizon, after the little village where they lived, seven miles from Fontainebleau. The most outstanding painter of this school was Camille Corot, the forerunner of Impressionism.

CHANTILLY. The château, built in 1560, stands at the corner of a lake. More than 200 years of effort by members of the same family, the descendents of the Marshall Duc Anne de Montmorency, made it into one of the finest French castles. During the 17th and 18th centuries additions were made and a formal garden of exceptionally noble design was created. The original part, called the *Petit Château*, contains intact the great library of the first Duke, exquisite woodwork and decorations, and much of his art collection, manuscripts, and the famous illuminations, *Très*

Fontainebleau

Château de Chantilly

Riches Heures (Very Rich Hours), a 15th-century masterpiece in Gothic-Flemish style by the Limbourg Brothers. About the middle of the last century another palace, the *Grand Château*, was constructed in Renaissance style behind the original building. Here paintings by Clouet, Raphael, Watteau, and other masters, also miniatures by Fouquet, can be seen in splendid surroundings.

The Château Country

From Orleans to Angers, a region called the "Garden of France," stretches the great château country. Between the Loire river and its tributaries, the Cher, Indre, Vienne, and Sarthe, many of the finest castles of France are to be found. Still, the lavish praise of the landscape and the picturesque villages, farmyards, and so on that one reads about in official travel folders does not seem justified. The rolling hills and plains are in reality monotonous, the distances from place to place are so long they induce boredom; the Garden of France is most fertile, no doubt, but it does not excite the imagination. The châteaux are a different story.

The château country begins beyond Orleans, the city made famous by Jeanne D'Arc's victory over the British. Its great Gothic cathedral was wrecked by the Calvinists in 1567 and rebuilt two centuries later in imitation Gothic style. Can imitation be as legitimate as the original? Putting all doctrines aside, we must admit that, imitation notwithstanding, the cathedral of Orleans appears most authentically Gothic. The city, much rebuilt after the last war, has little attraction, hence we shall proceed directly to the châteaux: Chambord, Blois, Cheverny, Chenonceaux, and Amboise.

CHAMBORD. The Palace, the largest by far in the Loire Valley is 813 feet long, 354 feet wide, and possesses 440 rooms. It is also the most splendid on the outside. The inside, however, is empty of décor and bleak, except for a spiral central staircase, and

Château de Chambord

The Roof, Chambord

several beautifully coffered ceilings. It was built by Francis I
over a period of 15 years with the help of nearly 2,000
workers and was the king's residence for the last years of
his life. The frontal view of the edifice is stunning, the façade
severely Classic up to the roof line. Here a French extravaganza
begins: A forest of ornate chimney stacks, bell turrets topped
by slender lanterns, and steep gables from which proud dormers
emerge—this roof appears in silhouette like the skyline of a
fabulous medieval city. Walking on top of it among its fantastic
structures is like being transported into a fairytale, where at
every turn dreamlike architectural wonders materialize out of
thin air.

BLOIS. Since the 13th century the château was the fortified
castle of a powerful line of counts; later Francis I made it his
residence. Its complex is made of 13th-century portions, including one wing built by Louis XII and another by his son-in-law,
Francis I. It combines three different styles in three of the wings,
Gothic, Renaissance, and Classic, and its great Flamboyant Gothic
doorway is surmounted by an equestrian statue of Louis XIII (a
modern copy). This doorway and the pentagonal frontal doorway
built by Francis I in the Renaissance wing, with its open bays
and oblique balustrades cutting across the horizontally arranged
fenestration of the façade in an extravagant sweep, are the most
interesting features of the château. Here again we find that although the French did not "invent" the Renaissance style, they
surely understood how to translate it into an idiom all their own.
The apartments of the château are empty of furniture, but their
interiors, graced by magnificently paneled ceilings and ornate fire-
places, are exquisite.

CHEVERNY. I asserted earlier that symmetry is apt to tran-

Château de Blois, the Gothic Wing

Château de Blois, the
Renaissance Wing

Château de Cheverny

Château de Chenonceaux

quilize the sensibilities into indifference. No matter how perfectly symmetrical a Gothic façade may be, its balance is modified by an important variant—sculptural adornments. Nothing disturbs the absolute regularity of Cheverny's façade, arranged in narrow horizontal divisions. The adornments are sparse; the ever-recurring oval niches holding conventional busts, the modest mansards, the domes topped by graceful belvederes—it is all in the severest French Classic style of the 17th century, and yet it is not monotonous. When we ask ourselves what accounts for our sustained interest in the edifice, the answer is its noble proportions: the rhythmic beat of the large and small dimensions within the framework of the wall. The château dates from the first quarter of the 17th century and is still in the possession of a descendant of the original builder, Count de Cheverny. Its interior is very luxurious.

CHENONCEAUX. Spanning the Cher on five arches, the château starts with a fortified tower on the bank of the river and leads over a bridge to a small castle built in what we may now call French Château style, dating from the beginning of the 16th century. It was further extended by the Grande Galerie built over

Château d'Amboise

Château d'Amboise, Chapel

Mont-Saint-Michel

the river and once belonged to Francis I. Henri II, his son, gave it to his mistress, Diane de Poitiers, who after Henri's death turned it over to his widow, Catherine de Medici.

AMBOISE. At the end of the 15th century, Charles VIII rebuilt the medieval castle, and later Francis I added a portion in Renaissance style. In the 19th century much of the very large complex was demolished; however, what is left of the original structure is impressive, standing on a high promontory of the Loire and dominating the town. Some of the rooms are beautifully decorated with Gothic furniture—obviously a more recent addition.

It was Charles I who invited Leonardo da Vinci to Amboise, where the master spent the last years of his life. His remains were transferred to the little chapel of the château, one of the outstanding examples of Flamboyant Gothic style in France. Indeed, it is a miracle that this fragile gem could have survived the ravages of time. Its tympanum and lintel carry Gothic sculptures that suggest Flemish workmanship. Unfortunately, its stained-glass windows, like all those in the Loire Valley, were blown out when the bridges of the river were dynamited during World War II.

Ile Mont-Saint-Michel

Famous throughout the world, the monastery belongs with the most spectacular sites in Europe, because of its location on an island as well as for the beauty of its architectural complex. It is made up of a group of severe Romanesque façades dating from the 11th century, varying in height and shape and forming a massive foundation for the burst of highly ornate Flamboyant Gothic buttresses that arise from the second story of the two-storied monastery. These fairytale structures (250 feet high) are surrounded by small houses, and the whole is encircled by medieval ramparts. From sea level to the top of the 19th-century spire is 500 feet. The interior of the cloister represents the finest example of Norman building. The galleries, courtyards, refectory, Hall of our Lady, Guests' Hall, Knights' Hall, and details of the architecture, despite—or perhaps because of their somber austerity and in part, oppressive weightiness, have a strange fascination.

The tiny island is located between Normandy and Brittany and is connected with the mainland by a causeway built late in the 19th century. Before that time it could only be reached at low tide over treacherous ground. However, since then conditions have changed, for today water reaches the island only twice a month, during the rising and the full moon periods; otherwise, sand flats surround the complex, with the sea not in evidence.

Since the 8th century *Mont-Saint-Michel* has been a sacred shrine, venerated by all, and even during wartime safe conduct was given to the pilgrims.

This factual account cannot possibly conjure up the fantastic spectacle of the island. Unless one is standing on the highest platform of the monastery it is impossible to realize that sand flats stretching as far as the eye can reach, broken only by an occasional glimpse of glistening water, can be such a tremendous sight.

Section 5 / Spain and Portugal

INTRODUCTION TO THE ART OF SPAIN

Reading older history books, one gains the impression that in Spain serious art started with the advent of the 15th century. In Italy, it is granted, art appeared earlier, since even Cimabue (who painted in Byzantine-Romanesque style) has been accorded high rank in the hierarchy of artists. But we must remember that this acknowledgment is of rather recent date.

Early Gothic art, however, is still referred to as "primitive" despite its obvious complexity, finesse, and superior craftsmanship —qualities that are anything but primitive. It is asserted, for example, that no Spanish painting to speak of was done before Luis de Morales appeared on the scene (born about 1500), because the country, under Moorish domination for centuries, had not developed a figurative art. The fact is that the Arabs were expelled from the north in 1085, at which time they retreated from Toledo. It is only in the southernmost part, around Granada, that they succeeded in maintaining their hold until 1492.

To realize the high esthetic level of Romanesque and Gothic statuary in Spain (late 13th to 15th century), one should visit the Museum of Catalonian Art in Barcelona. However, as this art is anonymous, modern glamorization techniques cannot work on it very well. Nevertheless, the crude murals of that era receive great acclaim because they are considered reminiscent of Matisse.

As for paintings in the so-called International style, the first room in the Prado is ample evidence that Spanish Late Gothic (15th century) art has great artistic merit. The term International is fully justified, for although it emanated from France, Gothic style was rapidly adopted by all of Western Europe—less so in Italy where Roman and Byzantine esthetic precepts managed to prevail.

Luis de Morales was the first known master to appear on the Spanish scene, followed by Juan de Juanes, Francisco de Ribalta, Juan de las Roelas, Jusepe de Ribera (who moved to Naples early in his life, Naples and Sicily being at that time Spanish possessions), and finally Francisco de Herrera, El Greco, Velázquez, and Zurbarán.

Of these painters only El Greco and Velázquez can be considered equal to the greatest artists of the epoch. But living in isolation, they remained largely unknown outside the borders of their own country.

El Greco and Velázquez had no successors. Later, the name of Bartolomé Murillo emerged to great prominence—especially during the 19th century, because the Victorian age had a penchant for sham. There is nothing wrong with Murillo's brush; the fault lies with his affectations, religious idealization, and false sentimentality. Because he rendered the human figure in conventional proportions, and observed the amenities of a well-ordered chiaroscuro, his style was considered Classic.

In the nearly one hundred years between the death of Murillo and Goya's rise as an artist, no painter of note appeared in Spain, and after Goya the art of that country went into total eclipse.

Madrid

The Prado. As regards architectural relics and monuments, Madrid does not invite exploration; it is the *Prado* we have come to visit, especially the Spanish masters who must be studied here to fully appreciate their greatness. Besides these, Bosch, Patinir,

Las Meninas. Velázquez

Prince Charles. Velázquez

Surrender of Breda. Velázquez

St. Jerome. Joachim Patinir

Dürer, Rubens, Van der Weyden, and lesser-known names are represented in superb works. How did they find their way into Spain? Records show that after the death of Queen Isabella in 1504, 460 pictures were listed in her collection—art collecting was a royal sport—and like her grandson, Charles V, she had a distinct preference for the Flemish. Charles's son, Philip II, a great patron of Titian, bought art wholesale; his favorite was Hieronymus Bosch. Velázquez, in his 20's, became court painter to Philip IV and was later the king's friend, mentor, and keeper of pictures—a more enviable position no painter has ever achieved!

When visiting a museum, should one start with lesser pictures or with the great works? I am inclined to believe that in order to establish in one's mind an example of excellence, while he is still fresh and receptive, it is best to start with the masterpieces. Hence we may begin with the *Surrender of Breda* (called in Spain *Las Lancas*). The large painting was done in 1635 and represents the surrender of the Dutch commander Justin, who turns over the key of the fortified city of Breda, which had endured a siege of eight months, to the Spanish victor, Spinola, on June 5, 1625. This was an insignificant event in the long history of warfare, an event that left a masterpiece never to be surpassed in all the history of painting. Try to recall other paintings of an official nature, dis-

Clothed Maja. Goya

The Family of Carlos IV. Goya

Baptism. El Greco   The Manikin. Goya   Eve. Dürer

plays of martial prowess, none will come up to this one by Velázquez. His is not a boastful celebration of a victory, but a deeply moving scene; there is a sense of the fateful woven into the fabric of the picture, but we cannot quite put our finger on it. There is the sky, for example—perhaps it has just been raining and the air has been washed clear. The clouds have thinned and late sunlight brightens the edges; we feel that a glorious day will follow the carnage. Does this sound like a sentimental illustration? Indeed, but Velázquez does not make it appear so. Behold the dramatis personae: Justin of Nassau bows to the Spanish victor, Marquis de Spinola, and the key of surrender is accepted with grace and humility. How subtly these figures are isolated, detached from the others by means of an ingenious design; how effective is the helter-skelter of heads on the right, pacified by the dark mass of horses in front of them. One could go on and on rhapsodizing about the virtues of the composition and its coloristic subtleties, but will it unravel the unfathomable that dwells within its fabric? And will it help to discover how hard Velázquez had to fight to realize his ideas? The lances, for example, had banners on them at one time, but he eventually overpainted these, for indeed, they would have brought a garrulous note into the composition. Many other changes were also made during the working period.

The unfathomable! How much of it dwells in the group portrait, *Las Meninas (the Maids of Honor)*! The over-all mastery in the use of pictorial means, the fact that it stands at the highest level any artist could attain, would not alone establish the painting in the galaxy of masterpieces. It is rather the imponderable that raises the realistic representation to the sphere of the transcendental. Does it sound facetious to say that even the dog in this picture has an aura of the supernatural? Yet no surrealistic devices were used to establish the mysterious relationship in *Las Meninas*.

Other outstanding paintings by Velázquez are *Infanta Margerita*, *Esop*, *El Bufon* (portrait of a court jester), *Don Balthasar Carlos on Horseback* and his portrait as a hunter, *St. Anthony and St. Paulus*, and a number of portraits of Philip IV. As to the *Weavers*, so highly praised by art critics because it supposedly presages Impressionism, it is merely reminiscent of certain 19th-century soft-focus genre paintings, conceived in a diffused light. Painted at the same time as *Las Meninas* (about 1657), its composition by comparison is confused, its colors murky, and the "naturalness" of the scene is rather trivial.

And now to Goya. The level of his work is so consistently high that he can be seen at his best in many European and American collections. However, the Prado possesses two categories of his paintings not to be found anywhere else: The group of youthful classic works for the Gobelin factory, painted when he was 31 years old, and the macabre series of fantasies, *The Witches' Sabbath*, which are his last paintings and very "modern" according to our present definition of the word. Both these examples bear witness to the fact that Goya's genius endured over almost half a century. The Gobelin series illustrating bucolic scenes—how different they are from the vacuous confections the best French painters of that time were able to produce (including those of Boucher and Fragonard). There is an earthiness and at the same time an aura of the symbolic in these representations that goes beyond the orbit of mere genre painting. *The Witches' Sabbath* is sinister, macabre; here Goya's pessimism seems to have reached its final crescendo. This tragic group could have been painted today. On the other hand—as could be expected—the much popularized *Majas* (especially the undressed version) have a sweet boudoir air about them, making it apparent that nude bodies were not his forte; he delighted instead in painting glistening material—the silks, brocades, and gold-trimmed uniforms—where his feeling for color and texture could find full expression. This sense is exploited supremely in the group portrait *The Family of Carlos IV*, a veritable Garden of Eden, unsurpassed in painterly brilliance.

And then there is the *Execution*, from which Manet has gathered his pictorial wisdom, and the many, many portraits, each a masterpiece, yielding in quality to no one—not even to

Rembrandt. In another room we find hundreds of his drawings; however, I fail to perceive the great merit ascribed to them by art critics. No doubt they are wonderful illustrations, and powerful social comments, but the graphic line lacks the high tension we find in Rembrandt's drawings, for example.

Next comes El Greco, the non-Spaniard, and the most Spanish of them all. Born on the island of Crete, he went early in life to Venice, where he is said to have worked in the studios of Titian, Tintoretto, and Bassano. In 1577 he moved to Toledo, accompanied by his uncle who held a beggar's license to collect money for the Pope. In Toledo, the Spanish "Lhasa" with its hundreds of churches and monasteries, El Greco ("the Greek"—originally named Domenico Theotocopoulos) gained enormous popularity. He failed, however, to impress Philip IV, who was himself an amateur painter tutored by Velázquez and who had only two loves: religion and art. At the height of his career El Greco led the life of a grandee, but with the changing fortunes of the country his fortunes, too, declined. At his death, his big house in the depopulated town of Toledo had scarcely enough furniture left to fill two rooms. Not much more is known of the life of one of the most glorious masters of the art of painting, whose name, forgotten soon after his death, was remembered again at the end of the 19th century.

All great art, no matter how ancient, contains elements that are forever modern. Whether these elements are recognized as such or whether we fail to comprehend them depends on the temper of the time, and only with the advent of Expressionism has the art of El Greco gained the full measure of appreciation. His Expressionism was consciously manipulated—no astigmatism seems to have impaired his vision, as has been suggested. He painted correctly proportioned portraits when the occasion required, and torturously distorted figures and landscapes for the sake of dramatization. Should we wish to categorize his art, we could call it manneristic, although his Mannerism had none of the weaknesses that characterized that style in Italy. Among his outstanding works in the Prado are the *Baptism, Pentacostes, Resurrection, Golgotha, St. John and St. Francis,* and of course, the portraits. More about El Greco when we reach Toledo.

The best of Ribera's and Zurbarán's works are here, though we can not assign first place to either one. The work of the former is too rhetorical; that of the latter, a master of simplification, is limited to tasteful decorative exploits.

Of the Italians, Titian's equestrian portrait of *Charles V* and his *Bacchanale* are first-rate. There is also a roomful of Tinto-

rettos, some excellent, some mediocre. The Flemish are represented first by Rubens, who spent nine months as envoy to the
court in Madrid and who, according to an account left by Velázquez, painted an incredibly large number of paintings for Philip
IV. Many of these were copies after Titian and Holbein, yet in
no way lesser artistic achievements. But the glory of all the
early northern masters is in the last two small rooms of the side
wing. Here we see Joachim Patinir's *St. Jerome,* a landscape of
fabulous distances such as only a Flemish painter was capable of,
and Albrecht Dürer's *Eve,* one of his best paintings. Quite Gothic
in design, *Eve* breathes the spirit of Biblical Paradise much more
convincingly than her Italian sisters who, even on paradisiac
ground, never forget their Parnassian cradle. Its companion
piece, *Adam,* was at this writing, still covered by a film of old
varnish and hence, is less impressive. Other memorable works
are Rogier van der Weyden's *Descent from the Cross;* two whimsi-
cally grotesque panels by Hans Baldung Grien (a contemporary of
Dürer), Brueghel's *Triumph of Death,* Hieronymus Bosch's *Adoration* and *Hayride*—all works of the first order. When entering
the last room we are literally transfixed by Brueghel's triptych,
the *Garden of Delights.* This is a garland of metaphors, a reel of
poetic fantasy and fabulous demonology so rich in inventive
imagery, so ensconced in cryptic connotation, it makes one feel
like a child witnessing marvelous goings-on—amusing, didactic,
and portentious at the same time. This is the garden of allure-
ments, the essence of erotic enchantment, a pageant of quasi-
religious *ars amandi*—yet all is steeped in blissful innocence; sin
does not dwell on this plane.

The foregoing do not exhaust the treasure of the Prado. Still
to be visited are the medieval paintings in the two main entrance
rooms on the upper floor and, downstairs, a small group of
thoroughly delightful Roman sculptures.

There is another collection of paintings in the **Academia de San
Fernando.** (If you found the Prado gloomy, wait till you see the
Academia.) Its only attractions are a few exquisite small Goyas,
a fairly interesting El Greco, and typical portraits by Zurbarán.

In fact, after the Prado, the art tour in Madrid is over. A
visit to the *Palacio Nacional* (the former palace of the kings) in
search of paintings would be anticlimactic, unless one is interested
in Rococo interiors. For those who admire armor, the *Museum of
Arms* is considered the finest of its kind. Outside Madrid, paintings will be viewed only in Toledo. After that we will concentrate
on cathedrals, monasteries, palaces, and the statuary which belong
to the architecture of the edifices.

MEDIEVAL SPAIN

Spanish architecture is quite different from that found elsewhere in Europe. To understand its national characteristics, one must realize that Spain was under Moorish domination for several centuries. In the 13th century, after the overthrow of Moorish rule and the subsequent acquisition of wealth, Gothic style on the French order was adopted and rapidly developed. Thus the earliest Gothic cathedral, the one in Toledo, was patterned to an extent after Notre Dame in Paris.

Other great cathedrals that show French influence were built in Burgos and Seville, the latter being the second-largest in Europe. However, the French influence extends to the structural plan only, not to the surface decoration which throughout Spain is extravagant, resplendent, and fanciful, often at the expense of the tectonic. Although this is frowned upon by the orthodox architect, we are concerned less with orthodoxy than with picturesqueness. Hence the flamboyant and curlicued should not be offensive to us.

Spanish architects did not eliminate walls to create more window space, as was done in the north; instead they maintained broad wall spaces and divided these by multiple horizontal lines, thus creating expanses which could be covered with a profusion of stone carvings. The courtyards of the monasteries (always attached to major churches) often show extraordinary imagination in the twists of their vaulted ceiling arches and in their fantastic columns, all of which becomes an endless source of delight to the beholder who does not have to worry whether these forms are "organic" or if the designs are rational. That these extravagant features were due to Moorish (and Oriental) influ-

Cathedral   Cathedral Transparente   Cathedral, Main Chapel,
                                                     lateral view

The Visagra Bridge

ences is obvious; it is apparent also in many instances that the exchange of decorative ideas was mutual: the Moors adopted some of the Christian features of building, and the Christians, in turn, borrowed from the Moslems.

Because of this diversity, we do not speak of a Renaissance style in Spain (unless it is an Italian replica), but call it "Plateresque." The Baroque is known as "Churriguerresque," after the leading architect of that period.

The *Escorial* is a famous place near Madrid and although it is listed as a "must" on many itineraries, one should well consider whether or not to spend a day on this trip, for it requires much hard footwork. Built by Phillip II late in the 16th century in Renaissance-Plateresque style, its imposing silhouette can be seen from a great distance. The connoisseur of architecture will point out the majestic proportions, the harmonious groupings of the various masses on a gigantic scale around its 16 courtyards, but these qualities do not compensate for the lack of décor, the bleakness of the exteriors and most of the interiors, and the forbidding monotony and somberness. In the 18th century Rococo decorations were added to the interior of the church and the royal apartments, and a number of important paintings are hung in the chapter house.

Toledo

If one contemplates making only a short trip to this country, a visit to Toledo alone will give the traveler an idea of medieval Spain at its richest, and acquaint him with El Greco's most sublime painting.

Situated on a steep, rocky hill and encircled by the Tajo River, Toledo was once looked upon as the "Rome of Spain." Conquered by the Romans, it was occupied in succession by the Visigoths, then the Moors; in the 16th century it was the seat of the Inquisition, and later, Philip II moved his court to Madrid. Reduced to

Despoiling of Christ.　　Burial of Count Orgaz. El Greco (Detail)
El Greco

provincial status, Toledo retained its original medieval look, largely Gothic, with a sprinkling of Renaissance and Mudejar architecture.

For us, the names of both Toledo and El Greco are closely allied, yet the fact that El Greco lived there does not mean that one must visit the town to study the master's work. In fact, the ritual of taking the tourist to the *Casa El Greco* (one cannot escape it when joining a guided tour) has something spurious about it, for the house may not have been the painter's abode; besides, it is filled with shoddy works that do his name no honor. After having seen the collection in the Prado, one should be fully aware of his stature, but the last and most brilliant major work from his hand, the *Baptism of Christ*, is housed in the *Palace de Tavera* adjoining the Hospital of San Juan Bautista. Other fine works by El Greco in Toledo are the *Assumption* in the *Museum of San Vicence*, the *Despoiling of Christ* in the *Cathedral*, and his largest painting, generally considered his most important, the *Burial of Count Orgaz*. This work is in the small, inconspicuous, gloomy *Church of St. Tomé* (its Plateresque golden altar, however, is quite impressive), and some 30 feet away from the painting (for it is fenced off and one cannot get nearer) one will always find a group of tourists seated in rapt contemplation listening to the perfunctory chant of the guide. Unable to approach the canvas for a closer scrutiny (there must be some marvelous painting in it), all we can say is that somehow it is a cold, academic work in spite of the genuine sentiment with which the scene is imbued.

In this city the student of art may learn a revealing lesson by comparing El Greco's early work with later treatments of identical subject matter. For example, an early work, the *Assumption* in the cathedral, is tight; while the one in the Pinakothek in Munich, a late work, is full of flight and spirit. And when we compare the *Baptism* of the Prado (painted about 1600) with that of the Tavera Palace (from about 1614), the latter shows much greater "freedom." Not that there is intrinsic virtue in a "free" handling of the brush—it all depends on the manner in which a particular artist best expresses himself. We could not maintain, for example, that the stiff, early Bellini's are of a lower order than the soft, almost Giorgionesque paintings of his old age. One might even successfully argue that the former possess greater allure.

Of the edifices, there is first the **Cathedral,** founded in the time of the Visigoths. Later converted to a Mosque, it received its Gothic shape during the 13th century, and still later Plateresque, Mudejar, and Baroque styles further diversified its appearance. Its interior is one of the most sumptuous in Spain, a veritable showplace displaying man's skill in converting stone, metal, and wood into sublime works of art. In fact, the profusion of stone statuary on every corbel, in niches, and in frieze fashion around the choir is unequaled in any Spanish church. Unequaled, too, is the choir, the black wood stalls carved in incredibly complex figurations, testifying to the enormous power and wealth of the church. The grandeur of the interior is heightened by 20 chapels and a Gothic high altar teeming with precious statuary sculptured in wood and reaching to the vaulted ceiling. But the most astounding experience in the cathedral is the Baroque intrusion right behind the *Capilla Major* in the ambulatory. Here the sculptor Narciso Tomé cut open groins of the vaulted ceiling and within the Gothic frame let loose a cascade of Churriguerresque volutes —clouds, cornices, angels, draperies—all in white marble, descending in a vertical swirl of such complexity as would make Bernini gasp. This retable is known as *Transparente*. Facing the clash of incongruous styles and the absurdity of such a violation, we are at a loss to form an opinion about it. And then there are the treasure chambers, the collection of reliquaries in precious gold and silver. Truly the cathedral is the most resplendent in all of Spain.

Other sites of importance are the *Church of San Juan de los Reyes* (Plateresque), *El Transito Synagogue* (elegant 14th-century Mudejar style), and *Santa Maria la Blanca*, erected in the 13th century and originally a synagogue. The white and black capitals of the columns which support Moorish horseshoe arches, and the magnificent carved wooden ceiling makes this structure the finest example of Moorish art in Toledo. All these edifices have been restored in varying degrees.

Aside from the beauty of the individual buildings, there is the medieval town itself, and one should not fail to take a leisurely walk through the gates and narrow streets, which have remained virtually unchanged for many centuries.

Seville

The *Cathedral* was first begun in Gothic style in 1401 upon the site of a Moorish mosque. In the course of time it acquired Renaissance and Mudejar additions, all set in close proximity— which makes it "impure" to the purist's eye, but a delight to anyone who can enjoy picturesqueness and structural variety. When circling the vast complex (next to St. Peter's in Rome it is the largest in Europe) with its seven portals, some Early Gothic, some Late, the diversity of architectural elements keeps the eye alert and enchanted. At night, illuminated by judiciously placed spotlights, it presents an unforgettable picture. The Gothic features of the cathedral are fanciful (Flamboyant Gothic in Spain partakes of the Mudejar), and the Renaissance structure attached to it is massive and very stern. As in all Spanish churches, the interior is dark; small stained-glass windows of the clerestory admit colored light into the somber nave and the side aisles, putting the faithful in the right mood for mystic contemplation. And then there is the *Giralda Belltower*, the largest in Europe. Made of pink bricks and bedecked with Islamic motifs, it is a masterpiece of grandiose design. It was built in the 12th century, but the upper part (the belfry) burned down and was rebuilt in the 15th century in Renaissance style, without impairing in the least, the beauty of the original structure.

In close proximity to the church is the dazzling Moorish palace —the *Alcázar*. Like all Moorish architecture, it is of no great

The Giralda

The Flying Buttresses

Façade detail

Central Nave, Seville
Cathedral

interest structurally, and the restless Islamic stucco lettering like icing on a cake, quickly tires the eye. Moorish designs, repetitious and mechanical in their symmetrical arrangement, lack inventiveness, hence interest, no matter how fine their workmanship. Moreover, most of the original carvings did not survive and what we now see are patterns pressed out of molds. The most interesting features in this Islamic architecture are some of the ceilings, which show an incredibly ingenious network of honeycombed segments.

The Renaissance addition to the palace, a part of the complex, is exquisite, and the adjoining park with its labyrinthine design is a delight. Every traveler should take the time to relax in this peaceful retreat. Adjoining the park and the palace are the reconstructed Moroccan quarters; "quaint" but obviously not antique. However, many houses in the city proper, even entire streets, have retained their original Moorish appearance. The

Alcázar, Salon of the
Ambassadors

Alcázar Interior

most ingratiating features of these houses are the tile-covered patios usually graced by a fountain in the center behind iron grillwork, these are always visible from the street.

The local museum is not of great importance. Some fine churches were destroyed during the Civil War. The few palaces bearing historic names are unimpressive from the outside and, at any rate, are not open for inspection. The finest of these palaces is the Casa de Pilatos, built during the 15th and 16th centuries in Mudejar style; its courtyard is especially impressive. This palace can be visited by special permission. Otherwise, Seville is a semimodern city, and what is sadder than the sight of river banks framed by grimy railroad tracks and forbiddingly ugly industrial installations?

CADIZ. A leisurely three-hour ride over flat land, through hilly regions thick with olive groves, over causeways flanked with naval installations and large modernistic housing sections, reminiscent of our Gulf of Mexico, will bring us to the very end of the peninsula and to the ancient town of Cádiz. It has a uniformly Moorish look, but its *Cathedral* is pure Italian Baroque, one of the finest of its kind in Spain. The slightly concave façade and the interior possess grandeur and simplicity at the same time, and the parsimony of ornamentation offers a welcome relief after the debauche of Mudejar and Churriguerresque ornateness.

MALAGA. From Cádiz we head back over rugged hilly country to the Mediterranean; on a clear day the contours of the African coastline become visible across the sea. The next stop is Málaga, a rather dreary town, but nothing more noble than its *Cathedral* has been built by man. It is in High Renaissance style, with Plateresque touches chiefly on the vaulted ceilings and minor façade placements. The latter represent a masterful arrangement of formal architectural components spelling order and harmony, and the same harmonious relationship rules the interior. The clustered Corinthian columns in their ingenious divisions (piers

View of the Cathedral (Cádiz)

Road to Málaga

Main Façade, Málaga Cathedral

Alhambra, Court of the Lions

atop the columns) are capped by a fantastic assembly of moldings forming graceful cornices and enveloping the intermediate orders with riotous zig-zag designs. There is also an organ loft four stories high. Faced with such a demonstration of perfection in scale and proportion, is our enthusiasm warranted? Haven't we, perhaps, grown tired of Churriguerresque fussiness overriding the fundamental issues of architecture? Perhaps, yet when we have become saturated with structural simplicity, we shall crave again the miasma of the ornamental.

En route to Granada, the road climbs through the Cuesta de la Reina mountain range, awesome in its wide open vistas and endless stretches of olive groves. On the crags, rocks, and atop ridges, one sees lonely farmhouses. Perfect in their shape, they seem to have a common bond with the ground in which they are deeply rooted.

We have driven along parts of the Spanish Riviera and have established the disquieting fact that the nearer to modern civilization, the more corrupt the building style becomes.

GRANADA. This town is situated in romantic hillside country, framed on the northwest by the snowcapped Sierra Nevada mountains. (The Alhambra Palace Hotel is the ideal place from which to experience fully the beauty of the landscape.) Though insignificant as a town, its relics are most remarkable. There is the *Alhambra,* one of the world's wonders. It consists of two separate parts: the palace of Carlos V and, adjoining it, the citadel of the Moors, the *Alcázar*. The first, built by a Spaniard in the Palladian manner, is a faultless but sober and unimaginative Renaissance edifice. Its most appealing feature is the circular courtyard, with a graceful colonnade.

The Alhambra ("the red," since it is built of red bricks), is said to be the most magnificent Islamic structure to be seen anywhere. Erected during the 13th and 14th centuries. The Alcázar, the oldest portion, is a conglomeration of courts and rooms, of which the most famous is the *Courtyard of the Lions*. If we did not know that these enchanting bronze animals came from Persia, we might think they were Byzantine, so strong was Oriental influence on the art of Byzantium. To describe and identify these rooms and courtyards would be futile; all we can do is to indicate the characteristic features of this exotic palace. First, there are the typical colonnades consisting of horseshoe arches supported by thin columns with Romanesque capitals. The roofs with their wide cornices are tile-covered as are the interior walls; there are colorful tiles everywhere. Some of the vaulted ceilings are honeycombed with stalactites of filigree stucco work, so ingenious in its delicate proliferations that words could never describe the effect. The exterior, which is covered by stucco ornamentation and perforated in front of the lacy windows, is a marvel of intricacy.

As we have seen, ornamentation can emphasize the character of a structure (as it does in Baroque buildings) or it can obscure it. Smothered under a deluge of fussy details, the fundamental structural features of the Islamic edifices are thoroughly obscured; hence the eye is compelled to immerse itself in the details of Arabesque calligraphy, and saturation sets in quickly. Most of these Arabesques are stucco replicas of original patterns that have been obliterated. Such ornaments, no matter what their character, always remain mechanical in appearance, for they are produced by means of molds and hence lack the artistic quality of patterns carved by hand. Originally these ornaments were cut into slabs placed on the ground (as in mosaic work) and were then affixed to walls and ceilings. Notwithstanding the artistry inherent in the carved material, the fact remains that Moorish ornamentation is stereotyped. Since it requires no creative imagination to execute, it can be carried out by any trained craftsman. As I pointed out previously, the Romanesque and Gothic stonemasons who carved the fantastic capitals, gargoyles, and devotional statuary were artists, even though no such designation existed during the Middle Ages. The most ingratiating feature of Islamic architecture is the courtyard surrounded by colonnades and graced by a fountain and pool in the center, emanating a feeling of cool restfulness and tranquillity.

On the same steep elevation, near the Alcázar, is the *Generalife* (pronounced Heneraleefay). This magnificent park and whatever remains of the original structures (once the sultan's summer residence), merit a close inspection.

The **Cathedral,** too, should be visited. It looks very much like a Renaissance palace on the outside; on the inside, its dignity and restraint in the use of detail is remarkable. It is divided by five naves of equal width (there are no side aisles) which gives the interior a much wider appearance and the massed rows of columns heightens still further the impression of grandeur. Some of the side altars, in Renaissance and Andalusian Baroque, are decorated with intricate wood carvings of the finest workmanship and design.

For an interior decoration gone mad (but with a wonderful system to legitimize the madness), for exuberance in Baroque and Churriguerresque ornamentation, for imagination that balks at no eccentricity, the **Cartuja Monastery** is unequaled. The marble veneer of the walls, brilliant in color and arranged in symmetrical patterns (by cutting sheets of the same block and then matching them laterally), are dazzling beyond belief. Man's complete domination over inert materials, his capacity to twist, bend, and mold them at will in any conceivable manner reaches its ultimate climax here.

CORDOBA. A three-hour drive from Granada, this ancient town was the first Roman colony and later one of the most splendid of the Islamic cities, as well as the seat of a great university. Today it is simply a provincial town with half the population it boasted a thousand years ago. Its only significant relic is the *Mosque* (Mezquite). The large complex is uniformly Moorish on the out-

Alhambra, Room of Abencerrajé

Interior of the Mosque

Sacristy of the Carthusian Monastery

Cathedral Interior
(Cordoba)

side; its low-stretched walls, fortress-like, are dark, gloomy, crumbling, ravaged by time. The 16th-century belltower within their enclosure is powerful, and its dark masonry blends well with the much older structure. The interior of the Mosque is a veritable sample case, combining a variety of styles from the Classic Islamic of the 9th century to the gaudiest of the Baroque, and with modern additions thrown in here and there for good measure. Yet the place is unique. In it grows a forest of about 850 columns made of marble, granite, and porphyry supporting two tiers of arches; once inside, one feels the need of a compass to find his way through the thicket.

The high point of the Mosque is the small 11th-century Islamic chapel, the *Mihrab,* in which Moorish and Romanesque elements are skillfully combined. The walls are carved of alabaster, and the mosaics of semiprecious stones glisten like tiny colored mirrors. The ceiling is a heavenly billowing marble shell, glowing with roseate colors.

BARCELONA. This city is not on our circuit, hence it has to be visited separately (see travel section). Its chief attractions are: *The Museum of Catalonian Art,* the *Cathedral,* and the *Gothic Quarter* which extends to the southeast. The museum has the finest collection of Romanesque and Gothic statuary in the country and some remarkable Gothic altar paintings. The Romanesque frescoes, however, highly praised by some critics because they are reminiscent of certain modern paintings, are merely crude and lack the artistry that is almost always present in sculptural work.

The cathedral, built during the 14th and 15th centuries, belongs with the greatest edifices in Spain, but its façade is unfortunately a 19th-century imitation Gothic. The Gothic quarter, however, in spite of extensive renovation, looks quite authentic and merits closer inspection.

Barcelona Cathedral Façade

PORTUGAL

Why should a traveler in quest of art visit a country that does not possess a single great repository of paintings or sculpture? Moreover, a country whose landscape (at least that seen from the popular tourist routes) is of no particular interest either? But as I said earlier, art is not limited to works framed and hung on the wall. As embodied in works of architecture, art is to be found throughout this country in great profusion and in a style impossible to see elsewhere.

Lisbon

Documentary evidence indicates to us that this charming town must at one time have been magnificent. But in the year 1755 a catastrophic earthquake and subsequent fire practically devastated the city, and in the conflagration great edifices and a vast accumulation of treasures including those from the East Indies perished. Whatever historic sites are left in the city proper date from the late 18th century or have been totally reconstructed. Only two buildings in the suburb of Belem (besides a few scattered and not easily accessible structures in the city), retain their original form. The *Tower of Belem,* a small fortress-like structure in Manueline style, adorned with the insignia of the Templars and typical Portuguese rope patterns carved in stone, is one survivor. The other, far more important, is the neighboring *Monastery of the Hieronymites* (Jeronimos).

Tower of Belem

Jeronimos Abbey

Hieronymite Monastery,
Church Interior

The basic construction is Gothic (although it was not built until the beginning of the 16th century), but the façade is a magnificent example of Manueline style. A splendid courtyard (always an important feature in the monasteries) and an arcade replete with sculptured ornaments and statuary are also in Flamboyant Gothic-Manueline design. Manueline (not discussed in the section on styles because it is confined to Portugal), is distinguished by excessive, frequently florid, ornamentation and elaboration of minute sculptural details. Another attraction is the *Coach Museum* in the suburb of Belem in which royal coaches of the 17th and 18th centuries are displayed. They are said to be among the finest of their kind in Europe.

The *Museum of Ancient Art* in Lisbon possesses a few paintings bearing august signatures (Holbein, Dürer, Bosch), but their quality does not justify a special excursion to Portugal—the Prado

Abbey Cloister

Polyptich. Nuño Gonçalves
(Detail)

offers much better examples of the work of these masters. As for the foremost Portuguese painter, Nuño Gonçalves (15th century), his much-praised polyptych, *Veneration of St. Vincent,* follows the Flemish school closely but does not quite come up to its exceedingly high standards. The museum also has a very large collection of porcelain, silverplate, works of applied art, and ancient ecclesiastic statuary, not of the highest quality.

The Country

SINTRA, on our itinerary is a few miles south of Lisbon and, en route to Oporto, we shall visit Alcobaça, Batalha, Tomar, and Coimbra. The charming resort town of Sintra has, in addition to its very beautiful location, one principal attraction: the *Palace of Sintra,* built in the 14th century as the residence of the country's early kings. The ruins of the Moorish castle atop the highest rocky hill offers a splendid view of the countryside, but the "Wagnerian" castle built by the German prince consort in the 19th century is a hodgepodge of every style, from the Dark Ages to the Victorian era—a "stupendous" spectacle one could easily overlook. **ESTORIL,** the famous seaside resort just outside of Lisbon, is commonplace.

ALCOBACA. The first stop on the way north this town has a monastery founded as a Cistercian abbey in the 12th century. Because of reconstructions in the 17th and 18th centuries, its exterior has lost its original character and now looks Italian

Cistercian Abbey of St. Mary

Terra cotta statue. (Detail)

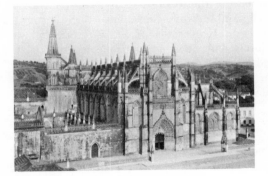

Batalha Monastery

Towers, Batalha
Monastery

Baroque; however, there are Romanesque and Gothic elements in many parts of the interior. The surprising feature of the monastery is its sculpture; the tombs of King Pedro I and his Queen, carved by an unknown 14th-century sculptor are of great artistic interest (one of the magnificent Gothic biers was heavily damaged by the invading Napoleonic soldiers), and the three over-life-size terra cotta angels (made late in the 17th century by anonymous monks) are imbued with that fine artistic quality usually found in the works of celebrated masters.

BATALHA. After one hour's drive over a hilly region, we face another splendid monastery. It was begun in the 14th century, but its façade, strongly influenced by the English Perpendicular style (an English builder worked on the monastery), was erected at the beginning of the 15th century. Various additions made half a century later by native architects in Manueline style with Moorish overtones, show a fecundity of ornamentation that baffles the imagination. The austere Gothic refectory contrasts with the

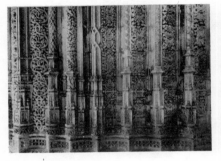

Monastery Façade (Detail)

Church Rotunda (Tomar)

Scene of the Monastery (Tomar)

Convent Cloister

lavish décor of the so-called Unfinished Chapels, and in spite of the variety of style the ensemble spells harmony.

TOMAR. The monastery of Tomar is of equal interest. Founded by the Templars in the 12th century, it displays astounding contrasts which, in spite of their incongruity, delight our senses. I have been militating against as well as praising, stylistic incongruities. Different but good styles need not be mutually exclusive; in Tomar, the complex structures retain their identity. The rotunda of the church (a characteristic feature of Templar architecture) is unique. The upper part of the monastery is in Manueline style and looks very much like an East Indian temple —obviously the builder must have been familiar with Indian architecture. The lower order of the monastery is of pure Italian Renaissance. The Manueline structures are adorned with fantastic rope pattern carvings and a variety of extravagant insignia typical of Portuguese 16th-century décor.

COIMBRA. Portugal's third-largest city and once its capital and university center, is situated in beautiful hilly surroundings. It can be reached in one hour's drive from Tomar. It has four principal attractions: the *Monastery of Santa Cruz* (founded in the 12th century and restored at the beginning of the 16th); the *Monastery of Santa Clara;* the 12th-century Romanesque *Cathedral;* and the *Museum Machado de Castro,* housed in a monastery and rich in statuary of the Romanesque, Gothic, and later periods. The Monastery of Santa Cruz has a pulpit of extraordinary refinement, carved in stone. The cathedral's stark, un-

Coimbra Cathedral   Santa Cruz Monastery

adorned façade hides a surprisingly elaborate, Gothic main altar carved in wood, and the Gothic façade of Santa Clara, although ravaged by time, makes us aware of the imaginative power poured into building at that time. The interior in Renaissance and Baroque style is decorated with enormous murals of ceramic tiles rarely seen on such a grand scale.

OPORTO. The city, bustling with commerce, lacks the charm that distinguishes the places we have just visited. However, a few remarkable edifices invite the traveler to take the ride of about 60 miles from Coimbra. The *Cathedral*, of a powerful Romanesque design, is situated on a hill, overlooking the entire city. It is graced by many Renaissance side altars and a stupendous Baroque

Monastery of Santa Clara

Tomb of the Holy Queen (Coimbra)

The Cathedral (Oporto)

main altar, carved in wood and richly gilded. One of the side altars (17th century) is all in chased silver work, a rare masterpiece. The interior of the *Church of San Francisco* is literally covered with the 17th-century wood carvings; not of high artistry, these will dazzle the beholder with the glitter of gold. More than two thousand pounds of gold leaf is said to have been used in the process. Lastly, a visit to the church and monastery *Da Serra do Pilar* should be made. The circular church in Renaissance style and the adjoining circular courtyard surrounded by a graceful colonnade make a picture of tranquillity and harmony. From its lofty position atop a steep hill, it overlooks an impressive panorama of the city and surrounding countryside.

S. Francisco Church Interior

S. Francisco Church

Section 6 / Switzerland, Germany, Austria

SWITZERLAND AND LIECHTENSTEIN

References to art in a country like Switzerland become equivocal, for there are grandiose "pictures" all around, nature being so inventive she tempts the artist to give up all intention of representation. Could this be the reason that this country produced no artist of importance in all of its history? Strange as it may seem, paintings of the most spectacular mountain panoramas were created in the Low Countries where a ground elevation of ten feet becomes quite conspicuous.

Churches in Switzerland are of no great interest, for Calvinistic austerity did away with all that is decorative and festive. However, the great Gothic cathedrals of Lausanne, Bern, Geneva, and Lucerne are worthy of a visit. The edifices, castles, and whatever other ancient buildings one encounters are also not the main reason for a journey to Switzerland. They are part of the landscape, and so is the rural architecture. When ancient, the style is always excellent, but this is much less true of the newer rustic buildings.

The Jungfrau

Lake Lugano

Mt. Pilatus

St. Moritz and Graubünden

In the realm of painting, collections of modern art predominate; as I mentioned earlier, it would be wasteful of time and effort to seek material abroad that is in plentiful supply at home. However, the **Kunsthaus** in **ZURICH** should be visited. Modest in scope, it possesses a few fine examples of old masters' works as well as some ancient statuary. This museum is also heavy on 19th- and 20th-century art, of poor quality, however.

A great collection, belonging to the Prince of Liechtenstein,· is housed in the *Vaduz Public Library.* It is only a small part of a considerable accumulation of masterpieces that were on display before World War II in the Liechtenstein Palace in Vienna. Some of the finest examples of Rubens' and Van Dyck's works can be seen here, and the little town of **VADUZ** is so enchanting that the short trip from Zurich (or Feldkirch, at the Swiss border, if you are traveling by train from Austria) is highly recommended.

Because all is tourism in Switzerland, the description of the suggested routes is contained in Part II, the travel section.

Zermatt with Matterhorn

Choir Stalls of the Stiftskirche

Genevra dei Benci.
Leonardo da Vinci (Vaduz)

The Triumph of Death. Pieter Brueghel
(Vaduz)

INTRODUCTION TO THE ART OF GERMANY

Very tragically, the number of antique edifices in large cities damaged during World War II was staggering; in many instances they were razed to the ground. Since then extensive restorations have been carried out, but these seldom recreate the original appearance of the relics. Of course, in a country as large as Germany, masterpieces of German architecture are still preserved in isolated localities; some of these are mentioned in the travel section.

As for paintings, statuary, and other works of art, the loss was not very extensive since a great many were removed for safekeeping. The difficulty of getting acquainted with German art collections lies in the fact that they are not centralized but dispersed throughout the capitals of the various provinces. These museums—one could not call them "provincial"—are important, and if their collections were all housed under one roof, the assemblage would be second to none in Europe. On our tour through the country, we will visit most of the principal repositories of art.

It should be noted that when referring to "German art," we mean also the art of Austria and Bohemia, even though the art of Germany proper shows local characteristics in various provinces.

Tradition, no doubt, is the mightiest foundation upon which art can grow and flourish. In Germany this precondition did not exist; hence in the early Middle Ages it had to borrow from sources outside its own boundaries. As early as the 13th century, many German craftsmen, such as church builders and sculptors, received their training in France. During that period painting was limited to illuminated manuscripts, stained-glass windows, and murals. During the 14th century, panel painting of monastic character was quite common, and what has survived shows a

French decorative influence in architectural detail and costume. Panel painting was intended exclusively for altars and was subordinate to sculptural work. Sculpture and architecture rather than painting dominated the early stages of Gothic art in Germany. It was primitive in nature because there was no underlying, well-developed style, with its concomitant esthetic discipline. It is characterized by the mystical and emotional; whether the reasons for this were sociological, as some maintain, is difficult to judge. As a rule (as practicing painters know) where there is a lack of fundamental knowledge of anatomy and perspective, "emotional" elements make themselves felt. Further, primitivism often shows up in an inability to achieve a coherent, harmonious composition.

Cologne, Vienna, and Prague were the centers of German art during the 13th and 14th centuries, and the most important works that have survived—all by anonymous masters—are few; among them are four panels in the Klosterneuburg Monastery near Vienna. In 1324 they were attached to the back of an enameled relic of a much earlier date, the so-called Verdun Altar. Other survivals belong to the Austro-Bohemian schools; because they are in the Byzantine tradition and follow the style of Giotto, they are generally superior to those of the Cologne school.

At the beginning of the 15th century, north and central German painting came under the influence of the Flemish school, with the result that its level improved greatly. Still, most of the painters, with a few exceptions, for example, Stephan Lochner, Hans Multscher, Lucas Moser, and Konrad Witz, remain anonymous. Today we refer to them as "Master" of this or that altar, or this or that biblical scene. Lochner and Multscher can be considered major artists. Both died shortly after the middle of the 15th century, to be followed soon after by Martin Schongauer of Colmar, in whose shop Dürer and Grünewald were supposed to have spent some time, and Michael Pacher, the Austrian, whose complex polyptych and retable can be seen in the parish church of St. Gilgen. Other of his important works are hung in the Pinakothek in Munich. The second decade of the 16th century saw the passing, at 85, of Michael Wohlgemut, who was Dürer's principal master. Thus ended the pre-Dürer era, during which only a few artists managed to raise the art of painting above the provincial level.

Strangely, during the decade 1470–1480, the illustrious German painters were born, the only ones who measure up to the great masters of other lands. They were Albrecht Dürer, Mathias Grünewald, Hans Holbein the Younger, Albrecht Altdorfer, and Lucas Cranach the Elder. They also had lesser contemporaries: Hans Burgkmair, Wolf Huber, Hans Suess von Kulmbach,

Christoph Amberger (an excellent portraitist), and Hans Baldung Grien, an original artist whose originality is often spoiled
by crudeness.

It is interesting to note that most of the early painters were
sculptors as well and that sculpture in Germany was chiefly in
wood and only rarely in stone or bronze. Also, in contrast to the
practice in Latin countries, sculpture was usually carried out in
raw wood rather than in polychromy, and even that of the late
16th century was Gothic in character. The best-known sculptors
of this era are Tilman Riemenschneider, Veit Stoss (whose
colossal, extravagantly polychromed work is in Cracow, Poland),
Peter Vischer (the bronzesmith), and the stone sculptor, Adam
Kraft. The leading sculptors of the Baroque were Balthasar Neumann and Raphael Donner, the Austrian.

Dürer's art is steeped in Renaissance esthetic, yet an element
of the Gothic is present in most of his paintings; in his graphic
work, Gothic ideas predominate. His genius in graphics surpassed even that of the greatest of his Italian contemporaries,
since Gothic iconography, the incident of décor, and the miracu-
lous craftsmanship that is woven into the fabric of Gothic art
are not within the precinct of Renaissance graphics. If we consider Dürer's paintings, even those with a strong bias for Italian
Renaissance could still not deny that he stands among the greatest
of his time.

Mathias Grünewald, endowed with a spirit more Gothic by far
than that of Dürer is, perhaps, the only artist whose genius
allowed him to express suffering without falling into the melo-
dramatic, contrived, ludicrous. In his work emotional and purely
pictorial elements coalesce into a grandiose union.

As a portraitist Holbein is second to none. The landscapes of
Altdorfer and Cranach often measure up to those of their Flemish
contemporaries, the highest praise one could bestow on practi-
tioners of this genre. In fact, they both were among the first to
use landscape as their main theme and with an intimacy to be
found only among works done centuries later. In the art of
Cranach we find, curiously, that a provincial style can, by virtue
of its naïveté and lack of conformity to the standards of the metropolitan milieu, be superior to a sophisticated conception.

It seems improbable to state that with the passing of these
masters—all of the same age—German painting ceased to function as a major force; nor can reasons be found to account for such
a decline. In the 17th century one name appears—Adam El-
sheimer, whose influence became widespread, especially in Holland.
However, his genre painting, once held in great esteem, was not
sturdy enough to retain its esthetic validity. The Baroque and

Classicistic styles were on the whole neither better nor worse than those elsewhere; yet they produced no artist of great stature. Competent but mediocre painters were plentiful during the 18th century, but none could shake off the academicism that engulfed German painting. After the period of neo-Classicism, which produced some estimable artists and lasted well into the 19th century, degeneration of taste and disorientation in esthetic probity became general, and to all appearances, irrevocable.

FREIBURG. Our first stop on the way north, is a town in the district of Breisgau at the foothills of the Black Forest mountains. Of the original town, founded early in the 12th century, only two city gates remain. The cathedral—the *Münster,* as it is called—was also begun at that time but in due course has taken on a Gothic appearance. Although war damage was extensive in Freiburg, the cathedral was spared. Of all German church buildings, the Münster is the earliest built in distinctively Gothic style, and its spire (dating from 1300) represents Gothic in its purest configuration. The 400-foot-tall structure is done entirely in open-work stone traceries, which have replaced the earlier, solid stone pyramid. The exterior of the Münster is noble if somewhat monotonous, but its statuary, especially that in the west porch, showing some traces of the original polychromy, is of a high order (many of the figures on the exterior, however, are copies of the originals, which are weather-worn and kept within the cathedral.) The sculptors are Hans Wyditz, Sixt von Staufen, and others hardly ever mentioned in history books, all of them artists of considerable stature. There is an altar by Hans Baldung Grien,

Freiburg Cathedral

Freiburg Cathedral (Detail)

The Porch, Freiburg Cathedral
(Detail)

his best painting, *Crowning of the Virgin,* set in a superb retable, as well as works by Hans Holbein, stained glass in the Heimhofer Chapel, a 13th-century bronze crucifix in the Boecklin chapel, and many other works of art. Other medieval edifices in the town are the *Town Hall,* the *Kaufhaus, Schwabentor, Baslerhof,* and a few Renaissance and Baroque structures. The earlier buildings, however, have been restored to such an extent that they can no longer be considered medieval.

Munich

Architecturally, the city is rather commonplace; it lacks charm, style and order. Its art collections, however, if not equal to the greatest in Europe, are remarkable at the very least. Old masters' paintings can be seen in the *Alte Pinakothek,* antique

Erasmus and Mauritius. Grünewald
(Alte Pinakothek)

Birth of Mary. Master of the
Life of Mary (Detail)

Karl V. Titian (Detail)

Fool's Paradise. Pieter Brueghel

sculpture in the *Glyptothek* now in the process of reorganization. Assembled in the *Bavarian National Museum* are ecclesiastic works and decorative art from the Middle Ages to the 19th century.

The **Alte Pinakothek** museum in Munich has the riches of a long history of art collecting by the ruling House of Wittelsbach and its successors. In the collection are paintings bought directly from contemporary artists by the first duke in the 16th century, among them Altdorfer's fabulous *Battle of Alexander*. The duke's heirs continued to amass works of art on a grand scale, often against the wishes of their taxpaying subjects; we can read a request addressed to the Prince in 1585 "to give up the pernicious purchase of curious and useless things," and even to sell the collection. Fortunately, the plea of the well-meaning citizen was not followed, and many art objects and antiquities were added to the store of art treasures. In 1684 a prince of the same line built Castle Schleissheim including his gallery, an inventory of which listed 1016 pictures alone. When the Wittelsbach line died out, the successors to the throne of Bavaria moved the gallery to Munich. Later, a large group of newly acquired early Flemish and German master paintings were sent to the museum, as well as

The Farm Courtyard.
Van Dahlem

Prometheus Myth. Piero di Cosimo

many of the art objects housed in various monasteries, after their secularization. The Gothic and the Flemish collections were assembled by the Boisserée brothers during the first quarter of the 19th century and were very much against the prevailing taste. We remember that Johann Wolfgang von Goethe, the most enlightened and knowledgeable man of the age, gave much attention to these Gothic paintings and statuary, but could not respond to them, steeped as he was in neo-Classic precepts.

As is to be expected, German art is represented by outstanding works. Many of these are housed in the downstairs rooms, which start with the Gothic masters, among them the *Laurentius Altar* by Michael Pacher (the sculptor and painter of the *St. Wolfgang Altar*). In spite of unfamiliar signatures (in art it is usually a much publicized name that arouses the admiration of laymen and experts alike), we must bow to Rueland Frueauf's *Man of Sorrow*, Hans Pleydenwurff's *St. Michael*, Martin Schaffner's *Wittelsbacher Altar*, works by Hans Wertinger, Bernhard Strigel, and other unfamiliar names.

The members of the Painters' Guild, only a generation before Altdorfer's birth, were evidently not sufficiently celebrated to have their names preserved for posterity. The Master of St. Veronika, the Master of the Life of Mary, the Master of the St. Bartholomew Altar, the Master of St. Severin—designations such as these were current as late as the 16th century, yet nothing is known of the lives of these great artists. When beholding their panels in the Alte Pinakothek, an old and troublesome question comes to mind: To what extent is the Gothic genius itself—the genius that coerced and guided the painters' minds and hands—responsible for the artistry inherent in their work? It could only be answered philosophically—or in effect, not answered at all.

The Flemish section (in the downstairs and upstairs galleries) is also teeming with important works. Remember: "Flemish" means not only the province of Flanders but what we know today as Belgium as well. The more accurate term, "Netherlandish," is today interchangeable with Dutch, hence we shall differentiate only between Flemish and Dutch. The term "Low Countries" includes both Belgium and Holland.

Having expended a plethora of adjectives in referring to 15th- and 16th-century German art, what more could be said about Flemish art of the same period? Simply that the best of it is unsurpassed. Unlike German, Flemish painting cannot be qualified as romantic or heroic; it shuns histrionics; it is more objective and detached; it is self-contained and reticent. All this points to the fact that formal issues in art outweigh any others. How gloriously these formal issues are resolved can be seen in Rogier van der Weyden's *Three Kings* altar and *Annunciation,* in Dirk Bouts' *Resurrection,* and Hans Memling's narrative *The Seven Joys of Mary* which reels off countless details in a cohesive framework of mountain and city vistas, rivers and ravines, bays, and promontories, leading to the farthest sea—all bound by a monumental design.

To realize the importance of design in a work of art, one has only to behold Brueghel's *Fool's Paradise.* Who but a Flemish master of the 16th (or 15th) century would dare to attempt such a composition and resolve it so successfully? And how often does one find a reference to a contemporary of Brueghel's, Cornelis van Dahlem? His masterpiece *Landscape with a Farm Yard* presages the entire school of Dutch landscape painting that was to arise a century later.

Another surprise awaits us in Munich. If one desires to study Rubens and Van Dyck at their best, one need travel no farther. There are more of these masters in the Pinakothek than in all of Belgium—if not yardwise, surely in point of quality. And when we consider quality alone, Ferdinand Bol's self-portrait and portrait of his wife are superior to Rembrandt's youthful works, which are of no great significance in this collection.

Seventeenth-century Dutch landscape painters—the priceless "Kleine Meesters"—who in the midst of plenty had to lead such wretched lives, are also here in force and are always a delight to behold.

The most "stupendous" German work is, perhaps, the previously-mentioned *Battle of Alexander* by Albrecht Altdorfer. I have often alluded to the fact that the "difficulty of doing it," or to put it in a different way, "the amount of talent" invested in a work of art, establishes its position on the scale of values more accurately than any other consideration. I also averred that a practicing painter conversant with the ins and outs of his profession always or almost always can, like an experienced surgeon, "diagnose" a case. The *Battle of Alexander* is an "almost" case. Take the sky, for example: to endow celestial space with so much imagination and poetry and to give it a cosmic dimension presents difficulties of the first order. It calls for the highest talent, as does the landscape, which though it derives its esthetic ideology from the Flemish, is nevertheless original withal. One-third of the lower part of the panel (which measures 63 x 47 inches) is filled with literally thousands of warriors, most on horseback, attired in their medieval best, all seen in sharp focus— a veritable sea of ants elaborated in the most minute detail, a tour de force, exasperating to behold. As a technical performance alone it is intricate beyond belief and, perhaps, unparalleled in complexity. Yet it is just this that weakens the grandeur of the conception, for the cosmic element in the landscape seems to reject the bothersome pressure of turbulent humanity.

It appears that technical wizardry was not one man's property. Joerg Breu the Elder equals Altdorfer's mastery in handling miniaturist details, but fails in his conception of the landscape, which lacks imagination; as does Ludwig Refinger's painting and Melchior Felselen's battle scene, which is poorly composed. All are in the same hall, and all bear witness to the fact that technical accomplishment if not guided by a superior talent will not elevate the artistry of a painting. Was Dürer at his best when he painted the monumental *Four Apostles?* In assuming a Renaissance stance and in removing himself from the German climate, his art fell into a· cold rhetoric. But not with others of his 25 works in this museum. The portraits in particular—among them his famous self-portrait of 1500 in which the young man of 28 saw himself not only as a representative of radiant manhood but as a historic figure as well—testify to his mastery of this genre.

Hans Burgkmair, Hans Holbein, Lucas Cranach, Hans Baldung Grien, and Mathias Grünewald complete the German section. Those who did not see the Isenheim Altar in Colmar will gain an inkling of Grünewald's greatness from his *Mocking of Christ* and *St. Erasmus and Mauritius.* Artistically these are perhaps the most satisfying of the German works, for they combine all the ingredients of great art.

Of the early Italians, Giotto, Fra Angelico, Masolino, and Fra Filippo Lippi appear with exquisite examples. So do Filippino Lippi and Piero di Cosimo—the surrealist one might call him, for his remarkable *Prometheus Myth* possesses the aura of improbability and a dissociation of ideas that lie at the core of the surrealist conception. Other noteworthy Italian paintings are *Madonna and Child,* labeled "Leonardo da Vinci" but not characteristic of him; a portrait by Giorgione that looks like a Giorgione but could be by someone else; Raphael's *Madonna della Sedia,* very popular, charming, and surely oversweet; Titian's very famous *Charles V,* a grand portrait worthy of his name, and his late *Crowning with Thorns,* a great work which is the mature climax of his art.

It would appear that mediocrity had been largely banned from the Alte Pinakothek. Of course, this is not so. There is always a picture postcard category: the "ideal" landscapes by Claude Lorrain, the "ideal" ragamuffins by Murillo, the "ideal" classicism of a Poussin, the "ideal" courtisans by Boucher, and the issues of a false heat produced in the name of art by so many of the minor Baroquists.

The **Glyptothek** under a reorganization since the war, only a small part of the collection in the **Prinz Carl Palais** is at present accessible. Of the Greek and Roman statuary and decorative objects which are the mainstay of the collection, the Aegina Marbles are considered to be the most important. Carved between 490 and 480 B.C. these once filled the pediments of the Aphia Temple on the small island of Aegina. They were bought in 1811 by the Bavarian king, Ludwig I, who entrusted their restoration to the Danish sculptor Thorwaldsen. The restorations—replacements of missing parts—have long been considered faulty because the impression of the whole is unfavorable. At present major work is in progress to do away with the additions and reduce the statuary to the fragmentary condition in which it was found. That this operation will immeasurably improve its appearance becomes at once apparent when viewing the pieces that have already been "re-antiqued." However, Thorwaldsen's restorations need not have falsified the original appearance. Not all that comes from ancient Greece is perfection. Restored, these figures are archaic and lifeless—though not everything that is "lifeless" is therefore esthetically inferior. When the work now in progress is complete, the fragmentary, as usual, will not fail to galvanize the beholder's imagination and conjure up in his mind a grandeur that the original work might never have had.

Bavarian National Museum (*Bayerishes National Museum*). When it was founded in 1855 by the Bavarian king, Maximilian II, the museum already had an important collection of medieval ecclesiastic art. Today it is perhaps unequaled in the size and quality of treasures from the 13th to the 16th century, especially those carved in wood. In point of creative imagination and sheer artistry of performance, what could intrigue the mind and stir

Aegina Marble, Restored
(Glyptothek)

Aegina Marble
Original
(Glyptothek)

Hellenistic terra cotta

St. Magdalen. Tilman
Riemenschneider
(National Museum)

Mary and Child. Anonymous (National Museum)

our emotions more deeply than the art of the. medieval man?
If Tilman Riemenschneider, to mention but one of the more familiar names, is not held in the same esteem as Phidias or
Michelangelo, only a bias for the Classic can be responsible. In
the National Museum, in addition to Riemenschneider, Veit Stoss,
and others lesser-known, a host of anonymous artists are present,
all of whom should be counted among the immortals.

Besides the medieval sculptures and paintings, terra cotta and
porcelain objects, armor, utilitarian objects, medieval tapestry,
and furnishings are gathered on the top floor. In the basement
there is a unique collection of ancient cribs.

Two of the old existing churches are of interest. The **Peterskirche,** once Gothic but now purest Baroque, is all white and
gold, light and festive, instilling gaiety and confidence. The second
is the tiny **Asamkirche,** named after its builders, the brothers
Asam, who created it in 1733 for their private use. It is a precious
jewel, all in Rococo, full of fanciful ornamentation, exquisitely
sculptured. Also in Rococo is the **Theatinerkirche,** in elegant white

Christ Figure. Erasmus Grasser

Peterskirche Altar

Old Residenz Theater
(Munich)

St. George, Treasure
Chamber (Residenz)

Jacobskirche,
Altar Detail
(Rothenburg)

stucco, rich and dignified. But the biggest of them all, the one-time Gothic *Frauenkirche* (the cathedral), is a sad reminder of World War II. Its original interior ruined, it has been re-done in a semi-modernistic style, with a few Gothic sculptures left standing forlornly here and there.

Rococo in its most spectacular and elegant dress can be seen in the small *Cuvilliés Theater* housed in the **Residenz,** the former winter home of the Bavarian kings. The exuberance of its sculptured and polychromed décor is beyond description. There is also the treasure chamber (*die Schatzkammer*). The seemingly endless number of precious objects assembled here puts the beholder in a quandary: Where does craftsmanship end and art begin? Why is a statuette such as the bejeweled, enameled, silver and gold, chased and intaglio work *St. George* considered merely an object of applied art, a goldsmith's tour de force and not the work of a creative artist? In the context of premachine-age art the modern designation "creative" often becomes ambiguous and arbitrary.

Just outside the city, to the west, stands the sumptuous Baroque palace, **Nymphenburg,** built between 1664 and 1675 and enlarged a few decades later. The Great Hall is decorated in Baroque, and some of the rooms in rich Rococo style. The palace is set in a park designed after Versailles, and behind it is a small hunting lodge known as **Amalienburg.** Built by Cuvilliés,, it represents the peak of Rococo style with characteristic designs of that style on the exterior—which is quite rare. Designs of this nature were first developed in France around 1720, and the Germans adopted them eagerly, at once bringing to the system an excellence unsurpassed by any other nation. Perhaps the native German propensity for detailed work was instrumental in this development,

Rococo Fountain (Residenz)   St. George   Herrgottskirche. Tilman
                                    Fountain   Riemenschneider (Detail)

so strikingly documented even in the small churches in certain
rural regions in the south.

ROTHENBURG OB DER TAUBER. This is one of the best-
preserved medieval towns in Germany. There is a Riemenschneider
altar in the *Jacobskirche,* and two splendid altars, one of them also
by Riemenschneider just below Rothenburg in the village of Det-
wang. Ten miles to the northwest in the *Herrgottskirche* of the
tiny village of Creglingen, his chief work is preserved—a 33-foot-
high altar combining a variety of figures in the round as well as in
relief, carved in linden wood within the framework of the retable.
This monumental work was done about the year 1510 and has all
the characteristics of Riemenschneider's mastery. The incredibly
subtle expression of the faces and gracefulness of the figures are
heightened by draperies—referred to by Goethe as the "thousand-
fold echos of form"—that seem to express the animation and
poetry of lofty thoughts. The staccato ripple of the draperies can
only be compared to those in the best of Dürer's engravings. The
incredible thing is that Riemenschneider, the German Michelangelo, because of his support of the Peasants' Revolt was put to
torture by the Bishop of Würzburg, his home town, after their
defeat. With his health broken his creativity ended. In the same
little church is a polychromed altar by Veit Stoss and one by a
Flemish master.

Nuremberg (Nürnberg)

Though heavily bombed in the war and with much of the ancient
part of this city destroyed or badly damaged, the original designs
of the dwellings have been meticulously observed in its reconstruction. But, they lack the patina of age so necessary to make the
buildings appear authentic. Nevertheless, for those in search of
the medieval, this city has much to offer, and, so important to
the traveler, all the sights can be visited in a leisurely one-day

Iron Grillwork, 14th
Century (National
Germanic Museum)

Cover of a Psalter,
10th Century

Portrait of Michael
Wohlgemut. Dürer

walk, which allows him to sustain the level of his enthusiasm.
The Germanic National Museum is the largest one of its kind
in the country, a gigantic accumulation of everything that represents German art, civilization, and history for a thousand years.
Although some of the illustrious names in German art are present,
it is not the paintings one would seek out here, for most of them
are of no great importance. It is the statuary and objects of everyday life and décor, that captivates our attention and admiration.
It is just the absence of the glamorous *"Mona Lisa* type" of work
that allows us to concentrate with never-ending wonderment on
the marvel of these so-called subsidiary arts.

Venus and Amor. Lucas Cranach

Parade Armor, 16th Century
(National Germanic Museum)

Whatever damage was done to the ancient churches has been expertly repaired and they now appear authentic. The oldest, *St. Sebaldus Church,* was built between 1223 and 1273 in Romanesque style as a pillar basilica with two chancels. A century later the Gothic east choir was added, and late in the 15th century the towers were finished. Like so many of the German Gothic churches, it is simple and austere on the outside, but its interior is all color and light. One might object to polychromed stone figures, for the texture of stone is not sympathetic to the effect of color applied upon it, but in this interior it is just the brilliant color and the glitter of gold that gives it the festive mood. Of the renowned relics there is the *St. Sebaldus Shrine* by Peter Vischer (from the beginning of the 16th century), cast in brass, it is a complex creation overburdened by a multiplicity of minutiae; a crucifixion group by Veit Stoss; the Schreyer-Monument, an early great work by Adam Kraft, and a multitude of less-known or anonymous works of equal merit.

The *St. Lorenz Church,* the largest in Nuremburg, was built during the middle of the 13th century and finished two centuries later. It is full of brilliant light that glorifies its treasures and its exquisite architectural detail at every turn. First there is the *Tabernacle* (Sacramentshaus) by Adam Kraft standing 60-feet-high against a pillar, left of the choir, a Gothic masterpiece of first order. The entire structure is supported by figures carved in stone representing the master and two of his assistants. The upper part of the structure was destroyed during the war,

St. Sebaldus Church. Tomb.
Peter Vischer

St. Sebaldus Church Tabernacle

St. Lorenz Church (Nuremberg)   Angelic Salutation (St. Lorenz)

now rebuilt by masons, who came of generations of masons employed by the church for centuries, it appears unscathed. From the hand of Veit Stoss, the *Angelic Salutation* (Engelgruss) is freely suspended from the ceiling, like a giant oval locket, delicately carved in linden wood. Although its figures are nearly seven feet tall, they are in too lofty a position to be studied in detail.

The *Church of Our Lady* (Frauenkirche) on the marketplace dates from the 14th century; it has an unusual Gothic screen façade with steep, stepped gables richly ornamented and crocketted. Tombs by Adam Kraft, the *Tucher Altar,* and many sculptures make its interior very attractive.

Also on the marketplace is the renowned Gothic *Beautiful Fountain* (Der Schöne Brunnen), carved in stone, gilded and polychromed, and brand-new in appearance. Despite all its splendor, however, the overrestored fountain looks garish; polychromed stone statuary seen in the open and close up does not look well. Next on our list is the *Dürer House* and the *Royal Castle.* The first impresses us as much more authentic than the Rembrandt House in Amsterdam, for example, and is structurally far more impressive. It is also filled with excellent copies of many of Dürer's major paintings, original woodcuts, etchings, and numerous facsimiles. The castle, no longer authentic in its main aspects, is still interesting architecturally, and from its lofty height it offers a dramatic view of the city of Nuremberg.

BAMBERG. This town is one of the few that did not suffer war damage. Its elegant patrician 16th-century dwellings and im-

Church of Our Lady and Schöner Brunnen   Albrecht Dürer House

mense cathedral are perhaps the only buildings that remained
unchanged since the 13th century. The *Cathedral* distinguished by
the simplicity and harmony of its structure, was planned early
in the 11th century by Emperor Henry II. Statues of King
Henry II and his Empress Kunigunde, stand outside the Adam
Portal. The cathedral is typically Romanesque, but its towers were
conceived after those of the Laon Cathedral and its sculpture
follows closely the style of the Rheims Cathedral. The sculpture,
more abundant here than elsewhere, is the most precious in the
country after that of the Dom of Naumburg (in East Germany).

WURZBURG. This is the city of Riemenschneider. He was born
here, and his work appears in nearly every church. It is found
in the cathedral (der *Dom*), on Neumünster, St. Burkard, the
Church of the Franciscans (*Franziskanerkirche*), the *Marienkapelle* (with the famous tomb of Konrad van Schaumberg), and
in the *Mainfränkishes Museum*. Würzburg was a bishops' See
from the middle of the 8th century. Originally, the bishops, who
were also the reigning Dukes of Franconia, resided in the *Marien-
berg Fortress*, where stands the oldest church of the region, one
of the few important buildings that escaped destruction. But the
showplace of the town is their Baroque residence built from 1720
to 1744 by the greatest German architect of the time, Balthasar
Neumann. Known as the *Residenz*, the edifice was hit during
the war, but the stairway hall, believed to be among the largest
and most resplendent in Europe, escaped major damage. The
entrance hall has a ceiling decorated by Tiepolo who has given
his painted figures sculptured limbs—it is indeed difficult to see
where the sculptured part of the legs terminates and the painted
portion begins. Such a violation of esthetic principles for the
creation of illusory effects could only have worked in the system
of Baroque architecture. Here it does produce the desired effect

of unlimited space. Another famous hall in the Residenz is the *Kaisersaal,* decorated in the frilliest Rococo.

WORMS. The *Cathedral,* built from the 11th to 12th centuries is an example of the purest unified Romanesque plan. It is a compactly built red stone pillar-basilica with two round towers and two choirs placed at each end (in a medieval building, "choir" refers to the body of the church from the crossing to the east, or altar end). Running columnar and blind arcading, combining power with grace, are the chief adornments of these most felicitously composed architectural components. The interior, however, is a 17th-century restoration carried out after it was damaged in a war with France. Now it contains a magnificent altar by Balthasar Neumann as well as Romanesque and Gothic sculpture placed in the church at a later time. Other points of interest are the *Museum of the City of Worms* (archeological and Roman excavations, also relics of the town's early history), two churches of the 11th and 12th centuries, *St. Martin's* and *St. Paul's,* and the large Gothic *Church of Our Lady* built during the 14th and 15th centuries. The town was heavily bombed, and the reconstruction of the sites was quite extensive.

FRANKFORT (Frankfurt). The bigger a modern city, the more difficult it is for the traveler to "pick his way" through acres of architectural abominations. Not that strictly utilitarian structures are ipso facto ugly. They are issues of engineering, not of art, and at best merely freeze up the imagination. In Frankfort the architectural absurdities by far outnumber the modern "erector set" structures. Much of the city was destroyed during the war, especially the old town with many historic buildings. Hence to try to seek out authentic Gothic or Renaissance relics here would be quite unreasonable. But the 14th-century *Cathedral* in spite of much restoration is not without interest, for it contains

Bamberg Cathedral

The Stairway Hall
(Residenz, Würzburg)

Worms Cathedral

Simonette Vespucci. Botticelli
(Städelsches Kunstinstitut,
Frankfurt)

Mocking of Christ. Bosch
(Städelsches Kunstinstitut)

some superb Gothic sculpture (as well as 19th-century imitations). The best vistas of the city are from the banks of the river Main; in silhouette the unfolding scenery is quite captivating.

There is one attraction for those in search of art—the collection of the **Staedel Art Institute** (Städelsches Kunstinstitut), which contains paintings of major importance. Among them is Van Eyck's *Lucca Madonna;* two equally exquisite panels in Gothic-Flemish tradition by the Master of Flémalle; an extraordinary composition, *Ecco Homo,* by Bosch; Grünewald's *St. Laurentius;* Altdorfer's *Adoration of the Magi;* and superb works by Cranach, Holbein, Bellini, Carpaccio, Memling, and those precious nameless primitives referred to as "Master of . . ." One of Botticelli's most attractive portraits is also here and is thought to be Giuliano de Medici's mistress, *Simonetta Vespucci,* glorified by the poet Politian as the "Goddess of Love." (It was he who suggested to the painter the theme for his *Birth of Venus.*) I have referred on previous occasions to the propensity of early Renaissance masters for portraits in profile, since such representations offer the great opportunities for the elaboration of linear patterns. Indeed, nothing could be more melodious than Botticelli's meandering delineations woven into this painting.

MAINZ. Once a Celtic settlement at a confluence of the Rhine and the Main, the city became the capital of a Roman province. In the 8th century it was the residence of the first German archbishop, and later the capital of the Holy Roman Empire.

Mainz Cathedral

The Roman Column
(Mainz)

It was at this later date (11th century) that *the Cathedral,* conceived largely in Lombard style, took shape and its east choir was erected. The west choir, in a trefoil form, followed a century later. It has a lantern tower (the loftiest in Germany) over each crossing and four other towers, built at different times. Many centuries passed in the making of the cathedral and a large number of restorations were carried out, but notwithstanding the variety of styles that are conspicuous here and there, ranging from Romanesque to Rococo, they all appear united into one grand design. In silhouette the cathedral is a complex, somber, imperious monument. Its interior is also somber, overrestored, cold, appearing empty. The statuary, in relief, of emblematic character, is placed on heavy piers which, in their massive squareness, somehow fail to rise. The main attraction in the interior is the black choir stalls. These are in sumptuous Baroque, carved in oak—indeed, in their rhythmic beat they suggest organ music. *The Cathedral Museum,* located in the cloisters, among other sculptures houses those by one of the nameless geniuses known only as the Naumburg Master because of his work in the Naumburg Cathedral.

One should also try to see the *Roman Column of Jupiter,* the *Romano-Germanic Museum* in the Electoral Palace, the *Picture Gallery,* and the *Museum of Antiquities.*

COLOGNE (Köln). This is a dismal place; disorder seems to be the ruling principle. After the bombing that completely destroyed the old city only some ugly prewar "modern" buildings remain, as dull as the later style of the 40's and 50's, and the common airport terminal variety so popular today. Miraculously the famous *Cathedral* suffered only minor damage.

The Classic paintings in the *Wallraf-Richartz Museum* and the fine collection of medieval statuary in the *Schnüttgen Museum* are of interest. Among the paintings those from the 14th and 15th centuries are well represented. Some of these are complex compositions, by anonymous masters of the highest rank, with their style based on the precepts of the Flemish school. Among the outstanding paintings one finds Stefan Lochner's *Last Judgment*, Bartolomäus Bruyn's Renaissance portraits, Dürer's *Piper and Drummer*, and Flemish and Dutch works by Rubens, Van Dyck, and Jordaens. If the last had limited himself to portraiture, he might have come close to Frans Hals, who never failed to capture the character of his sitters. Rembrandt is also at his best in the *Portrait of a Scholar*, but his last self-portrait is in such poor condition that its artistic merit cannot be evaluated. Again, the Dutch Kleine Meesters—what an enormous production of exquisite works there was in Holland during the 17th and 18th centuries— Averkamp van de Velde, Van Goyen, De Witte, and many more are here to honor these presently unfashionable artists.

The upper floor of the museum is devoted to 20th-century art, with Germans dominating the scene. Poor taste and an unabashed lack of talent are rampant. It is as if the German Expressionists made a deliberate show of their ineptness.

In the *Schnüttgen Museum,* housed in the remodeled ruins of the one-time Romanesque *Cecilienkirche,* all is aptitude, refinement, and in the best of taste. Statuary, ivory carvings, objects of bronze from the 9th through the 16th century delight our senses at every turn.

As can be expected of the richest city in Germany until the 16th century, Cologne's cathedral has great distinction. Next to those of Seville and Milan, it is the largest Gothic structure in Europe. The Gothic design adopted in Cologne in the middle of

A Reliquary Bust
(Schnüttgen Museum,
Cologne)

The Awakening of Lazarus. Anonymous
(Schnüttgen)

Cologne Cathedral

Maria in Kapital Church (Cologne)

the 13th century closely followed the plans of Beauvais and Amiens, and the early windows were copied from the Sainte Chapelle in Paris. The lower section of the nave and the choir are 14th-century. The upper part, the west front, and the towers were finished in the 19th century. In spite of the long duration of building and the many restorations that were carried out even before the more recent calamity, it has a uniformly Gothic look. It is a beautiful edifice, though somewhat monotonous, and its towers are too powerful for the rest of it. But this is compensated for by a massiveness emphasized by the shortness of the nave and transepts. The whole appears like a giant pyramid; rising from the ground, its pinnacled surface suggests a waterfall cascading from a precipitous height. Other churches, once distinguished by pure Rhenish-Romanesque designs, are either in a state of complete disrepair or restored to a degree where their ancient characteristics have vanished.

AACHEN. The name of this town is closely linked with that of Charlemagne, King of the Franks, Emperor of the Holy Roman Empire. His throne and his burial place are in the *Cathedral,* which for six centuries served for the coronation of German Kings. Erected between 796 and 804, it was the most important building of the epoch and at one time the emperor's palace was attached to it. The core of the cathedral, known as the *Octagonal,* closely follows the pattern established in San Vitale in Ravenna. Much of its marble paneling as well as some of the Byzantine capitals surmounting the external pilasters were actually obtained from the palace of Theodoric, who founded his kingdom in that city three centuries earlier. Although the edifice was rebuilt in the 10th century, it retained its eastern look as Byzantine artists working on various projects along the Rhine were employed. They established a Byzantine-German style to which we now refer as

Aachen Cathedral

Ottonian (after Otto I, Emperor of the Holy Roman Empire). These eastern artists exerted great influence on bronze casting, ivory carving, stained-glass manufacture, and the art of illuminated manuscripts. It is believed that the bronze balustrading that fills the opening of the galleries and the bronze doors in the interior date from that time. The treasury of the cathedral is very rich in early German metalsmith work. The building, as such, has undergone many changes through the ages: the choir was built in the 14th century, and in addition to the original Byzantine and Romanesque features, Flamboyant Gothic and even Baroque appear picturesquely combined. Fortunately, the war damage did not seriously affect the structure.

The *Sauermond Museum* contains 12th- to 18th-century statuary and 15th- to 16th-century Flemish and German panels, much of it of great distinction.

Berlin

Now located in Dahlem, a suburb of Berlin, the splendid *Museum Dahlem* was known before World War II as the *Kaiser Friedrich Museum*. Its foundation was laid only after the Napoleonic wars, when Prussia gained immensely in power, but art collecting really started under King Frederick the Great (18th century). An ardent admirer of French culture, the king acquired chiefly French contemporary pictures, and since the Rococo period did not favor the art of painting, his Lancrets, Paters, Bouchers, and so forth do not amount to much. Later he also obtained works by Rubens, Van Dyck, Tintoretto, and Veronese. At the

Mars, Venus and Amor. Pierro di Cosimo
(Dahlem Museum, Berlin)

beginning of the 19th century the Berlin collection had only 300 paintings, which were scattered all over royal residences in Prussia. The original museum was officially established in 1823, and only after the founding of the German Empire in 1872 did it begin to gain international importance, chiefly because of its efficient organizer, the great German scholar Wilhelm von Bode. But like all scholars, he, too, suffered from his own bias. At the end of the last century he would not accept El Greco for the museum and staunchly declined to acquire paintings done "before the invention of art"—among which he grouped all work prior to the Italian Renaissance.

Even after having visited the famous museums in Europe, one cannot help but be overawed by the wealth of this collection. In fact, on this occasion it becomes difficult to comprehend that there was enough genius around in so few centuries to fill so many museums with works of such importance. If there ever was a doubt about Altdorfer's claim to greatness, his *Flight to Egypt* would dispel it. He was the first German landscape painter who could stand side-by-side with the Flemish, although they began painting landscapes as an independent art form at an earlier date. Flemish influence is obvious in Altdorfer's work, but there

Portrait. Rogier van der
Weyden (Dahlem
Museum)

Portrait. Petrus Christus
(Dahlem Museum)

Man with the Gold Helmet.
Rembrandt (Dahlem)

Jacob Wrestling with the Angel. Rembrandt (Dahlem Museum)

Portrait of George Gisze. Holbein (Dahlem)

Madonna. Van Eyck (Dahlem)

is something essentially German, even something provincial, in his conception of nature. There is also a certain weakness in most of his creations (though not in the *Flight to Egypt*) in that the figures animating the scene appear as an afterthought, an appendage, as it were. It would seem that the intimacy of his insight into the grandeur of nature robbed him of the focus needed to concentrate on humanity dwarfed by the majesty of the place it occupies. There are eight of his paintings in the museum.

Konrad Witz was born 80 years earlier; steeped in Gothic discipline, he was much influenced by the school of Van Eyck. His, also, is an uncommon feeling for landscape, where incidental details are subordinated to a larger scheme of space seen in depth. Several of his best paintings are here. As can be expected, German masters are represented in the museum with their foremost works: Dürer's late portraits (*Holzschuher* and *Muffel*), steeped

Burial of Christ. Vittore Carpaccio (Dahlem)

St. Matthew. Tilman Riemenschneider (Dahlem)

Portrait. Master of the Flémalle
(Dahlem)

Portrait. Domenico Veneziano
(Dahlem)

in Renaissance tradition, and others such as *Madonna with the
Finch,* painted during his second stay in Venice in 1506. Holbein
the Elder and his more famous son, who became a court painter
in London, are here, and among the latter's portraits that of
George Gisze has never been surpassed. Lucas Cranach the Elder,
the arch-provincial (in this case, the father outranks the son),
was also enamored of landscapes—and who could make a tree more
tree-like or had his flair for painting these wicked-looking "slinky"
nudes (*Venus and Amor Stealing Honey*)? Martin Schongauer
and Hans Multscher complete the German elite gathered at
Dahlem.

The Flemish contingent is no less august, and I should like to
mention first the *Portrait of a Young Girl* (1446) by Petrus
Christus, believed to have been a pupil of Van Eyck, which I prize
most of all the portraits of that period, not for the sentiment
implied in the painting, but for the disposition of its design.
Compare it with Domenico Veneziano's equally famous, totally
Renaissance *Profile of a Young Woman* painted at about the same
time; when we weigh one against the other, we shall have to admit
that only a bias for the Gothic would make one lean toward the
former. The Flemish masters are of such outstanding quality that
one is hard put to name "the best." Here is Van Eyck's portrait
of *Giovanni Arnolfini* (the one of the *Marriage of Arnolfini* is in
the National Gallery in London), and it is not the "psychological"

penetration of the subject that is so compelling, but the manner of its formal design. There is also: Hieronymus Bosch's *St. John on Patmos* amid a landscape that only he could have invented; Van der Weyden's much-reproduced *Portrait of a Young Woman,* and his *Nativity;* Hugo van der Goes' monumental *Adoration of the Magi;* and two panels—enchanting as ever—by Geertgen tot Sint Jans, the genius who died before reaching his 30th year; and not to be forgotten, Jan Gossaert's (better known as Mabuse) *Gethsemane* and *Virgin and Child.*

One might expect the Italian section to show weakness. Not at all. Besides the work by Domenico Veneziano (sometimes attributed to Pollaiuolo), Fra Filippo Lippi cannot, even in his native Florence, be seen to better advantage than in his *Adoration of the Child,* which once hung in the Medici-Riccardi Palace. The same can be said of Francesco del Cossa's *The Autumn* and Piero di Cosimo's *Venus, Mars and Amor;* the latter possesses great poetic charm as well as his usual whimsicality. Botticelli, Andrea del Castagno, Luca Signorelli, Mantegna, Titian—all are here in their best dress, and when Bronzino assumes in his portrait of *Ugolino Martelli* a selfconscious heroic stance, he does it with impeccable taste and great authority. And who could fail to be profoundly moved by Carpaccio's *Burial of Christ?* Here surrealistic thoughts are woven into a fabric of poetic sentiment.

The Holland collection is as fine as the Italian. It contains 25 Rembrandts—the largest number in any museum of Europe. And if not all are important or even good Rembrandts, some belong with his best portraits, notably the *Man with the Gold Helmet* and *Portrait of Hendrickje Stoffels.* Rubens, Vermeer, De Hooch, and a host of the Kleine Meesters are here, delightful, all. It is strange to meet Gerard Terborch's *The Concert* in Dahlem. A print of this painting hung in my room when I was a small boy and it never ceased to worry me: the figure of the lady visible above the spinet seemed to be a lifeless dummy stuck against the wall—it gave me a weird feeling. Only many, many years later did I learn that this was a late 19th-century over-painting, covering up a gentleman who originally sat at the spinet.

AUSTRIA

Most of Austria possesses unsurpassed natural beauty. This is not simply a personal impression but is the generally held opinion of seasoned, discriminating travelers. Moreover, the country is rich in relics—churches, castles, monasteries. Few have retained their one-time Gothic style, for Baroque predominates in this country. The Baroque style followed the Gothic, while the Renaissance scarcely touched its architecture. It is not difficult to predict that the art-conscious traveler, when in the charming city of Vienna will find the Museum of Art History is a high point in his journey. Hence we shall start with this great repository of paintings.

Museums and Edifices

The **Museum of Art History** (Das Kunsthistorisches Museum). This once-imperial collection is housed in a pompous, typical late 19th-century palace, and although its range is not wide, the general level of the paintings is very high. Established by the Emperors of Austria, it mirrors their taste. Thus one will find no work of the 13th and 14th centuries or of the early Italian Renaissance, and no English or French art. However, the museum is well endowed with examples of the Spanish school (after the Prado in Madrid, it possesses the largest number of works by Velázquez) as well as Flemish and Late Renaissance paintings. The collection was started by Emperor Maximilian, whose portrait by Dürer from a drawing made in Augsburg in 1519 is owned by the gallery. Maximilian's daughter, Margaret of Austria, was the one-time leading collector of art in Europe, as was the Emperor's grandson, Rudolph II. In fact, the latter could be considered one of the most voracious collectors of all time. It is because of his efforts and those of his descendants that the museum owns the most important of Pieter Brueghel's paintings. In fact, a trip to Vienna would be worthwhile if only to study these works. Because the Austrian and Spanish Hapsburgs had close family ties, there are numerous portraits by Velázquez in the gallery. But they were thought little of by the monarchs; displeased with the likenesses, the emperor dispatched his own court painter to Spain to produce more "authentic" pictures.

Return of the Herd. Pieter Brueghel
(Kunsthistorisches Museum)

The Hunters in Snow. Pieter Breughel

Conversion of Paul. Pieter Breughel

Susanna. Tintoretto

Needless to say, the favored court painter is now in total oblivion.

Though Brueghel is today recognized as one of the greatest artists, this was not always the case. As late as 1894 his *Dulle Griet* (now in the Van der Bergh Collection in Antwerp) was bought for $100. His compositions are anti-Classic; they lack the grand scheme of the Renaissance masters; there is still much of the Gothic spirit in them (considered by classicists a negative feature); his themes are didactic and the images often grotesque —"peasant Brueghel" he was called, and this was not meant as a compliment. Since it is assembled in one large hall, we have the opportunity to steep ourselves in his *oeuvre*. Each of the large panels tells a story of the human condition; on the surface it is a common one, but in Brueghel the common always harbors the symbolic. In what way is the symbolic in Brueghel so re-

The Little Fur. Rubens

Princess Margaret Theresa. Velázquez

markable? Its operatives employ all the means which in lesser hands would become trivial. Debarred from esotericism, the particular is sublimated into the universal, and the universal harbors in its folds man's eternal predicaments—his collective irrationalities, his heroism, folly, lawlessness, piety, and demonism. These human conditions are represented with such a power of imagination, inventiveness, and originality, and with pictorial means so grandiose, that words can hardly describe the magnificence of his panels. Brueghel's technique is very simple. These panels are painted in an essentially *alla prima* manner following the precepts of Bosch—eminently suitable to narrative subject matter.

Velázquez, unlike Brueghel, was not plagued by inner demonism; behold, for example, the portraits of the Spanish royal children in two small side wings of the museum. One is reminded of Renoir at his best, so impressionistic is the 17th-century master's brush; it constitutes a great lesson for the art student in illuminating an epigrammatic technique that relies on the essentials of representation.

Single-figure pieces (other than formal portraits) have a charm and persuasiveness of their own, besides being found quite rarely with painters like Rubens, Tintoretto, or Correggio. Rubens' *Little Fur* is no doubt his most ingratiating performance of this kind, as is Tintoretto's *Susanna*. In the same category belong Titian's *Nymph and Shepherd,* in romantic Giorgionesque overtones, and Correggio's *Jupiter and Io* and *Ganymede,* which once decorated a room in the castle at Mantua. Another famous Rubens, the *Ildefonso* altarpiece (painted for the Jesuit Church in Brussels), is splendid work, but its Baroque opulence somehow does not sit well with us today.

Other works of importance are Dürer's *Adoration of the Trinity,* Giorgione's *The Three Philosophers,* Raphael's *The Madonna of the Meadow,* and Vermeer's *The Artist in the Studio,* one of the largest works by this master. These paintings are the *pièces de résistance,* but there are also a great number of "minor" works worthy of close study.

There is a collection on the lower floor of the museum which is not as important to those whose main interest is painting. There are sculptures from early Roman times to the Baroque, as well as a variety of objects classified under the general term "Applied Art." I have often felt a certain uneasiness when referring to that category of art of the past, for the term minimizes the esthetic value of these creations. These works of décor (also an inaccurate designation, for all art objects primarily serve the purpose of decoration), such as ornate vessels fashioned of every conceivable material and other precious items to embellish the status of men in high social position, are of the finest quality, as was to be expected in a country whose rulers were at one time among the mightiest in Europe. To describe the appearance of these artifacts would be a tedious and futile task. Chronologically they range from the Egyptian, Roman, and early Christian eras to the High Baroque, which in Austria covers the first part of the 18th century. Crystal, marble, bronze, silver, wood—these raw materials have been transformed through the miracle of skilled artistry, into objects whose beauty places them with the works of the immortals.

Academy of Fine Arts (Die Akademie der Bildenden Künste). 17th- to 18th-century paintings assembled in the Academy are also not negligible, although there are no world-renowned masterpieces among them.

Those interested in ecclesiastic statuary should not miss the *Museum of Austrian Baroque and Medieval Art* (Österreichisches Museum für Barock und Mittelalterliche Kunst) in the *Lower Belvedere*. Except for some Gothic panels the paintings in these collections are of no great interest.

In the *Albertina* one will find the largest and most important repository of drawings and prints in Europe. However the rare items are not on exhibit. These can be seen only by special appointment.

Museum of the City of Vienna (Historisches Museum der Stadt Wien). This museum is very near the Karlskirche and should be on the traveler's list for one purpose—to view a few of the original statuary that once graced both the façade and the tower of St. Stephen's Cathedral. Badly weathered and in a fragmented condition, these monuments, because of their ambiguous appearance, have a magic appeal, for today the mysterious, the equivocal—rather than the explicit—in art incites our imagination.

Austrian Folk Art Museum (Österreichisches Museum für Volkskunde). Beholding the ancient art of the peasants, in this collection of folk art, one realizes that it is no less sophisticated than that of the upper classes. It shows great sensitivity because it lacks the "finish," the slick finish which is the result of over-elaboration by those concerned with status in life. In other words, folk art, guided essentially by the same style as the more luxuriant art produced for kings, has one basic virtue, that of simplicity. Simple things, as experience teaches us, are less liable to go wrong.

Although Vienna does not outrank the city of Paris in over-all design, the Austrian capital is ingratiating because of its relaxed atmosphere and the abundance of Baroque and Biedermeier architecture. (Biedermeier, a typical Austrian style, dates from about

1820 to 1850. It modified the haughtiness of Empire style characteristic of the neo-Classic Napoleonic period and made it fit into a middle-class milieu.)

Particularly charming is the central district with its squares: Die Freyung; die Burg; and Josephsplatz, with the famous Baroque complexes of the *Albertina Museum*, the *Spanish Riding School*, the *Reichskanzlertrakt*, the *Redoutensaal* (the ballroom), and the magnificent *Winter Reitsaal* used for the celebrated performance of the Spanish Riding School. The environs of the *St. Stephen's Cathedral* also retain their 18-century flair, and of course, there is the Opernplatz with its unmatched *Opera House*.

Another masterpiece of Baroque architecture is **The Belvedere,** two separate palaces (the upper and the lower) erected for the Prince of Savoy by Lucas von Hildebrandt in the early 18th century. They are divided by an enormous formal garden planned after Versailles. From the same period comes the **Palace of Schönbrunn,** the former summer residence of the Austrian emperors. Some of its interiors are decorated with the original Rococo furnishings from the time of Maria Theresa, Empress of Austria (whose daughter married Louis XVI), while others are in severe Empire style.

St. Stephen's Cathedral (Stefansdom) stands in the very heart of Vienna; because of its location and characteristic tall, slender steeple, it is considered the symbol of the city. The steeple, finished in the 15th century, tapers directly from the base (there is no evidence of a shaft), which weakens its effect. When the tower was erected, the steep roof of the church was covered with glazed tiles; what we see today is a modern replica. The church was built first in Romanesque style, then changed to Gothic, but a part of the original façade incorporated into the later structure is still in evidence. The interior, of German design, is referred to as *Hallenkirche* (hall church). Raising the vault of the side aisles and increasing the height of the pier arches and side walls, made the interior more spacious. The clerestory disappeared and the

Belvedere Castle (Vienna)

Schönbrunn Palace Courtyard (Vienna)

St. Stephen's Cathedral (Vienna)

The Chancel, St. Stephen's (Detail)

flying buttresses were no longer required. Such devices as a rule deprive an interior of its variety, but because of the relatively small dimensions of the edifice, the interior did not lose in interest; on the contrary, it became more intimate, elegant, and harmonious by far, and the delicacy of its detail, by making it much more conspicuous, was greatly enhanced. St. Stephen's is truly the finest church in all of Austria.

St. Charles Church (Karlskirche), a masterpiece by the great Austrian architect Fischer von Erlach, is an edifice of great originality and architectural imagination. Here Roman, Renaissance, and Baroque ideas are daringly combined. Strangely, in

St. Stephen's Cathedral Interior

Karlskirche (Vienna)

Vienna, there are not many churches of particular interest. Some minor edifices are either overrestored, or emptied of their ancient relics; and others are hidden away in suburbs.

The Country

THE ROAD TO SALZBURG. The first stop on the trip to Salzburg should be the ancient village of *Dürnstein*, located on the Danube amid the enchanting landscape of the Wachau. Only fragments of the medieval castle in which Richard the Lion-hearted was held prisoner in 1193 remain. This former Gothic monastery dating from the early 15th century has taken on—as has practically every important edifice in Austria—a Baroque look. I do not mean to belittle this look, for there is nothing more charming than Austrian Baroque, nothing that engages the eye more pleasurably, nothing that makes us feel equal to the occasion, not cowed by it.

Our next stop is *Melk* (where we cross the river by ferry) and its abbey, the largest and most imposing Baroque structure in Europe. Founded in the 11th century and reconstructed from 1660 to 1726, it stands high on a promontory and dominates the landscape for many miles around. Just six miles off the main road, outside the tiny village of *Mauer*, stands a little church founded about 1300; its side altar, said to have come from the workshop of the renowned sculptor, Veit Stoss, is a masterpiece of late Gothic art. Equally splendid is the main altar, built in high

Dürnstein Abbey

Altar Detail (Mauer)

Baroque. As we know, Gothic style was at one time considered regressive, so the little church was given an up-to-date touch (luckily the style of the middle of the 18th century was a good one). When visiting these out-of-the-way villages, one can hardly conceive that so much sophistication could have flourished in a simple peasant milieu.

Enns is our next stop. It was founded in the 11th century, and the plan of the main square appears to date from the same time, but the façades of the houses around it are three to four centuries younger. With the 16th-century bell tower in the center, rising imperiously over the low dwellings, it is a solemn sight. If time permits, the abbey of *St. Florian,* with its magnificently designed staircase, is worth a visit, as is a second abbey in *Kremsmunster,* some 15 miles away.

On to *Traunsee* and the *Salzkammergut.* In this sub-alpine region, nature is pre-eminent and the man-made, no matter how enchanting, takes a back seat. Now our road leads through *Gmunden, Bad Ischl, Strobl,* and finally *St. Wolfgang.* It is ironic indeed that it has taken the gay operetta (*"The White Horse Inn"*) to make this extraordinary village familiar to the public. Its *Hallenkirche* (15th-century Late Gothic, plus the usual Baroque ornamentation) contains an altarpiece by Michael Pacher, one of the greatest Austrian masters working in this field late in the 15th century. The polyptych consists of 16 paintings on four separate panels, a painted predella, and a carved retable. The little church, its courtyard, the neighboring houses, and the lake form an inseparable unit, never to be forgotten. On such occasions the importance of a homogeneous setting becomes apparent as does the fact that in a poor composition, the incongruous can vitiate the beauty of an ensemble and impair our enjoyment of it.

The road in St. Wolfgang comes to a dead end. Hence to continue to Salzburg we shall double back to Strobl, then around the lake, through *St. Gilgen,* over the pass to *Mondsee,* spending two leisurely hours amidst a fabulous landscape. In the village of Mondsee is another church—Baroque, of course—that could be the pride of any metropolis. On to Salzburg, over old country roads, through ancient hamlets—or over the less-interesting speedway.

Salzburg

There can certainly be no doubt about it, this is *the* most beautiful city in Europe; here nature and man conspired to produce a masterpiece combining grandeur and soul-satisfying loveliness. As to its "composition"—although one expects to find all members coordinated under a ruling principle in a well-balanced arrangement, in nature the interest can be found more often than not in the fortuitous and capricious. These qualities account for variety, and variety offers surprise—the sustaining element in everything visual. In Salzburg one experiences these sensations at every turn. Lest we lose ourselves in ecstatic pronouncements, here are some statistics: The majority of the houses in the old city through which the river Salzach winds its leisurely way are from the 15th century, although their mortar-covered stone façades do not show it; as is to be expected, some are decorated with Baroque and Rococo ornaments, but within, the medieval look remains unchanged.

The "crown" of the city is its imposing medieval fortress, the *Hohensalzburg;* it grows out of the high rock and dominates the valleys around it. Built in the 11th century and much enlarged in the 15th and 16th centuries, it served as the seat of the reigning archbishops. The fortress itself, its courtyards and battlements, the view over the surrounding valleys and the distant mountains, together form a work of art beyond compare.

Other edifices are the *Residence,* built in the 12th and rebuilt in the 17th century; *Hofmarstall,* with portal design by Fischer von Erlach (17th century); and the elegant *Hofmarstallschwemme—* the horses' fountain—on which no effort was spared to give the horses a regal watering place. *Schloss Mirabel,* with its gardens, Baroque limestone statuary, grotesque *Dwarf Garden* and the *Pegasus Fountain,* has been much altered in the course of two centuries. The palace has a grand 18th-century staircase decorated with cherubs. At one time it was the seat of the bishops, who had by then left the gloomy fortress. Finally, *Schloss Hellbrunn,* outside the city, with its fantastic palace gardens and ingenious Baroque fountain works, will give endless delight to anyone weary of modern technology.

View of the Hohensalzburg

Mirabel, Dwarf Garden Figure (Salzburg)

Pegasus, Mirabel Castle

Staircase, Mirabel Castle

The Cathedral (Der Dom). When first erected, the Romanesque building could accommodate 10,000 people, at a time when the city had but 8000 inhabitants—such was the ambition of the ruling bishop of the province. Over the centuries the cathedral has entirely changed its medieval character. Today, it appears in a palatial, late Italian Renaissance style, although parts of the severely Romanesque structure are recognized unexpectedly here and there. Its interior, cool, light, and aloof, does not invite metaphysical contemplation—its splendor is too self-assured and worldly, but the entire powerful complex of the cathedral with its adjoining courtyards and palaces is awe-inspiring. In strongest contrast, a few hundred feet away, stands the **Church of the Franciscans,** built in the 8th century. It still possesses some original structures; the nave is Romanesque-Gothic, the lofty choir dates from the 15th century, and the high altar is a Baroque masterpiece by Fischer von Erlach, the builder of the Karlskirche in Vienna. His **Collegian Church** in Salzburg must also be numbered among his important works, as are the **Dreifaltigkeitskirche,** the **St. Johannesspitalkirche** and the **Ursulinenkirche.** In *St.*

Mozart Platz and the Dome (Salzburg)

The Cathedral Interior

Franciskanerkirche Altar (Salzburg)

Peter's, with its ancient cemetery, the 9th century meets the Rococo, without disturbing our esthetic equilibrium. To describe the place in words seems a foolhardy endeavor.

Salzburg is often referred to as the City of Mozart, and never was there a more appropriate name given to a place. *Mozart's House* is right in the center of the old city. Do not fail to climb the three flights of stairs to the modest flat.

The Country

THE ROAD TO INNSBRUCK. After leaving Vienna, paintings and statuary cease to occupy the traveler. From here on he will be concerned with ancient architecture and in connection with it, the landscape, which must here be looked upon as art in its most sublime form. For one who reacts to all visual experiences on an esthetic level, it is often impossible to remain within the narrow confines of semantics and consider as art only that which has a frame around it or which stands on a pedestal. Thus the journey to Innsbruck will have as its chief inducement the Alpine landscape. (For details of the trip see Part II.)

INNSBRUCK. With but few exceptions, as in all the larger settlements, the old city alone is of interest; the outlying districts are drab. However, the area once enclosed by the city walls, with its 14th- and 15th-century dwellings and pointed arcades, still exudes the air of the Middle Ages. Some remarkable buildings can be found in the old city, many virtually unchanged such as the graceful *Goldenes Dachl* (golden roof). Others, equally ancient, are now unabashedly dressed in fanciful Rococo fronts. Together with the squares and fountains, they are framed by the snow-covered mountain peaks. In places like this, the traveler can hardly work up a desire to seek out art collections—walking the cobblestone streets and gazing at relics that seem to date from an unfathom-

Helbinghaus (Innsbruck)

Das Goldenes Dachl (Innsbruck)

Hofkirche (Innsbruck)

ably remote past is all one wishes to do. Nevertheless, two visits should be made: the *Folk Art Museum* (Das Museum für Volkskunde) and the *Court Castle*.

Folk art is often looked upon with condescension, but to experience the beauty in the everyday life of the simple peasants and town folk of times gone by, the exacting craftsmanship, innate good taste, and art that went into the making of household goods and decorative objects, a visit to this collection should not be omitted. Here the mysterious interrelationship between style and art reveals itself to us, and the overriding importance of a viable style-ideology that directs man's handiwork, making it noble or shoddy, becomes manifest at once.

Court Castle (Dass Schloss), as it appears in Dürer's watercolor, done in 1495 when he stopped in Innsbruck on his way to Italy, was once medieval—turrets, arcades, moats, bays. Today, it is in typical Maria Theresa Rococo style, although the skeleton of the original structure has not been totally obliterated—it shows up surreptitiously here and there in the Gothic groined and fan vaulting. The reception halls and apartments are adorned with an imperial splendor, no different from that of the Schönbrunn palace in Vienna. However, our chief attention will be given to the Court Chapel and the church. The Silver Chapel, as it is known, because of the embossed silver reliefs on the altar, and the exquisitely sculptured sarcophagi of the archduke and his wife from the 16th century, are remarkable, but the interior, containing the mausoleum of the "Last Knight," Emperor Maximilian I, is unique. It is not just a tomb of a great potentate, but a fantasy, solemnizing a mythical knighthood. The architectural variety of the church hall with its 23 bronze statuettes of saints (the Emperor's "kin folk"), 20 bronze busts of Roman Emperors (also

Tomb of Maximilian I
(Innsbruck)

Parish Church,
Heiligenblut
(Kärnten)

Heiligenblut and View
of the Grossglockner

illustrious "family members" of the knight), and the view from the gallery down into the church interior is extraordinary. Here 28 giant knights and ladies—ancestors, close relatives, and historical figures cast in bronze—solemnly surround the sepulcher. Some of the designs for the figures were made by Dürer, and other great masters collaborated in casting this group of Late Gothic statuary. As technical achievements alone, these must be considered rare works of art of their kind, although the names of the master craftsmen who fashioned them are not celebrated in art history.

Angel. Tilman Riemenschneider (Jacobs-kirche, Rothenburg)

Section 7 / Italy

INTRODUCTION TO THE ART OF ITALY

Should one plan to visit but one country in Europe in search of art, Italy would be the first choice, for here the best in art flourished for more than two millenia almost without interruption. The "best" is not limited to Italy, but nowhere else can it be seen in such profusion and diversity. Because of this overwhelming wealth, only the generally known artists, architects, and sites will be mentioned in this introduction, for to list all the important ones would require a great many pages.

To begin with, there is native pre-Roman art, the Etruscan, which flourished from about the 6th to the 3rd century B.C. The sculptures are predominantly in terra cotta, but there are also some in bronze, usually funerary in nature. They have a strange, almost surrealistic mood about them, a compelling ritualistic suggestiveness and remoteness and not infrequently a grotesquerie. It appears that Etruscan image-makers must have been well thought of, for their work is found far from Etruria, as well as in Roman and Greek colonies.

Roman art is patterned after the Greek, and although much of it is a direct copy or a close approximation of Greek examples, we cannot relegate it to second place. In fact, in portraiture, it is unequaled. Forms of realism differ. If we compare Roman realism with that of later periods, the vast difference between them becomes obvious.

There can be no doubt that extensive painting was practiced in ancient Rome, as the murals from Pompeii, Herculaneum, and a few other surviving examples testify, and their quality is often excellent. Yet for some reason Roman artists did not enjoy high standing in society, for their names are not recorded.

After the fall of the Western Roman Empire, Constantinople (founded by Constantine in 330 A.D. on the site of the ancient city of Byzantium) became the capital of the new empire, and with it began the development of Christian art, which was to last for almost a thousand years before secular art reappeared. In Italy, Sicily, and Greece there remain a few Byzantine abbeys and churches, as well as magnificent mosaics, some of which date from the 6th century, but there are no paintings or statuary in evidence except for icons and small, but exquisite objects of ivory, bronze, and enamel.

The art of the 11th century seems to have limited itself to church building, of which the Cathedral Group in Pisa is the finest example in existence. Statuary and paintings appear late in the 12th century, but by anonymous masters; the 13th century, however, teems with stellar names: Cimabue, Duccio, Giotto, Daddi, Niccolò Pisano, Arnolfo di Cambio. During the 14th century Gothic art centered chiefly in Siena and Florence. Among the many masters of that time, the best-known are Andrea Orcagna, Gentile da Fabriano, Giovanni Pisano, Pietro and Ambrogio Lorenzetti.

Although the Romanesque and Gothic schools lasted from the 12th to the 14th century, in Italy the influence of the Byzantine-Romanesque was stronger than the Gothic, and the borderline between these systems is often blurred. The Gothic traits that managed to prevail during the 14th century largely vanished with the advent of the Early Renaissance at the outset of the 15th century.

We can consider that the Renaissance began by the year 1400, although Gothic—or, perhaps more accurately, archaic—traits still persevered with painters like Fra Angelico, Antonio Vivarini, Simone Martini, Masolino. With Masaccio, however, Renaissance style emerged in its true configuration. Fra Filippo Lippi, Gozzoli, Bellini, Pollaiuolo, Mantegna, Donatello, Verrocchio, and the architects Brunelleschi, Bramante, Alberti, Palladio conjure up the magnitude of a style that was to continue through the 16th century with Luca Signorelli, Botticelli, Leonardo da Vinci, Filippino Lippi, Raphael, Michelangelo, Giorgione, Titian.

Next came the Mannerists and the Baroquists; their advent in time cannot be precisely established, for in periods of transition crosscurrents do not always allow accurate dating or classification. The greatest names of the post-Leonardo period were Tintoretto and Veronese (Baroque), then a host of Mannerists—Bronzino, Parmigianino, Pontormo—and Late Baroquists—Tiepolo, Guardi,

Salvator Rosa—yet how many names did I fail to mention? This brings us to the end of the 18th century—and the end of greatness in Italian art.

Milan

Milan, the northernmost city in our progressive journey south, need not be the first one to visit, for it certainly ranks after Florence and Rome in works of art and architecture. However, there are four major museums—the *Brera, Museo Poldi-Pezzoli, Museo del Duomo,* and the *Biblioteca Ambrosiana*—as well as several churches—the *Duomo, Santa Maria delle Grazie, Basilica di Sant' Ambrogio*—and edifices—the *Castello Sforzesco* and the buildings around the *Piazza dei Mercanti.* For a metropolis this size, places of interest are few indeed, but this is a modern city, whose sober, mercantile aspect is ever-present.

Museums

Brera. Although not to be compared with the Uffizi, this dreary palace harbors one of the great Italian collections of paintings. It also leaves in us the recognition that mediocrities were plentiful even at a time when the art of painting was in its heyday. Run-of-the-mill works abound (chiefly of the 17th century), hence it is best to pass them by quickly and head directly for the master-

Adoration of Madonna and Child.
Piero della Francesca

Marriage of the Virgin. Raphael

pieces. Let us begin with Piero della Francesca's *Adoration of the Child with Saints* and *Duke of Urbino*. Wherein lies the greatness of a work of art, we ask ourselves in front of this picture. In some instances we are at a loss to pinpoint the locus of spirituality. With Piero it is the monumentality, the grand simplicity of conception, the utter solemnity of the actors he puts on his stage, that arouses our admiration. Yet the significance of these paintings is not thereby explained. We could add that the manner of composition is different from that of any of his contemporaries, but to attribute it to his originality is as close as we can come to divining his "secret." However, we know that originality is not necessarily the secret of greatness; some of the best painters, Raphael for one, cannot be called "original."

Other masterpieces in the Brera are Carpaccio's *Sposalizio* and *Presentation at the Temple,* Crivelli's *Madonna della Candeletta,* Mantegna's *Dead Christ,* Giovanni Bellini's *Pietà,* Tintoretto's *Finding of the Body of St. Mark,* as well as a Lorenzetti, many Gothic masters, and a host of the "unknowns" who left works of excellence. As might be expected, one finds nearly all of Leonardo's followers in the Brera, and their work is pretty weak. It appears that the master did not have a good influence on his pupils.

As for Raphael's famous *Nuptials of the Virgin,* celebrated in a roped-off niche and still very much in the style of his teacher Perugino, it is of an astonishingly technical perfection for anyone so young (he was 21 when he painted it), but its shortcomings are glaring. Many of the figures maintain an identical stance, the heads display unvarying, vapid expressions, and, most disturbing, the entire picture has a frigid, glassy air. Moreover, its surface has not been freed from the yellowed obscuring film of an old varnish. Then there are the enormous Paolo Veronese canvases. Whoever admires his stupendous display of silk, brocade, precious stuffs, and over-robust anatomy will find it at its best in the Brera. Bernardino Luini's large transferred frescoes arouse in us a curious thought: As soon as a certain type of painting is deprived of its polychromy and hence its illusionistic quality, it gains immensely in appeal—provided, of course, that the work is well composed. Luini's oil paintings, oversweet and full-blown in color, stand at a much lower level than his bleached-out flat murals; these, indeed, are remarkable.

Museo Poldi-Pezzoli. The tenement-like exterior and entrance portal of this palace are deceiving, for it contains a formerly private collection of importance. Amid an incongruous company of bric-à-brac ranging from medieval armor to 19th-century *chinoiserie* are a few sublime works of the *quattrocento.* Foremost among them is Pollaiuolo's *Portrait of a Young Woman;* through

Pietà. Giovanni Bellini

St. Jerome. Bartolomeo
Montagna

it the Renaissance spring speaks to us with sentiment but without sentimentality and with a charm that has not yet become stereotyped. It has no trace of the ostentatious and extravagant that were to appear a century later in much of portraiture. The school of Leonardo is also well represented and by its best work.

The **Biblioteca Ambrosiana,** housed in a conglomeration of structures built over several centuries, contains, after the Vatican, the largest collection of manuscripts, palimpsests, and incunabula. In the adjoining Pinacoteca is a display of graphic art and drawings, among them Raphael's masterly cartoon for his fresco in the Vatican. A special room devoted to Leonardo da Vinci contains three of his paintings that, alas, lack distinction; encased in a glass strongbox is his famous *Codico Atlantico,* encompassing the bulk of his manuscripts. As for paintings, many by Leonardo's followers demonstrate clearly what happens to minor painters who try to follow in the footsteps of a master whose talent far surpasses theirs. The technique in question here was a form of chiaroscuro called *sfumato* ("smoke" in Italian), developed to perfection in Leonardo's work. Like smoke thinning out imperceptibly as it rises, so the transitions from light to dark were to create the mysterious light-shade effects so characteristic in the master's work. Straining their limited faculties, his followers, among them d'Oggione, Boltraffio, da Sesta, Solari, instead of "mystery" merely created a contrived illumination.

Museo del Duomo. Some of the earliest statuary and fragments of stone ornaments from the cathedral are kept here, together with architectural plans, diagrams, and wooden models of the church. More than any other documents, these make one realize the immensity of the task and the genius of the builders and sculptors who created this sublime edifice.

The **Castello Sforzesco** epitomizes the power and the splendor of the Lombard Renaissance. Newly installed, relics, statuary, paintings, furnishings—all the trappings of the 13th to the 18th centuries—are presented and glorified in these lofty halls with extraordinary showmanship and unsurpassed taste in the combining of ancient décor and a functional manner of display. A special installation is accorded Michelangelo's celebrated *Pietà Rondanini*. But although the heads of the figures are expressive (mainly because of their unfinished state) the last work of the master is in my view a failure. First of all, the right arm of Christ could not possibly belong to his body. The sculptor must have become aware of the error, for he detached the arm, leaving it dangling as an incongruous appendage. Nor does there seem to be a compelling reason for the lower part of the figures to be polished while the upper part is rough-hewn—unless we consider that the work was unfinished. Why do I expound on this incident? Simply because official criticism invariably. considers the last (or late) works of artists as being of greatest excellence—in many cases without justification.

As for the history of the castle, it is a turbulent one. Reconstructed on the ruins of an older fortification in 1450, it was later enlarged and equipped with luxurious apartments. Leonardo da Vinci, Bramante, and other great architects worked on the building in which a succession of *condottieri* of the Sforza family lived

Pietà Rondanini.
Michelangelo
(Castello Sforzesco)

Castello Sforzesco, First Court

until 1525. The last of the Sforzas was Ludovico, known as "Il Moro," in whose service Leonardo spent 14 years. At the end of the last century the architect Beltrami conscientiously re-established the original appearance of the fierce-looking fortress, which consists of two rather unprepossessing courts, obviously designed for utilitarian purposes, and an elegant one, called appropriately the Ducal. In all, the Castello Sforzesco belongs with the most memorable museums in Italy.

Churches and Other Historic Edifices

As for the city itself, the historic and artistically interesting structures are located in the neighborhood of the Duomo. West from the Duomo is the *Via dei Mercanti;* entering through arcades we face a group of medieval edifices—the *Palazzo della Regione* (13th century) and, opposite, the *Palazzo dei Jurisconsulti* (16th century). The *Palace of the Scuole Palatine* and the *Loggia dei Osii* (14th century) complete the group of ancient communal buildings. On the *Piazza del Duomo* are the splendid Renaissance façade and courtyard of the *Arivescovado Palace* and the *Royal Palace,* originally from the third century, but now in neo-Classic style, as is the famed *Teatro alla Scala* on the *Piazza della Scala.*

The **Duomo,** in the very center of the city, is a Late Gothic structure that was begun in 1386, but its façade is an incongruous 19th-century concoction of Gothic and Renaissance elements. It is unique among Gothic churches because of its design, which causes the squat structure to eject, as it were, lacy spires in open marble work, as well as pinnacles and buttresses in seemingly endless profusion. To view this amazing and bewildering forest, there is an elevator to the roof, where one can take a walk of nearly a mile over several levels. The interior of the Duomo is very dark, so that it is difficult to see the rich ornamentation. The groins of the ogive ceiling, for example, are overlaid with stone lacework; the

Duomo Square (Milan)

Cathedral (Detail)   Cathedral (Detail)

ever, most of these are removed from proximate sight. Although
many are of older date, those on the exterior seem Baroque. To
realize the high artistic merit of some of the statues one should
visit the *Museo del Duomo,* located in the *Palazzo Reale* at the
south side of the cathedral.

The history of The **Basilica of Sant' Ambrogio** goes back into
the 4th century, but its present shape, with the cuspidal façade
and sloping arches, the interior arches supporting the heavy ribs
of the groined vaulting, are regarded as the earliest Lombard
examples of Romanesque church buildings and date from the 10th
to 12th centuries. The most noteworthy relics in the church are
the Romanesque pulpit and the altar, decorated with a 9th century
relief made of gold plate.

Santa Maria delle Grazie is a Gothic structure, reconstructed by
Bramante late in the 15th century; it has a rather lusterless interior. A passage leads from this church to two cloisters, one also
by Bramante and another in the refectory where "Leonardo's"
Last Supper can be seen. I put the name in quotes advisedly, for
the great mural started to deteriorate during his lifetime, and by
the 17th century very little was left of it. What we see today is
entirely the work of restorers.

The Country

VERONA. En route to Venice our next stop is Verona, where we
re-enter the medieval climate. Once an Etruscan city, it became

Basilica Sant'Ambrogio

Bridge of Castelvecchio e Mastio
(Verona)

a Roman colony in the first century B.C. A well-preserved amphitheater and double gate—*Porta dei Borsari*—still bear witness to its remote past. Later, the kings of Lombardy made the city their capital, and the Lombard style, all 12th century, influenced the early architecture of Romanesque churches in other countries. A few of the outstanding relics are: *San Zeno Maggiore*, with extraordinary bronze reliefs on the door panel dating from 1130; the church *Santa Maria Antica* and next to it the *Gothic Tombs of the Scaligere* (the early rulers of Verona), one of the finest examples of Gothic art in northern Italy; the *Piazza dei Signori;* the *Ponte Scaligero*, built over the river Adige in the 14th century on Roman remains (destroyed in 1945 and lately rebuilt). Verona, as we all know, was the locale of the Romeo and Juliet affair, a most appropriate setting for such a wildly romantic story.

On the banks over the ancient bridge are the fabulous *Giusti Gardens.* Cypresses, some five hundred years old, border the walks leading to the summit of a hill which offers a view of the entire countryside.

VICENZA. Vicenza is the birthplace of Andrea Palladio, the great architect whose art influenced the Classic style of building in all of Europe, and particularly that of 18th-century England. The prototypes of his style appear in most of the palaces in Vicenza. Among them is the *Villa Rotunda* (based on the design of the Pantheon in Rome), the *Loggia del Capistrano,* and the two-storied arcade that encases the medieval basilica. Also in Vicenza stands *Palladio's Olympic Theater*—the embodiment of classic design—which was built as a permanent stage setting. Here the illusion of depth rendered by a tricky perspective creates an extraordinary spectacle.

PADUA. By the 13th century this ancient city had one of the most famous universities in Europe; Galileo was among its teachers. Today we are attracted not only by its medieval buildings but by some remarkable works of art, such as the frescoes by Giotto

Palladio's Olympic Theatre (Vicenza)   The Basilica (Padua)

in the *Arena Chapel*, Giovanni Pisano's masterpiece, *Madonna and Child*, and, in front of the *Basilica of Sant' Antonio*, Donatello's equestrian statue of the condottiere Gattamelata. The Giotto murals are in a better state of preservation than those found elsewhere, and in their representation of the human drama they constitute one of the earliest departures from the rigor of the preceding Byzantine school. Boccaccio wrote of him: "There is nothing in nature that he would not imitate so well as to deceive our very senses." Which shows how relative are assessments of art—Boccaccio could not witness how close an approximation to natural appearances was achieved by painters a hundred years hence.

As for Donatello, his was the first life-size equestrian monument executed in bronze since Roman times. Viewed against the background of San Antonio with its Byzantine domes (reminiscent of St. Mark's in Venice) and Early Gothic façade, it is a wonderful sight. Just 25 miles from Padua lies the most improbable city in the world—Venice.

Venice

While traveling in Europe in search of beauty, the tourist too often encounters such difficulties that he may no longer be receptive when he finally reaches his goal. To put oneself instantly in a condition of enchantment, switching from low to high gear on the spur of the moment, and then to reverse the course when returning to normal, is neither easy nor pleasurable. When visiting Venice, where enchantment operates consistently in high register, one need not be intermittently galvanized into self-mesmerization.

Places, like works of art, engage our emotions in different ways; antiquities evoke admiration for their esthetic merits and craftsmanship, but few instill nostalgia. In Venice nostalgia meets us at every turn. Once I wrote: "to be awakened every hundred years, to be able to wander about the streets of Venice." And who has not experienced the delight of having lost his way in the labyrinthine streets of Venice? The most improbable city, it has not always delighted discriminating visitors. People of "exclusive" taste do not like to find themselves riding in the same boat with just anyone. Authentic poets, the (as usual) misguided estheticians, architects of orthodox leanings, had much quarrel with this city. "A folding picture post card in itself," a writer once described it. Obviously the negative reactions have psychological reasons: The compelling obligation to fall into rapture. This compulsion is apt to arouse iconoclastic instincts in some viewers, inviting them to opposition, or at best to synthetic indifference. In the eyes of the purist, the accent on the picturesque pollutes formal issues, and some critics refer to the "barbaric architecture" of Venice. To men steeped in the Classic, the Gothic has always seemed "barbaric," or at best irrational. We remember Goethe's frustration before the magnificent collection of Gothic art assembled by the Boisserée brothers (now dispersed in many German museums) when he studied it to form an opinion on early German art.

A BRIEF HISTORY OF THE CITY. In the 6th century the banks of the lagoons were populated by fishermen; they moved through the shallow waters by means of single-oar flatboats, the prototype of the present gondola, in use since the early Middle Ages. The successive waves of the Avars, Goths, and Huns passed by the early inhabitants of that region protected by the maze of lagoons. By the end of the 8th century they had already formed a maritime confederacy under a doge and established nominal allegiance to Byzantium. At the dawn of the Christian era, a skiff carrying John, later known as Mark, sought shelter from a storm in one of the lagoons, and, after he was martyred in Alexandria, the Venetians adopted him as their patron saint. In 878 his body is supposed to have been captured from the Turks and brought to Venice by two Venetian merchants. The first church dedicated to his name was partially destroyed by fire in 976, and in its place arose St. Mark's as we see it today, practically unaltered.

During the 12th century, Pope Alexander III consecrated the Venetian dominion by instituting its "Marriage with the Sea," a festival celebrated ever since. Venice broadened its powers successively by maritime victories, particularly those over Genoa; through participation in the Crusades, serving as a supply and shipping center; by its share of the enormous booty connected with these enterprises, as well as through legitimate trade with Adriatic and Mediterranean countries. But after serious political reverses, the discovery of America and the concomitant changes of trade routes, Venice began to decline in importance; its glam-

Rialto Bridge

our, however, has never dimmed. For the past three centuries
the City of the Lagoons has remained the most widely admired
and most visited place on earth, and the throng of travelers who
seek out its beauty never diminishes.

Museums and Churches

St. Mark's (San Marco) has been called variously an "Oriental
bazaar," a "satrap's den," "half-pleasure house, half war-tent."
It has been judged to be in "very bad taste, both inside and outside," and so on and so forth. Such pronouncements have been
made by illustrious literati, architects, and connoisseurs of all
sorts because of a particular prejudice. This edifice does not
seem to conform to any definite standard of taste; nor does it
follow any architectural orthodoxy. The simple fact, however, is
that in originality, imagination, and picturesqueness it remains
unparalleled in the realm of building. And, being essentially
Venetian based on Byzantine and Gothic style how could it fail to
be in good taste?

If we consider what has gone into the construction of St. Mark's,
this edifice is truly a miracle. It is made of brick, but the core
disappears completely under the veneer of marble alabaster,
jasper, porphyry, vert antique, which like most of the countless

St. Mark's and the Ducal Palace (Venice)

Tetrarchs (Venice)   Ducal Palace and Campanile

objects of décor—columns, statuary, reliquaries—represent
plunder from all over the Mediterranean world. The four great
horses (what function might they have standing on the façade?)
were stolen during the sack of Constantinople in 1204 (the Byzantines, in turn, carried them away from Rome, and Napoleon had
them removed to Paris; they came back after his fall). The great
altarpiece in gold, jewels, and enamel is also a "souvenir" from
Constantinople, and the four Moorish knights, carved in porphyry
and hugging the corner of the church next to the entrance of the
Ducal Palace, came from Syria; they are of the 4th century. The
precious columns, scarcely two alike (the study of their capitals
alone would be a considerable task in itself), were collected in
Asia Minor, Africa, Greece, and wherever the rapacious adven-
turers could lay their hands on them. A contemporary account
tells us that the loot was unceremoniously dumped from ships in
big heaps on the Molo (at the side of St. Mark's) to await its
utilization.

To understand the seemingly haphazard in the decoration of
the church, the helter-skelter of materials put to use in an extravagant manner, the history of St. Mark's must be known. Had all
this happened at any other time, in any other place, it would not
have "worked"; the *genius loci* of Venice makes it work. This
improbable building with its five lead-covered Byzantine domes
and five arched doorways has remained unchanged in its salient
features since the 11th century, although it received many additions during the following 300 years. Its early mosaics, from the

12th and 13th centuries, are all superb, as are all mosaics of that age; those from the 15th century are less interesting and those from the 17th century are downright ugly. Comparing them, it becomes obvious that as soon as this ancient technique is not guided by the principles inherent in the Byzantine style, its artistic value diminishes and it becomes at best insignificant in its attempts at naturalism.

Of the countless details on St. Marks' façade and in the interior, one can speak only in broad terms; it would be futile to describe it in detail. The façade especially is exceedingly elusive—it is never the same; it changes with the hours of the day and night as its colors and shapes respond to the mood of the sky as well as to the change in our own receptivity. One must go up on St. Mark's roof; when walking between the turrets, pinnacles, balustrades, parapets, and statues, the spirit of this building somehow comes nearer to us.

Then there is this mighty *campanile,* but its appearance is totally "technological"—it is too straight, too smooth, it is modern despite the fact that it corresponds accurately to the original belltower built in 900 and restored in the 14th and 16th centuries. What we see today is a reconstruction dating from 1902.

Palazzo Ducale (The Doge's Palace) was the seat of the rulers for 11 centuries. The last doge, Manin, was deposed by Napoleon. The main part of the edifice, the front of which dates from the second half of the 11th century, has come into being in stages, beginning with the 15th century, and apparently without any definite plan. The original architect is unknown, hence it must be assumed that the co-operation of many masons has left us with an unequaled masterpiece, notwithstanding some objections raised by doctrinaire architects who quarrel with the building's "lack of architectural logic." The façade facing the San Marco Basin and the Piazetta is Gothic with Oriental overtones, but the side toward the Rio di Palazzo (connected with the Bridge of Sighs) is in severe Renaissance; it is the work of Antonio Rizzo, an architect and sculptor of highest rank.

It is quite true that the lower arcade of the Palace with its clipped columns appears awkward, but this is through no fault of the builders: the level of the ground had to be raised, thus reducing their original length by 15 inches. The two-storied arcades with open quatrefoils, cusped arches, columns, and the delicate balusters are rich and varied in design; together with the large, unadorned expanse of wall above them, they form an exquisitely balanced design. A source of endless wonder are the capitals of the portico and loggia columns and the statues at the corners of the building. Many of the original carvings, however, because of their poor condition have been replaced by accurate copies, but in sculpture, copies, as I have pointed out, can be indistinguishable from the originals; all that is lacking in this case are the marks of age that, of course, always ennobles works from the past. The names of the sculptors responsible for these masterly Gothic carvings are known, but one would be hard put to find them in art books, since they are looked upon as mere "craftsmen." The same can be said of the polychrome portal of the palace adjoining St. Mark's, the *Porta della Carta* (government proclamations were posted on it), which is also a great work of art. All of it except the figures of the doge and the lion, which are modern, date from the 15th century.

Through this Gothic gate we enter the courtyard, much of it designed by Antonio Rizzo. The complexity and variety of architectural forms, the ever-recurring arches, the fenestration, and great Byzantine domes in the background offer a sight for which all the admiration we could summon is inadequate. Right in front of the entrance is the Giant's Staircase, so-named because of the over-life-size mythological figures on its top landing; these, however, are commonplace. Besides the marvelous decoration of foliage carved into the stone, the staircase, as well as the Foscari Arch facing it, designed by Rizzo, are supremely beautiful, as are the figures of Adam and Eve on the façade. Adam, combining Gothic and Renaissance features, is a copy of the badly deteriorated original, now kept indoors; Eve is wholly Gothic, and of her we can say without exaggeration that she belongs with the greatest sculptural works. The same cannot be said of the other statues of the arch.

From the Loggia we come upon the resplendent golden staircase which leads into the halls of the Palace. To describe the interiors is hardly possible—actually, it is difficult to register them permanently in our minds even after repeated visits. That these are the most sumptuously decorated interiors goes without saying, but in addition to the carvings in wood, marble, and stucco, covering the walls and ceilings are paintings by great masters. However, these confront the beholder with a real difficulty—a common one whenever the frame of a painting outdoes the picture. In other words, the elements of décor absorb our attention to such a degree, they do not allow the paintings to assert themselves. Besides, the fact is that only certain types of paintings lend themselves to forming a harmonious whole with the setting of which they are a part.

The paintings by Tintoretto, the greatest Italian Baroque master, because of their emotion-laden contents and dramatic presentation are not "decorative"; Titian at times does better in this respect. But the best of them all is Veronese; here is a decorative artist par excellence. His paintings are one with the décor of the halls, as are those by Giandomenico Tiepolo (the son of Gianbattista Tiepolo). Moreover, the paintings in the Palace have been worked over by a variety of restorers for a period of 200 years; hence many of these cannot be really considered "originals."

To begin with, in the room called "Avogaria" is Bellini's early *Pietà,* with two saints obviously added later by Tintoretto, whose own painting in the same room is mediocre. In the "Quattroporte" we find a fine painting by Tiepolo and some minor Titians; in the "Anticollegio" (the Waiting Room of the Ambassadors) are fine works by Tintoretto, Veronese's splendid *Rape of Europa,* and a Bassano. In the "Collegio" (the Hall of the Great Audiences) Veronese dominates, and in the Hall of the "Pregadi" (the Hall of the Senate) paintings by Tintoretto and his assistants testify to the fact that they never got beyond the apprentice stage. The largest hall of them all, the "Maggior Consiglio" (the Great Council), has the largest painting ever done on canvas, Tintoretto's *Paradise.* This was executed with the aid of assistants, and the master evidently did not wish to pay wages for competent help. But the composition is stupendous. Acres of canvas hang in this hall, and the best of them are those by Veronese. It must be stated that all the paintings in the Palace were done on canvas, not in fresco on walls, and that their poor state of preservation (often invisible under the restoration) was partially due to the unfavorable climatic conditions, chiefly the moist, salty air.

Thus far we have described the "heart of Venice," St. Mark's, and the Palazzo Ducale; now to the museums.

Galleria dell' Accademia. This Gallery is housed in a group of 14th-century structures. What is particularly rare is that almost all of the paintings are Venetian. These are of such a high

Miracle of the True Cross. Carpaccio

Madonna and Child. Bellini

Venus at the Mirror. Titian
(Ca' d'Oro)

order that one is hard put to it to keep one's enthusiasm from running wild. If I have been repeatedly stating that all collections start invariably with the splendor of the Gothic (or Byzantine) masters, those gathered in the Accademia are deserving of an even stronger superlative. And this holds true from room to room, even though the names of the masters are not in the "glamorous" category. In the Gothic ensemble, Lorenzo Veneziano, del Fiore, Lambertini, and so on, are not stellar names; rarely do we hear the names of Marco Basaiti or Cima da Conegliano, but here all are represented by large canvases of great distinction. As we enter hall after hall and the side rooms, Bellini's mastery shines from every wall. Here is also Giorgione's *Tempest*, the best authenticated of all of his works. It is a charming piece, but the exaggerated admiration bestowed upon it is certainly not due to its artistic uniqueness, but rather to the mystery that surrounds the name of the artist—and the subject of this particular painting.

Crucifixion. Tintoretto

Pietà. Bellini (Accademia)

In the same location one will also find Mantegna's great master-piece, though on a small scale—*St. George*—and Piero della Fran-cesca's *San Geronimo*.

But the second hall has perhaps the greatest treat for us, as here Tintoretto's work can be seen in all its glory. To comprehend his genius fully, he must be seen in the Accademia and in the Scuola di San Rocco. None of his contemporaries were capable of composing pictures with such originality and vigor; the mastery in the use of dramatic light and shade relations, the exaltation of human form combined with a technique that employs strong delineations—a dark and light calligraphy for a sketchy rendering of a painting's subsidiary elements were his inventions. Although he learned much from Titian, he followed a different school of thought—he was the Baroquist par excellence. A few of his most outstanding works are the *Miracle of St. Mark, Adam and Eve, The Crucifixion, Deposition*—but why go on with "certain" titles? All the Tintorettos, as well as the Titians, and Veroneses, should be carefully studied in the Accademia; all are on a grand scale and of highest quality. As we proceed further, Late Baroque painters appear. These—Luca Giordano, Bernardo Strozzi, Piaz-zetta, and Gianbattista Tiepolo—are impressive. There are also delightful minor works by Bernardo Bellotto, Canaletto, and Pietro Longhi. Then the tenor of the show becomes attenuated; but not to release the visitor on a low note, the Accademia provides an exit with fanfares. There are more Gothic works, a goodly number of lesser-known masters at their best, and then the *pièce de résistance*, the Carpaccio series: *Presentation of the Ambassa-dors, Legend of St. Ursula, Lion of St. Mark's, Healing of the Demonical*—all fairytale visions of Venice, presented as "simple illustrations." Nor does one have to wrest from them the secrets of their artistry—they are simply incomparable. At the exit Titian's *Mary's Presentation at the Temple* bids us a glorious farewell.

Museo Correr, at the end of the Piazza opposite St. Mark's, is a palace filled with treasures. One would do well to pay little atten-tion to the lower story, where armor, maps, coins, and various bric-à-brac are assembled, and proceed upstairs. It is not easy to realize that in this museum—little-known even to the well-traveled public, the greatest artists are represented, though on an intimate scale. To name but a few, there is Bellini in his early archaic style, Vivarini, Tura, Carpaccio, Antonello da Messina, and of course, early Venetian-Byzantine panels, the *tondi oro* (pictures with gold backgrounds). One cannot help but concede that these achieve deeper spirituality than much work by sophisticated Renaissance masters. The Flemish school is also present—Pieter

Visitation. Bellini (Detail. Museo Correr)   Portrait. Lorenzo Lotto

Brueghel, Dirk Bouts, Herri met de Bles. In addition, Gothic
wood carvings and diverse sculptures make the visit to the Correr
a great esthetic experience.

Scuola San Rocco. "Scuola" designated a charitable organization, and the one of San Rocco was set up in such splendor that
one wonders if there were any funds left for the poor after the
palace was completed. Its interior alone, without the paintings,
is sensational, but if we consider that the walls of the halls and
of the staircase are covered with enormous Tintorettos—the best
that have come off his brush—this palace should be a "must"·on
our itinerary.

There are other palatial museums along the Grand Canal. *Museo
del Settecento Veneziano* in the *Palazzo Razzonico* is not a
"must"; its décor is Rococo, and there are minor works by Longhi
and Giandomenico Tiepolo, as well as an unusual figurepiece un-
convincingly attributed to Guardi, the arch-Venetian, whose best
work is not present in Venice. Next in order is the *Ca' d'Oro*, so-
called because the façade was once gilded. Its interiors are

Palazzo Rezzonico Interior

Japanese Armor (Palazzo Pesaro)

Crucifixion. Tintoretto (Scuola
S. Rocco)

S. Maria Gloriosa dei Frari

gloomy; on a dark day it is impossible to view the paintings, statuary, and furnishings. A remarkable carved staircase and an enchanting courtyard with monuments grace this patrician mansion. Lastly, the *Palazzo Pesaro* contains a Far Eastern collection, chiefly armor, costumes, works of applied art, and some graphics.

Besides St. Mark's, the following churches should be on our program: *Santa Maria della Salute, Santa Maria Gloriosa dei Frari, Santi Giovanni e Paolo* right next to the Ospedale Civile and facing the Colleoni monument, and *Santa Maria dei Miracoli*.

Santa Maria della Salute has a very original exterior characterized by powerful scrolls buttressing the drum of its main dome. This elegant Baroque structure was designed by the renowned architect Longhena. Its interior, except for the fantastic main altar in the apse, is rather restrained.

Santa Maria Gloriosa dei Frari. Everything seems to be different in Venice! The common experience is that paintings do not register very well in churches, because their effect becomes secondary to statuary and miscellaneous ornamentation. But not so in this sublime Gothic edifice, built in the 13th century and rebuilt 100 years later. Here, the clarity and harmony in the disposition of minor and major architectural components, the uncluttered interior of pink bricks, lends a superb background to the statuary (among them Donatello's *St. John* carved in wood) and the paintings, free from ecclesiastic trappings appear, as it were, in their natural habitat. Thus Titian's altarpiece, *The Assumption*, one of his most important works, is seen to best advantage, as is the

Interior, S. Giovanni e Paolo

Ospedale Civile

Madonna of the Pesaro Family and Bellini's tryptich, *Madonna and Saints.* In this church Titian is buried; his tomb, as well as that of the sculptor Canova, are here; his mausoleum, a pompous neo-Classic self-glorification in marble, injects a jarring note into the noble interior.

The second Gothic structure, **Santi Giovanni e Paolo,** resembling the former church but less elaborate, perhaps, was built during the 13th century on the Campo of the same name. The church, its façade never finished, adjoins the former Scuola Grande di San Marco, now the *Ospedale Civile* (a hospital). Its dreamlike façade (finished at the end of the 15th century) belongs with the finest Venetian Renaissance adaptations of Gothic forms. In it polychromy and sharply delineated volumes have been used to create the illusion of space; here sculptural as well as pictorial elements coalesce into a glorious ensemble. And to top it all, in front of this building stands Verrocchio's *Monument of Colleoni.*

Proceeding west from the Piazza to reach the Fundamente Nuove landing for the boat ride to Torcello, one arrives in less than ten minutes at the Campiello dei Miracoli (campiello means "little square") with the small church **Santa Maria dei Miracoli.** Built during the last quarter of the 15th century, the marble facing of the exterior, the many-colored inlays of the interior, the coffered vault, raised choir, and domed apse represent the culmination of the noble Lombard design.

Verrocchio's Colleoni. The bronze monument representing the famous condottiere (1400-1475) was made between the years 1481 and 1488, but the casting was done, after Verrocchio's death, by his pupil Lorenzo di Credi in 1496, who also designed the splendid pedestal. In his will Colleoni left funds for the erection of the statue and stipulated that it should stand on the Piazza in front of St. Mark's. But the city fathers decided otherwise, and per-

S. Maria dei Miracoli   Verrocchio's Colleoni

haps it was a good decision, for the solitary, austere surrounding lends grandeur to the greatest equestrian masterpiece of all time. The monument represents not only a high point of artistry, but the spirit of the Italian Renaissance—its power, pride, and supreme self-confidence. On the spacious Campo, in mid-air, defying any intimacy with the viewer, stands this effigy of Bartolomeo Colleoni. It is good to sit down in one of the two cafés facing the monument and ponder futilely over the passing of time and circumstance.

The Country

TORCELLO. By vaporetto from Fundamente Nuove pier, it is a 45-minute ride (with stops at Murano and Burano) to Torcello. On the small island stand a few houses and a Byzantine *cathedral*, founded in 639 and partially rebuilt in the year 1008. The *campanile* dates from the 9th century. Adjoining it is the 9th-century church, *Santa Fosca*, an octagonal structure surrounded on five sides by an arched portico. The apse of the cathedral contains a most remarkable mosaic—an enormous single figure of the Virgin, all in blue, against a gold background. On the opposite wall the largest mosaic in existence tells the story of the Last Judgment.

S. Fosca (Torcello)   Mosaics of the   Byzantine Screen (Torcello
                             Cathedral   Cathedral)
                             (Torcello)

Both date from the 12th century; thus they are contemporary with the oldest mosaics in St. Mark's and artistically their equal.

One should stay on the island for a few hours to drink in the enchantment of the place. Here, bucolic tranquillity, the air of remoteness in time and space, envelops the traveler in a mantle of gentle melancholy, carrying him away from the hectic reality of Venice—the most unreal place in Europe.

FERRARA. It is hardly believable that at one time the small sleepy town of Ferrara was an intellectual and artistic center almost unequaled in all of Europe. The greatest names in literature, painting, and music enjoyed the patronage of its ducal rulers, the Este family, who, beginning in 1208 had their court in the town for 400 years. After their decline, the *Castle of Ferrara* was used (among other purposes) as a tobacco factory, and only recently some of its mural decorations by Cosimo Tura and Dosso Dossi were discovered beneath a layer of calcimine. The exterior of the 13th-century *cathedral,* with its three-gabled, arcaded front is fairly well preserved but the interior is a 19th-century renovation.

BOLOGNA is the city of arcades; they radiate from the center of town, giving it a medieval look. It once boasted 200 fortresses, red brick towers of immense height. Two of these remain, although they are no longer quite perpendicular. In fact, even today there is something martial about the place. Bologna was also a center of learning, and its university, founded in 1119, is the oldest in Italy; Dante and Petrarch were among its students. A few monuments will occupy our particular attention: the Gothic *San*

The Cathedral (Ferrara)

Fountain of Neptune. Giambologna

Bologna University

The Two Towers,
12th Century

Petronio church, with a masterful Early Renaissance façade by Jacopo della Quercia; *San Francesco,* a 13th-century Gothic church, and the *Fountain of Neptune* by Gianbologna and Tommaso Laureti, in full-blown Baroque. The city is also teeming with great palaces, among them the *Mercazia, Palazzo dei Notari Pallavicini, Bevilacqua,* and *Podestà Communale.*

RAVENNA. In the 6th century, when Rome sank into insignificance, Ravenna was an important seaport that monopolized the religious and cultural life of Europe for 200 years. Today we travel to this out-of-the-way place only to visit the few remaining edifices: the church of *San Vitale,* with the Mausoleum of Galla Placidia; the basilica of *Sant' Apollinare Nuovo; Sant' Apollinare in Classe,* the ancient port three miles north of Ravenna, is very much like the original port; and the *Baptistry* on the Piazza Duomo, with its colorful marble inlays and mosaics.

Basilica of San Vitale

San Vitale Interior (Ravenna)

The church of *San Vitale,* consecrated in 547, is, like most Byzantine structures, deceivingly unassuming—one might say drab—on the outside. Within, however, it is a veritable jewel case. Multicolored marble inlays and mosaics cover the entire wall space; among them are two large 6th-century mosaic panels, one representing Emperor Justinian with his courtiers and the other, the Empress Theodora surrounded by her ladies-in-waiting. Were it not for the glitter of the tesserae, these panels might be taken for precious embroideries. The small adjoining mausoleum is, if possible, even more colorful; blue light enters through windows covered with alabaster panels, creating an aura of mystery.

Adorned by mosaics a century older than those of San Vitale is the 6th-century basilica of *Sant' Apollinare Nuovo.* These four edifices are the earliest of the Byzantine era in the Western world, and they alone justify a trip to Ravenna, which is now a dull, provincial town.

Florence

It has been said that Florence was not only the birthplace of post-medieval art but of art history as well. In other words, Florence was the center of the art world in the 15th and 16th centuries, surpassing even Antwerp in importance; nowhere else was art patronage so active, and nowhere else were artists looked upon as leading citizens. Art was part of daily and official life to such a degree that the name of the ruling house of Medici became synonymous with art patronage, from Cosimo de' Medici to his grandson Lorenzo, known as "Il Magnifico." In consequence, Florence is literally teeming with architectural relics, splendid monuments, churches, and repositories of art. Yet in its total aspect, the place fails to satisfy the eye—there is no order or consonance among its components. Its layout is chaotic. The main square—the Piazza della Signoria—symbolizes the prevailing confusion: the Palazzo Vecchio, with the fountain of Neptune awkwardly appended to its flank; the Loggia dei Lanzi, crowded with poorly placed statuary; and other incongruous statues strewn around the square are a picture of disorder. From which vàntage point on the crowded streets and most of the squares can one behóld the cathedral, the campanile, the palaces, and churches? Unity, the most important element in a composition, is absent in the city. The exceptions are a few squares—Santa Croce, Sant' Anunciata, Santa Carmine, Santa Novella—these are balm to the appreciative eye.

Museums, Edifices and Bridges

It is often quite difficult to differentiate between a museum and a palace or a church, for in Florence all are repositories of art— museums in the truest sense—and the difference lies chiefly in the size of the collection. The largest of these is housed in the Uffizi.

The *Uffizi*. The building was originally the seat of government, and paintings were housed in the Palazzo Pitti, the Medici residence. The importance of precious works of art was recognized early in Florence, and at the beginning of the 17th century an edict was issued forbidding the export of important works. The gallery as it appears today dates only from 1737, and unlike other great museums it did not have to go far afield to gather the best. That the best was homegrown becomes evident as soon as we enter the museum, as the first halls set the pace for the assembly of paintings that Italian genius produced in its early era: the 13th century. Duccio, Cimabue, Giotto, and the "unknowns" create a mood of festive reverence. In the next four halls are Gentile da Fabriano, Lorenzo Monaco, Taddeo Gaddi, Simone Martini, Bernardo Daddi, Ambrogio Lorenzetti—all stellar names, steeped in the most sublime medieval spirit, carried by a style that gave artists license to use wings and to raise themselves to the sphere of the wondrous.

Allegory. Bellini (Uffizi, Florence)

Venus with the Lap Dog. Titian

Birth of Venus. Botticelli

Judith. Botticelli

Duke of Urbino. P. della Francesca

Nativity. Hugo van der Goes   Tobias and the Three Angels.

With the 15th century sublimation became more earthbound; for example, Piero della Francesca's portraits of *Federigo da Montefeltro and His Wife*. As usual, faced with Piero's work, we ask ourselves wherein hides the spirituality of a work of art; from which dimension does it emanate; and what imponderable configurations imprison its essence. Paolo Uccello, Domenico Veneziano, Fra Angelico—what gives their painting its magical appeal? Not their genius alone, but also the genius of a time that gave their art its form and substance.

In Rooms 9 through 14, Early Renaissance presents its most ingratiating creations. Among them Sandro Botticelli's *Primavera*, which is in dire need of cleaning; but despite the heavy layer of grime that dims its surface, one senses its unearthly

The Baptism. Verrocchio   Madonna Enthroned. Duccio

beauty. *Birth of Venus,* very clean and crisp, is a tempera work executed like a mechanical decoration; nevertheless, it, too, speaks to us through its delineations, and more melodiously meandering lines have never been created. Here also are Hugo van der Goes' *Nativity,* a marvel which only an early Flemish master could have brought about; Francesco Botticini's *Tobias and the Angel;* a splendid Lorenzo di Credi; and many Botticellis.

Next we see Verrocchio, Leonardo, and Signorelli (Room 15). Leonardo's sketch of *St. Jerome* is very dark, but it is every inch a Leonardo, whereas his *Annunciation* could have been done by many others. And now Bronzino (Room 18): is he a Mannerist? Nominally, perhaps, but this term carries pejorative connotations, and the "iron-clad" portraits by this master have great merit in spite of the somewhat artificial, heroic poses. Continuing with side rooms 20 through 22, which present the German school, crude on the whole, with the exception of a self-portrait by Dürer and his *Adoration of the Magi,* one of his most successful works. Did Bellini paint the *Allegory* (hanging in an adjoining room)? Steeped in the spirit of Giorgione, this enigmatic painting has a surrealistic air about it and clarifying its meaning would not increase our admiration. Like poetry, certain pictures reveal themselves more fully if not clearly understood. Such is the case of this great work, whose authorship is doubtful.

On we go to face Michelangelo's hard, sculpturesque *Holy Family,* a darkened Raphael, and then Titian at his best: *Flora* and *Venus Recumbent.* Even the trivial Palma Vecchio and the Mannerists Jacopo Pontormo, Parmigianino, Rosso Fiorentino, and Francesco Rossi appear with estimable works. Tintoretto can be seen to much better advantage in Venice, and the 18th-century Baroque contingent, Tiepolo, Guardi, Magnasco, is of the usual sort. The Dutch school is not too well represented, and even the Rembrandts and Ruisdaels are rather pedestrian. In Hall 41, Rubens appears with enormous compositions, and although one may not care for these essays in florid fleshiness, they are among his best of this genre.

The **Pitti Palace** is the second-largest repository of paintings in Florence and the most difficult to digest. It is overcrowded with potboilers, paintings hung in total darkness on the window side, paintings covered by ancient grime, hung three and four rows deep, often out of sight, paintings (predominantly of the 18th century) often so inferior and tasteless that it hurts. Yet some of the most memorable works appear in this lowly company: Raphael's *Madonna della Sedia, Cardinal Bibiena, La Velata, Tommaso Inghirami;* superb Titians—*La Bella, Pope Julius II, Concerto;* Ghirlandaio; Rubens—two of his rare large landscapes;

Eleanor of Toledo and her Son. Bronzino   Pietà. Michelangelo (Accademia)
(Pitti)

Fra Filippo Lippi; Sodoma. Thus despite the hardships, the Palazzo Pitti is worth a visit.

The *Museo dell' Accademia* also has an important collection. Although its paintings do not measure up to the Pitti, it possesses a group of Michelangelo sculptures, among them *David,* a replica of which stands in front of the Palazzo Vecchio.

Medici-Riccardi Palace. Only a few of the richly furbished rooms in this Renaissance edifice are open to the public, but its chief attraction is the chapel decorated with Benozzo Gozzoli's fabulous murals. These belong with the most ingratiating creations of the Early Renaissance. Here again it is the style of his age that aided the painter in making the works so satisfying esthetically. A style imbued with the festive, the joyful—all that belongs to the vernal time of life.

The *Bargello,* known also as the *Museo Nazionale,* is a splendid

Fresco detail. Gozzoli (Medici-Riccardi)

Renaissance palace. It houses statuary of all description, dominated by the genius of Donatello. His work is in the main hall.
Other rooms are filed with 14th-century ecclesiastic statuary,
10th- to 15th-century ivory carvings, enamels, vessels of gold,
silver, majolica, and crystal, ornamental objects dating from the
time of Byzantium, as well as small early Italian paintings of
excellent quality. On the top floor Benvenuto Cellini's extraordinary work demonstrates that by the middle of the 16th century
Mannerism affected sculptors as well as painters.

Antique statuary, countless vessels, implements, and fragments
are crowded into the endless rows of rooms of the *Museo Archeologico*. But quantity takes precedence over quality. Only a few
objects of beauty attract our attention in the enormous agglomera-
tion of Hellenistic, Roman, and Etruscan remains. Strangely, the
art of the ancient inhabitants of Tuscany is not well represented
in Florence. It is only in the Villa Giulia, in Rome, that we are
confronted with the best of Etruscan sculpture.

The *Palazzo Vecchio* stands in the very heart of the city on
the Piazza della Signoria. The Piazza once was a civic center
where public speeches were given and the decrees of government
delivered. Built as a fortress at the end of the 13th century, the
Palace is a great mass of masonry and perfect in its stark truculence. Its upper story contains a gallery for defense, from which
rises an imperious 308-foot tower crowned with an open belfry.
The battlement has a mighty overhang of almost six feet supported by heavy corbeling. From the portait of Solderini, chief
magistrate of Florence, painted in 1510 by Piero di Cosimo and
depicting the Palazzo in the background, it appears that these were
once beautifully decorated. This picture is now in the National
Gallery in London.

The interior of the Palace was redecorated in the 16th century,

St. George. Donatello
(Bargello)   Entrance to the Bargello   Palazzo Vecchio

and its luxury is extravagant. In its beautiful courtyard stands Verrocchio's lovely *Boy with Dolphin.* Even the most retentive mind could not take in room after room and hall after hall. The stucco and woodcarving, the ceilings, friezes, and doorways— decorated by the great Renaissance masters Bronzino, Pontormo, Ghirlandaio, Benedetto de Maiano, among others—are dazzling to say the least.

As for the **Piazza della Signoria,** it is a picture of confusion. The disorder begins on one side of the Palazzo Vecchio with the hideous statue of the *Neptune Fountain* (already ridiculed by Michelangelo) only to be joined by the statues in the exquisite *Loggia dei Lanzi* (14th century), an open-vaulted hall of Roman-esque design but Gothic in décor. Within, an assembly of ruffians in marble and bronze vie with one another in various acts of mayhem. The fact that illustrious sculptors were at work here and that there are excellent Roman copies of Greek statuary does not help matters; having been shocked by the gross *Hercules and Cacus,* how can one quickly adjust one's sensibilities to the *Judith* by Donatello (in front of the Palazzo)? Small surprise that Michelangelo's *David* (a copy of the original in the Accademia) seems to scowl contemptuously down at the lawless crowd. It is easy to see how a good work of art can suffer when it is put in poor company.

The *Palazzo Vecchio* is a relic of the Middle Ages. With the Renaissance, a different conception of architecture, one that relied on Classic tenets, came into being. In fact, in no other country did the thoughts and sentiments of the Roman past express themselves with such force and vitality as in Renaissance Italy. In Florence alone, 30 splendid palaces were built in 25 years (1450-1475), all in accordance with the precepts of Classic design: harmony, balance, coherence. To use the words of the great preceptor of Renaissance esthetic, Leon Battista Alberti: "The business and office of these qualities is to put together members differing from each other in their nature in such a manner that they may conspire to form a beautiful whole." But to the beholder not conversant with the probities of Classic architecture, these early palaces do not have much eye appeal. The palaces were also fortresses and because they were castellated outside, they appear closed to discourage uninvited "guests." Hence the fronts of these buildings are heavily rusticated, which adds to their severity. In keeping with the nature of the structure, the façades are arranged along horizontal lines; moldings and simple friezes divide the stories, and all is topped by a strong cornice. There are practically no decorative embellishments to soften the stern look, but harmony is maintained by the proper relationship between the stories and their fenestration within the wall space.

Palaces belonging to this category are the *Pitti* (Brunelleschi) ; the *Medici-Riccardi* (Michelozzo, a pupil of Brunelleschi and Bramante), built for Cosimo de' Medici; and, finest of all, the *Rucellai Palace* (designed by Alberti). With this last, the architect introduced a new type of building. The vertical accents are produced by classical pilasters arranged in superposed stages. The rustication is flattened and more delicate than usual. Because builders were generally restricted in exterior design, they constructed interior courts graced by columnar arcades, whose style was derived from the courtyards of medieval monasteries.

Of the old bridges over the Arno, only one remains—the **Ponte Vecchio.** This venerable landmark (it was in existence before the year 1000, and Dante used to cross over it), once served the Medici as an overground passage from the government offices at the Uffizi to their residence in the Palazzo Pitti. Benvenuto Cellini had his shop here as the covered bridge then housed as it does now, gold- and silversmiths' shops—none of this makes it noble, however, though it is very picturesque. To be sure ancient architectural forms are rarely, if ever, bad, but age alone is not an unfailing guarantor of beauty.

The next bridge down river is **Ponte Santa Trinità,** and it may well be the most beautiful bridge of its kind in the world. Here, with extreme simplicity, three delicate spans express perfect rhythmic sequence. Santa Trinità, with the four Baroque figures standing on its corner, is like an enchanting melody frozen in stone. The bridge, originally of the 13th century, was destroyed by a flood and rebuilt in 1569. Destroyed again during World War II, it was reconstructed and its original design, material, and workmanship matched with great accuracy. Lacking only are marks left on the stone by the ravages of time.

View of the Ponte Vecchio

Churches

Santa Maria del Fiore, generally referred to as the *Duomo* (cathedral), is one of the largest and, in construction, most perfect of edifices. It was started at the end of the 13th century (by Arnolfo di Cambio), and 50 years later Brunelleschi built the dome crowned by the graceful lantern, then the biggest in existence. The technique of construction was also highly original; the thrust of the enormous octagonal dome is resisted by three projecting limbs with apsidal termination, while from the opposite side the nave is formed by four immense bays. The outside walls of the Duomo are inlaid with marble in black-and-white geometric patterns. For some reason the façade remained unfinished until 1875, at which time a neo-Gothic front was added to the structure—and not to its advantage. The interior of the Duomo is barnlike and architecturally unremarkable. But it contains important works of art by Donatello, da Maiano, di Credi, della Robbia, and Michelangelo.

The original cathedral, now the octagonal *baptistry,* faces the Duomo; according to tradition it was once the temple of Mars. Built in the 11th century in Tuscan-Romanesque style, it has the characteristic striped black-and-white look, produced by alternating two-colored marble veneer. This fashion is generally referred to as Pisan, for it was the Pisan sailors who brought it from their Arabian exploits. The inside of the dome is covered with Byzantine mosaics. There are only a few statues, among them Donatello's weird *Mary Magdalen,* his last work done in wood. On the outside, flanking the wall of the building, stand two magnificent Roman sarcophagi.

And now to the celebrated work by Lorenzo Ghiberti, the *east doors,* looked upon as a miracle of Renaissance sculpture. Made of bronze and originally gilded, they are composed of ten separate panels with scenes from the Old Testament in low relief, set in richly decorated bronze frames. The work reveals the sculptor's technical and artistic resourcefulness. Michelangelo, who was not easily given to praise of his colleagues, admired it greatly; he even used some of the designs for his own compositions—but this happened 50 years after Ghiberti's death. Yet as an integral part of the architecture, the doors appear too fussy, demanding close scrutiny by the beholder; they cannot be seen in one all-encompassing glance, so that one may judge the total effect. The *south doors,* on the other hand, with bas-reliefs by Andrea Pisano and rendered with the scantest of means, are most effective in their simplicity of design and clarity of purpose.

The third member of the group is the *Campanile,* the bell tower

View of the Cathedral   Santa Maria Novella

designed by Giotto when he was 68 years old and later finished by
Talenti. Luca della Robbia and Andrea Pisano also worked on the
decoration. The square monolithic tower is supremely beautiful;
inlaid with pink, green, and white marble veneering and mosaics,
replete with bas-reliefs and delicate open tracery, it is fussy all
over, to be sure, but the details coalesce nonetheless, testifying
to the Tuscan genius for décor.

Facing the apse of the Duomo is the *Museo dell' Opera del
Duomo,* in which outstanding sculptural work is exhibited. Fore-
most among the statuary is Arnolfo di Cambio's *Pope Bonifatius
VIII,* sculptures by Andrea Pisano and Donatello, terra cottas by
Luca della Robbia, and many other antiquities of great precious-
ness.

Another church with marble inlays characteristic of the Roman-
esque-Tuscan period (13th century) is *Santa Maria Novella,* a
14th-century structure which contains a famous fresco by Masaccio, as well as frescoes and paintings by noted masters; most of
these, however, are in a poor state of preservation. Adjoining the
church is a lovely cloister with a Spanish chapel built by order
of Duchess Eleanor of Toledo, a member of the Medici family.
San Miniato al Monte, situated on a hill far from the center (hence
seldom visited by tourists), is an older structure in dark green
and white marble incrustations applied in geometric designs. The
exterior has great elegance, as does the interior and the fabulous
pulpit dating from about 1207.

San Lorenzo is another important church. Façade unfinished
and walls now crumbling, it was built by Brunelleschi in 1425. Its
Medici Chapel contains Michelangelo's tomb of Lorenzo de' Medici,
with the famed statues of *Night* and *Day, Twilight* and *Dawn.*
The splendor of the ensemble in its architectural framework is

Façade, S. Miniato al Monte   San Lorenzo

overwhelming and we sense without being prompted by the weight
of official opinion, that these are great works. Yet we are hard
put to warm up to the smooth, glossy, somehow slick statuary
and the Roman hero effigies of Lorenzo and Guiliano (incidentally,
this one was merely a cousin of the Lorenzo called "the Magnificent").

Santa Croce is a Gothic church constructed by Arnolfo di
Cambio, but it has been much altered in the course of time, and
its façade is a well-conceived 19th-century imitation. The most
noteworthy objects in this spacious church, distinguished by a
splendidly decorated wooden roof, are the pulpit by Benedetto da
Maiano, a masterpiece of its kind; the tomb of Marsuppini by
Desiderio da Settignano; and many other tombs, some of great
artistic significance. Among the artists who contributed to the
adornment of this church were Donatello, Orcagna and the della
Robbias. The Giotto frescoes in the *Bardi Chapel* have recently
been much restored, hence their original appearance cannot very
well be judged. Outside, in the courtyard of the cloister, the
Pazzi Chapel (by Brunelleschi) is structurally interesting. A

Sta. Croce   Basilica di Sta. Croce

Pazzi Chapel

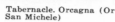

Tabernacle. Orcagna (Or San Michele)

Detail. Masaccio (Church of the Carmine)

vestibule with a richly decorated vault leads into the rectangular interior, the central part of which is capped by a Byzantine dome resting on pendentives. It is pure Early Renaissance of the most perfect kind. The church of *Santo Spirito* is of similar construction. Its plain, unadorned but beautifully contoured façade hides a splendid interior.

On the exterior of *Or San Michele,* foundations of which were laid in 1337 (it was to serve as a shrine and a grain storage), statues of the leading masters of the time are set in Gothic and Renaissance niches. This church also contains Orcagna's indescribably precious tabernacle, a marble work executed in the Cosmati technique of incrusted meandering bands of mosaic.

The *Brancacci Chapel* (part of the much later and insignificant *Church of the Carmine*) contains murals by Masaccio, Masolino, and Filippino Lippi who both worked in the chapel after the master's death. In spite of all this collaboration, the frescoes are Masaccio's own, but their state of preservation is deplorable. They were venerated by a generation of great masters of the Renaissance, who derived much inspiration from the new ideas embodied in them. These new concepts were expressed in the relatively realistic treatment of the human figure, endowed with a hitherto unknown monumentality achieved by eliminating unessential details and concentrating on the large form. Besides the humanization of man in point of physiognomy and anatomy, Masaccio introduced into his compositions a unifying chiaroscuro half a century before it was generally adopted by Florentine painters.

From Florence to Pisa

Since it is not included in the tours covered by long distance tourist buses, it is best to visit Pisa on a round trip from Florence.

Cathedral and Leaning Tower (Pisa)

After Florence, Pisa may be anticlimactic; hence we will limit our attention to the **Cathedral Group.** Not that the city lacks interest; far from it, although compared to its former status as a major maritime power (during the 10th to 13th centuries) today it seems just another provincial town.

The *Cathedral,* the *Baptistry,* and the *Leaning Tower* represent the most remarkable group of ecclesiastic buildings in all of Europe. These date from the 11th to 13th centuries, and set apart from the rest of the city, they form a unity and completeness seldom seen in edifices crowded amid an incongruous company of totally unrelated structures.

The style of the buildings is Romanesque, characterized by the use of colored marble in alternating bands—obviously of Moorish origin—or in paneled veneering that points to Byzantine influence. The most characteristic features of these structures are the external columnar arcades in superposed stages—a decorative element of great elegance. The circular baptistry with its lofty dome is adorned with slender columns supporting arches of incredibly delicate design. As if our appetite for beauty were not fully satisfied, the interior of the baptistry offers a still greater sensation. Here stand four half figures by Niccolò Pisano, whose art is second to none. These figures—St. John, St. Mark, Moses, and David—twice life-size, were removed from their tiers, 140 feet above the ground, on the façade. The sculptures are simply overwhelming. Many years ago I wrote of them: "The celestial sculptors collaborated on these works—the rain, the wind, and the burning sun. Mercilessly they have pitted and eroded them; they have effaced all the superfluity and burdensomeness, obliterated all such temporality as marks the image of man." Also in the baptistry there is a pulpit by Pisano, and in the Duomo, one by his son Giovanni. Both are works of art of unsurpassed beauty, as are the statues that adorn the church.

The Leaning Tower of Pisa—is there a more touristy, more

admired image than this one? Is it because of its oblique position, or because in some instances even the unschooled eye can be touched by an object of great beauty? Evidence shows that it was supposed to lean (although the slant increased with time). Perhaps the builders were aware that theirs was a supreme masterpiece, and that it would please everybody forever. There is nothing like the recurring theme of the Tower's helicoidal open arcades, and there never will be anything to rival its beauty.

Adjoining the Cathedral Group is the *Campo Santo,* the ancient cemetery; it suffered considerable damage during the last war, but its famous 14th-century frescoes representing the *Triumph of Death,* done by anonymous masters, have been saved.

From Florence to Rome

All the important sights en route cannot be included in one trip by a tourist bus (this is explained in Part II); however, we shall discuss all these sights on the following pages in the order in which they appear on the way south.

SAN GIMIGNANO, a few miles off the main road to Siena, is an oddity. From afar, its towers remind one of the New York skyline. Thirteen of the original 73 family fortresses are still left, but they had already lost their defensive purpose by the 16th century, when there were 25.

SIENA. In the 13th and 14th centuries this city was the greatest rival of Florence. But in 1348 the Great Plague destroyed half of its population, ending its pre-eminence in painting and architecture. The foremost representatives of the Sienese-Gothic school were Duccio, Simone Martini, and Ambrogio and Pietro Lorenzetti (both died of the plague in 1348). These as well as minor masters were—and still are in certain quarters—referred to as "primitives," because their art contains no reference to realistic facts as regards perspective, and anatomy, or, generally, to the verisimilitude achieved by the painters of the Renaissance. This enchanting art can best be studied in the Uffizi in Florence. However, when in Siena one should visit the *Museo dell' Opera del Duomo* (next to the cathedral) with its Gothic paintings and statuary and of course the collection of the ***Palazzo Pubblico.*** As a city, Siena, like all medieval places that survive, is somber; its houses, built as fortresses, are sinister, and walking the narrow, gorgelike streets, one feels uneasy—without armor.

Of Italian secular Gothic buildings, the ***Palazzo Pubblico*** is one of the most beautiful architecturally; it is also luxuriously adorned. Its façade conforms to the semicircular shape of the Piazza, which impresses us very much like a theatrical stage

Towers (San Gimignano)   Arezzo

awaiting some extraordinary dramatic goings-on. A slender campanile—asymmetrically placed and resembling that of the Palazzo Vecchio in Florence—rises from the body of the palace like a graceful exclamation mark; its shaft of red brick is crowned with battlements of white marble. The interior of the palace is replete with works of art, among them murals by Lorenzetti and the curious and well-known equestrian portrait of a knight (Giudoriccio da Fogliano, the victor of a battle against Florence), in which both horse and rider are clad in checkered raiment.

The magnificent **Duomo** was started in 1245; the sumptuously ornamented and figured polychrome façade is the work of Giovanni Pisano, as is the pulpit. The exterior design combines three high gables fronting three aisles, deeply recessed portals, pinnacled turrets, and a large, circular window. The interior is faced with alternate courses of black and white marble, and the floor is made of intricate cosmatesque marble inlays.

Palazzo Pubblico   Cathedral Façade (Detail)

AREZZO. We travel to Arezzo for one reason; to see the frescoes by Piero della Francesca in the plain, unassuming church of *San Francesco*. These murals, painted during the period 1452 to 1466 and occupying three walls, represent his chief work: *The Dream of Constantine, Victory of Constantine over Maxentius,* and *The Visit of the Queen of Sheba to King Solomon.* The paintings are traditional, not innovations as were Giotto's; we see in them an influence of Uccello, Masaccio, and Piero's teacher Domenico Veneziano. But the poetry and nobility of these compositions, their crystalline clarity, solemnity, and monumentality, are Piero's own. Yet, all these epithets do not explain the enigma of their appeal. Can the poetry of a painting be adequately interpreted by verbal equivalents?

PERUGIA. Once an Etruscan stronghold, it is perched atop a rock 1350 feet high; during the Middle Ages it sported 700 towers serving those interminable family feuds so popular in the better towns of Umbria and Tuscany. During the early Renaissance, the Umbrian school of painting flourished here, with Perugino (Raphael's master) and Pinturiccio its chief exponents. Of interest to us is the *Palazzo Communale,* which is similar to the Palazzo Vecchio in Florence. On the square in front of the palace is one of the most noble of fountains, the *Fontana Maggiore;* it is adorned with figures and reliefs by Giovanni Pisano and Arnolfo di Cambio, the greatest names among the Italian medieval artists. Reached easily from the square is the *Augustan Gate,* built by the Etruscans and rebuilt in 40 B.C.

ASSISI. A few miles away is a small, insignificant town, but its 13th-century church is among the most renowned places of pilgrimage. It is dedicated to St. Francis who was born in Assisi. Built on two levels, the complex consists of a large convent, a tower, and interconnected lower and upper basilicas. Historically important frescoes adorn the church, the most famous of them Giotto's *Scenes from the Life of St. Francis.* The second fresco, on the upper level—unfortunately in a very poor state of preser-

Fontana Maggiore (Perugia)

St. Francis Basilica (Assisi)

vation—is by Cimabue. In the lower church is Pietro Lorenzetti's moving *Descent from the Cross*, also *Madonna and Child*, and Simone Martini's fresco *Life of St. Martin*. On the main town square stands the graceful *Temple of Minerva* dating from the time of Augustus.

ORVIETO. Another of those fierce Etruscan hillside towns in Umbria, its medieval houses and palaces are practically unchanged through the ages. But what interests us here is the cathedral (begun in 1290), and in it Luca Signorelli's great mural. The façade of this church is its special glory, for it is in large measure the work of the Cosmati school, executed by Lorenzo Maitano. Cosmati work derives its name from the family of renowned marble workers by that name, who in the 13th century revived the ancient technique of mosaics. It employs small particles of precious marble, porphyry, and other colorful stones, usually arranged to form meandering bands and ornaments in a style of work generally referred to as "Opus Alexandrium," or parcel mosaics. However, the designation "Cosmati-work" is more popular in Italy, where it produced some of the most precious surface effects on twisted columns, tombs, and small architectural structures, but seldom on such large surfaces as the façade of the *Duomo* in Orvieto. Other great masters also worked on the reliefs of this façade, among them Andrea Pisano and Andrea Orcagna. In the simple interior with its wooden roof is Signorelli's fresco work, the *Last Judgment*. It is an epos in heroic muscularity and

The Cathedral (Orvieto)

Campanile (Viterbo)

clearly presages the art of Michelangelo. Next to the Duomo, in a small museum is a superb collection of sculptures.

The last town on the way to Rome is **VITERBO,** called the "city of beautiful fountains." It also has many interesting houses with street arcades and open stairways and, like all large Gothic places, a *Palazzo Pubblico* resembling the prototype in Florence. Here ends our journey through medieval Italy.

Rome

As everyone knows, it is called the "Eternal City," and more than 2½ millenia of historical continuity may well justify this claim. That its history—like all histories—was sometimes glorious and sometimes not, is understood; however, the accretion of ups and downs left a monumental heritage beyond compare. Today, Rome is a hodge-podge of anything and everything, but whereas under ordinary circumstances this is deprecatory, in Rome it is glorious. Here the rules of ordered design simply do not apply, and no one could be successfully challenged when calling Rome the most beautiful city in the world.

Which is its most important site or the most noteworthy art collection? The logical answer would be the Vatican, the Terme Museum, and the Forum Romanum. The Vatican (although an independent state) embodies the essence and the magnificence of Rome, and whatever has been preserved of antiquity can best be seen here in the two sites mentioned.

As for collections of paintings, Rome cannot measure up to Florence; nor is it reasonable to seek out the medieval in this city. In its large design, Rome is Baroque, and even the planimetric order of the Renaissance is energized to the point of assuming thoroughly dynamic configurations.

THE VATICAN. Of interest to us are: *St. Peter's* church, the adjoining *Sistine Chapel,* the museum-apartments around the Belvedere Court and the Court della Pigna, the *Library* and

St. Peter's (Rome)

finally the *Pinacoteca* Museum. It is obvious that to survey this
vast territory in a day's time would be a grueling task, even
should one give only a passing glance at the mass of art treasures.
Hence, repeated visits will be necessary. Moreover, the distance
from St. Peter's and the Sistine to the museums is too great to
be covered comfortably on foot.

St. Peter's should be our first visit, for here the magnitude and
the power of the Vatican in its historic context are revealed. The
construction of the church, designed by Bramante, started in 1506
and was finished 100 years later after many changes in the original plan. In 1546 Michelangelo was assigned to the work and gave
the structure its most important feature—the colossal dome
which stands on the massive drum flanked by coupled Corinthian
columns and measures 140 feet in internal diameter at its base
and 405 feet to the top of the lantern. Unfortunately, after
Michelangelo's death the nave was lengthened by two bays, at
which time the mediocre façade was constructed. This added
length makes the dome disappear when seen at close quarters,
altering the proportions of the edifice and thus nullifying Michelangelo's plan. Indeed, seen from within the incomparable colon-
naded portico built by Bernini (1629–67), with its two fountains
and the obelisk which came from Heliopolis and once stood in the
circus of Nero, the dome looks dwarfed.

In the Vatican everything is on a gigantic scale, from Bernini's
majestic portico and the four rows of powerful columns (180 of
them), to the interior with its vast coffered vault and the dome,
which, when seen with one's head turned skyward, does precisely
what its planners intended it to do—reduce the human scale to
naught. Architecturally the most grandiose of all the churches, it
has in its interior a rather gaudy 17th-century décor lacking in
originality and refinement. However, it must be quickly added
that the qualification of "refinement" is, in this instance, really
inapplicable. For the impact of St. Peter's is the result of a
design aimed at suggesting overwhelming power and authority,
and within the confines of these self-asserting ideologies, everything is "right" here.

As for the art objects housed in the church, Arnolfo di Cambio's
(1232–1301) bronze statue of *St. Peter* might be looked upon as
the most interesting by those who, like this author, have a
penchant for archaic statuary. Pollaiuolo's bronze statue of *Pope
Innocent VIII* and Michelangelo's youthful work, the *Pietà*, are
very Renaissance, but they do not fully testify to their creators'
artistic potential.

Beneath Michelangelo's dome stands Bernini's *Baldacchino*, containing the high altar. Here again, in the magnificent structure

we can realize how great was the architect's genius for Baroque design. Curiously, he was rarely successful in his sculptures, which more often than not are sentimental, or bombastic.

An impression of St. Peter's would be incomplete without a "tour" to the top. The first part can be made by elevator that reaches the top of the church, which is closed on the east by a balustrade of gigantic statues of saints. To the west one faces Michelangelo's awesome dome; on this level is a staircase, whereby one enters the interior of the dome, ascending gradually to the first gallery. This is our second stop and it is the most rewarding, for seen from this precipitous height, the immensity of the church interior is revealed in all its grandeur. There is a second gallery, some 65 feet higher, and finally, the sturdy "mountaineer" may reach the outside gallery which runs around the lantern on top of the dome by climbing the "snail," a narrow helicoidal passage between the inside and outside shell of the dome. Those accustomed to air travel will be less impressed by the bird's-eye view of the city than by the construction of the church, which with all its complexity makes a modern skyscraper seem a mere erector-set affair.

Sistine Chapel. There is a danger, when writing on works like those in the Sistine, of bogging down in a morass of clichès. But the official verdicts are true—the *ceiling* and *The Last Judgment* by Michelangelo *are* the greatest artistic achievements in art history, they *are* overwhelming in their majesty, their dramatic significance, the power of their creative imagination. Yet a qualification seems in order, for in the claptrap of writings on art, unsubstantiated claims as to the greatness of this or that "masterpiece" abound, and the only way to recognize greatness

Sistine Ceiling. Michelangelo
(Detail)

Sistine Ceiling. Michelangelo (Detail)

(without being influenced by one's personal preferences) is to consider the *difficulty of doing it*. And this difficulty is by no means of a physical nature; it encompasses all the imponderable complexities such as imagination and originality which in Michelangelo's frescoes are implicit in the figural compositions—that is, in their formal interrelationship. In the Sistine, a description of the scenes, titles, and so on seems irrelevant and inconsequential.

The side walls are also covered by frescoes. Although they are by great Renaissance masters (Botticelli and Perugino among them), they suffer in the presence of Michelangelo's work to such an extent that one finds it difficult to concentrate on them.

Vatican Collections. Further exploration of Vatican City will not prove easy, for the complex suffers from gigantism and from a hypertrophy of splendor. After leaving the Sistine, it is necessary to circle the area in order to reach the entrance to the Pinacoteca. Because of the distance (about one mile), it is advisable to avail oneself of a conveyance for this purpose to avoid fatigue before starting on what will prove to be an interminable march.

The *Pinacoteca* is the Vatican's picture gallery; the collection housed in the lavishly decorated halls, however, is not among the best in Italy. In the first two halls, 13th- and 14th-century paintings, usually referred to as "primitive," start us off. Far from being primitive, they impress by their superb craftsmanship and their Byzantine or Gothic character. Most of the names here are largely unfamiliar, even to those conversant with art history, but Giotto, Gaddi, da Fabriano, Gozzoli, and Filippo Lippi are among them. Other notable works are Melozzo da Forli's mural (transferred to canvas) and his poetic angels playing musical instruments, in the Fourth Hall. The enormous Eighth Hall contains a group of Raphael's large paintings—sweet, somehow hard and polychrome, and coldly rhetorical. But the Gobelins done in Flanders after his designs are magnificent in their subdued, muted colors. Here we are confronted by a baffling thought: How can a work by common craftsmen (the weavers) have greater esthetic appeal than that of a genius? Partially it is because Raphael composed the design, and in art, the quality of design (composition) is of surpassing importance. As we proceed, Titian and Veronese appear chronologically, followed inevitably by the later Baroque painters; at this point rhetoric takes over and tedium overtakes us.

In the *Library Halls* there are no books in evidence, but the décor is dazzling. The apartments of the Borgias are gloomy and resplendent. Upstairs are the *stanze* (the rooms of the Pope). Here Raphael's genius for design appears in all its power. The

The School of Athens. Raphael

frescoes were commissioned by Julius II in 1508 on the recommen-
dation of Bramante, who thought so highly of the painter that he
made him the successor to his architectural works. But only some
of the paintings are wholly (or even largely) from his brush. The
first is the *Dispute of the Sacrament* (1509–11) in the *Room of
the Segnatura.* Here the symmetrical arrangement of the main
portions of the composition impairs the interest of the whole.
Not so in *The School of Athens,* perhaps the most successful and
grandiose of all his murals. But when Leo X ascended to the papel
throne after the death of Julius II in 1513, he burdened the painter
with so many commissions that more and more assistants had to
be called upon to collaborate. The *Fire in the Borgo* (1514–17)
in the next room is wholly of Raphael's design, although the execution is not. The fourth *stanza,* containing the *Battle of Constantine,* remained unfinished at his death in 1520, and much of it
looks as if it were done without even the benefit of his designs.
Moving through these rooms, it is with relief that we are at once
able to realize where the hand of a great master wrought and
where mere routine prevailed. In the last of the papal rooms,
however, it is not a question of mere routine, but of outright
ineptness, combined with a taste of such low order that we
quickly turn away—these are the late 19th-century potboilers,
once looked upon as great works of art.

We continue on through the *Hall of Maps,* where all is fresco
and very elegant, the *Hall of Tapestries* (a "hall" is equivalent
to about a city block), and finally the *Hall of Sculptures,* where
we face such a prodigious accumulation of statuary to make concentration on this or that object very, very difficult. We have
just put behind us a "forced" march of two hours.

Museums

The Vatican museums were described in the preceding chapter;
there remain the Museo Terme, Museo Capitolino, and Villa

Roman Sculpture,
2nd Century (Terme)

Sculpture (Museo Terme)

Museo Terme Entrance

Giulia, all displaying statuary; the Museo Borghese, and Palazzo Barberini, where paintings can be seen. In Rome, those whose interest is antique sculpture will be gratified beyond expectation, for nowhere else is it present in such prodigious quality and quantity.

Museo Terme, located on Piazza dell' Esedra, a short distance from the railroad station, is unlike any other museum in Europe in that the principal building is contemporary with the objects it contains. The building, once the baths of Diocletian (into which a Carthusian monastery was later incorporated), is now in ruins, but the broken arches and walls together with the arcaded court-yard of the monastery provide an incomparable background for the monuments, creating a mood that no formal museum could induce. Hellenistic and Roman statuary, much of it copies of Greek originals, fill the cavernous halls and courtyards. There is so much beauty around that to draw the onlooker's attention to the more popular objects would be unreasonable.

Museo Capitolino (on the Piazza del Campidoglio) also provides

Birth of Venus, Greek Relief (Terme)

Amor and Psyche
(Museo Capitolino)

a magnificent foil for its treasures. It is one of the three structures, all authentic Renaissance palaces, with the design attributed
to Michelangelo. The collection is top-heavy with perfunctory
Roman portraiture, but this need not occupy our attention. There
is enough fine statuary around to merit a visit to this museum as
well as to the one facing it (Palazzo Conservatori). Even if
the gigantic head and parts of the body of Emperor Constantine
are not great works of art, the courtyard with these fragments
and other marbles will not fail to enchant us.

Villa Giulia, located in the Borghese Gardens, was a country
house built for Pope Julius III in the middle of the 16th century
and since 1888 it has been a museum of Etruscan art. The
installation of the collection is of the most modern, functional
kind and has largely obliterated the Renaissance elements of the
interior. Appreciation of Etruscan art has not been widespread
enough to make it generally known. Indeed, it is, at times, crude,
often grotesque, and on the whole, fantastic. In these respects, it
is "modern"and hence pleases contemporary taste. The collection
contains a vast number of terra cotta figures, Tanagra figurines,
friezes, statuary, vases, vessels, weapons, and household utensils.
It should not be missed by anyone who is capable of appreciating
an art which, although possessing classic overtones, is paradoxically often anti-Classic. It should be noted that although the
Etruscans were conquered by the Romans, their craftsmen continued to find employment all over Italy, Sicily, and other Greek
and Roman colonies.

Museo Borghese was built in the 17th century as a country villa
for a Borghese cardinal, and it gives a vivid picture of the luxury
with which the aristocracy of the period surrounded itself. The
gallery has many Roman and Hellenistic sculptures, also those

The Capitoline Venus

Rape of Proserpina.
Bernini (Borghese)

La Fornarina. Raphael
(Palazzo Barberini)

Palazzo Barberini

by Bernini and Canova. The work of the first borders on the ludicrous—*Apollo and Daphne,* the *Rape of Proserpina,* and *Truth,* are potboilers in the truest sense, but Canova's pseudo-Classicistic statuary is merely devitalized. There are a few first-rate paintings in the large collection: Lucas Cranach's *Venus;* Titian's *Sacred and Profane Love,* one of his best early works reminiscent of Bellini; Raphael's *Deposition* and *Portrait of a Lady;* Piero di Cosimo's *Adoration;* a fine Rubens; a Vermeer; a Dürer; and Correggio's *Danae.*

Palazzo Barberini was built in 1625 for Pope Urban VII. It is a typical Baroque building, on which Maderna, Borromini, and Bernini collaborated. Among its paintings are a few conspicuous masterpieces: Raphael's *La Fornarina* (the baker's daughter, reported to have been his mistress), undoubtedly one of the most ingratiating Renaissance female portraits; a Filippo Lippi, a Piero di Cosimo; Holbein's *Henry VIII;* a small El Greco; Titian's famous *Philip II* and his *Venus and Adonis,* unfortunately much deteriorated.

Roman Remains

We start with the ***Castel' Sant' Angelo*** and the *Sant' Angelo Bridge.* Emperor Hadrian built the castle as his mausoleum in the year 139 A.D., and several later Roman emperors were buried here. From the beginning of the Middle Ages, the fortified complex served as a prison and as the citadel of Rome. From the 14th to 16th centuries, a succession of popes changed and rebuilt the interior of the castle and installed luxuriously decorated apartments in its upper stories. Today, it serves chiefly as a military museum. The interior of the fortress is of interest; however, to inspect it would be hard on the feet, so we will be content to admire the dynamic truculence of the exterior. The bridge, also built by Hadrian, is of a piece with the castle. Its

Sant' Angelo Bridge and Castle

imperious, weighty mass remains strangely buoyant thanks to eight angels flanking its balustrade literally lending wings to its five massive spans.

Pantheon. Considered the symbol of Rome, it is one of the best preserved of the ancient Roman edifices. Once a temple dedicated to the seven planets, it was built in the first century B.C. and its rotunda was enlarged about 100 years later. In the 7th century it was converted into a church and still later, into a fortress. Now stripped of statuary, ornaments, marble paneling, and the gilded bronze plates of the dome, its former splendor has vanished. The oddest feature of the interior is its single source of daylight, the large, open "eye"—the *oculus* placed in the center of the dome.

Trajan's Column, standing over 100 feet tall on the now virtually obliterated Forum of Trajan, was erected in 113 A.D. Its winding marble relief representing scenes from the emperor's wars is the best-preserved Roman sculpture of its kind. It is surmounted by a 16th-century bronze statue of St. Peter.

Forum Romanum. Next to the Parthenon in Greece, this is the most important antique site in Europe. The Forum dates from the 1st to 4th centuries A.D., although long before this the site was the market and gathering place of the Romans. After the

The Pantheon

Pantheon Interior

fall of the Empire, over the centuries, its temples and statuary were relentlessly destroyed. In a report of 1518 by Raphael, who was appointed by Pope Leo X as custodian of antiquities, we read: "Modern Rome in all its splendor was built entirely with lime made from antique marbles." Magnificent in its over-all scope, the site can best be viewed from the terrace behind the central palace of the Campidoglio. In fact, the panorama of the Forum with the Palatine Hill in the background is more impressive seen from a distance than from close by, for it is the picturesque quality of the ruins, not the detail of the fragments, that captivates us.

From the terrace of the Palazzo Senatorio, the portico of the *Temple of Saturn,* the most ancient building on the Forum, which has eight of its original ten granite columns, and the *Arch of Septimius Severus* can be seen. To identify other minor fragments is rather futile, hence we shall mention two of the most interesting arches, those of *Titus* and *Constantine.* The first stands on the highest point of the *Via Sacra;* it was built in the 1st century to commemorate the victory over the Jews; the second, nearest the Colosseum, dates from the 4th century, but its lavish decoration, marble statues, reliefs, and ornaments were taken from other, older structures. At the north end of the Forum stands the last, and greatest, architectural achievement of the Romans—the *Basilica of Constantine.* The building measures 265 by 195 feet, and its large coffered vaulting represents an important innovation in building technique. In the main apse once stood the colossal statue of Constantine, the head, feet, and other fragments of which are preserved in the courtyard of the Palazzo dei Conservatori on the Campidoglio.

Colosseum. The building was so-named in the 8th century, and it fully deserves the epithet. More than any other edifice, this elliptical colossus conjures up in our mind the power, debauchery and barbarism of ancient Rome. But it is not the dimension alone

Arch of Septimius Severus

Arch of Constantine

that impresses us (it once seated 8,000 spectators), it is the
rhythmic beat of the majestic architecture, much imitated by
some of the Renaissance masters. Today we see only one-third of
its original size as the rest was used for building material by
anyone who cared to cart it away. It was only in the 18th century
that Pope Benedict XIV consecrated the building and thus stopped
further depredation.

Churches and Palaces

Sant' Agnese in Agone (on the Piazza Navona) was completely
reconstructed by the great architect Borromini in 1657, and its
beautifully contoured façade and sumptuously decorated interior
represent Baroque at the height of its virtuosity and inventiveness. The same can be said of *Il Gesù,* the principal church of the
Jesuits in Rome, which was built a century earlier and served as
the prototype of all Baroque churches. Instead of the traditional
design, we see a high, barrel-vaulted nave with short transept
below the dome and very small side chapels. *Santa Maria in
Aracoeli* (beside the Campidoglio), on the other hand, has a
history dating as far back as the 6th century; its present shape,
however, dates from the middle of the 13th century, and its façade
was never completed. Facing the Forum of Trajan, the *Santis-
simo Nome di Maria* is an impressive 18th-century structure, and
farther down the eastern slope of the Capitoline Hill, between the

Il Gesù Church

Moses. Michelangelo

Temple of Vespasian and the Arch of Septimius Severus, the *Santi Martina e Luca*, built in 1640, must be counted among the finest of Roman edifices.

Three more churches remain on our list; the first is *San Pietro in Vincoli*, planned as a mausoleum for Pope Julius II; it was to be built by Michelangelo, but the commission was never carried out. However, his over-life-size *Moses*, designed to be the central figure of the complex monument, is now placed in the rather dull interior of the church. Viewing the statue of Moses in the original, surrounded as it is by subsidiary figures which detract from, rather than add to, its effectiveness, one cannot help but ask: Where did I see this war-horse before? But at the same time one is aware that it represents the culmination of Renaissance sculpture.

The history of *Santa Maria Maggiore* is a long one. Founded in the 5th century, it was repeatedly enlarged and reconstructed. It has a 14th-century campanile, the tallest of its kind in Rome, and a Baroque façade that dates from the middle of the 18th century. The most interesting feature of this church is its solemn and noble interior.

Santa Maria degli Angeli, to the right of the Museo Terme, was designed by Michelangelo, but has 18th-century additions. Its interior is reminiscent of the Pantheon—architecture in its purest sense. The enormous, monolithic granite columns in the transept add to the effect of grandeur.

It is perfectly obvious that there is no greater pomp than that found in the Vatican apartments, halls, and libraries. In their luxuriant décor, the Museo Borghese and the Palazzo Barberini are smaller Baroque palaces. The *Villa Medici*, a short distance from *Santa Trinità dei Monti* (above the Spanish Steps), hides one of the most enchanting garden fronts to be found in Rome behind a sober façade turned toward the city. The villa was built in 1544 and was owned by cardinals, a pope, and the Grand Duke of Tuscany. Napoleon bought it in 1801, and it has since housed the French Academy of Art in Rome. It is of interest to note that among its former tenants were Velázquez, Delacroix, and Berlioz, and in 1630 Galileo was held there as a prisoner of the Inquisition.

Piazzas and Fountains

No matter how far we travel, nowhere but in Rome does one find so many felicitous elements of city design—the piazzas, many of them graced by fountains. Rome and its Baroque foun-

Fountain, Piazza Navona

tains! What is the secret of the gushing fountains that always enraptures our senses?

First there is the famed *Piazza Navona* with its three fountains, two of them by Bernini. The one called *Dei Fiumi* (of the rivers) in front of the Sant' Agnese with the obelisk, is the most spectacular. The second is known as *Del Moro;* it represents a Negro wrestling with a dolphin. Every building on this square dates from the same epoch, hence its perfect harmony.

On the *Piazza della Minerva,* in front of the noble Renaissance façade of *Santa Maria sopra Minerva,* stands a marble elephant (designed by Bernini), carrying a small Egyptian obelisk on its back.

Next we come to the **Piazza del Campidoglio,** the oldest political and religious center of Rome. The original buildings and temples disappeared during the Middle Ages (some fragments were unearthed not long ago where Santa Maria in Aracoeli borders the Piazza), and what presents itself to us now is the essence of Roman High Renaissance. Michelangelo designed the structures in 1540, but the execution was left to other architects. Ascending the monumental flight of shallow steps, we face the **Palazzo dei Senatori;** to the right is the **Palazzo dei Conservatori** and to the left, the *Capitoline Museum.* A wealth of ancient statuary is preserved in both of these. In the center of the square stands the equestrian statue of the *Emperor Marcus Aurelius* still showing

Campidoglio

Marcus Aurelius

Neptune's Fountain (Capitolino)   Courtyard (Palazzo dei Conservatori)

traces of the original gilding. It is one of the very few remaining bronze relics of its kind and is in a perfect state of preservation. Its beautiful pedestal is said to have been designed by Michelangelo. The flight of stairs, flanked below by figures of Egyptian lions (the originals are preserved in the Capitoline Museum), terminates with two colossal figures of Castor and Pollux on both sides of the balustrade, together with two subordinate statues. They are from different locations and are Roman copies of Greek originals.

MORE FOUNTAINS. On the Piazza Barberini, a commonplace metropolitan square, Bernini's *Fontana del Tritone* and the small *Fontana degli Api* (Fountain of the Bees) are charming, and so is the *Fontana della Barcaccia* (the Boat Fountain) in the *Piazza di Spagna,* a work of Bernini's father. Together with the **Spanish Steps** (a masterpiece of Baroque design built in 1725), the Roman obelisk, and the Santa Trinità dei Monti in the background, it is one of the most ingratiating sights in the city. The Spanish Steps —they seem to issue from the church like a river, circling the obelisk and the bulwarks of the balustrades, cascading down in two streams to meet midway in a gentle confluence. What is the fascination in a flight of steps? Why do so many people just sit on them, pausing as it were, before rushing from the 18th century into the maelstrom of the modern city below?

Finally there is the **Fontana di Trevi.** The most extravagant of them all. Many sculptors worked at this stupendous project, which, it is said, originated from a sketch by Bernini, but was finished 82 years after his death. I call the project "extravagant," a weak attribute, indeed, to qualify the most audacious of sculptural fountains. Fantastic waterworks were particularly favored during the Baroque building period, and many of them have been designed with great imagination; yet none has been conceived on such a monumental scale as the Fontana di Trevi. In a tiny square, surrounded on three sides by "ordinary" buildings—if an 18th-century building can be called ordinary—the fountain issues from

Trinità dei Monti and the
Spanish Steps

Fountain of Trevi

the façade of the Palazzo Poli. In fact this façade metamorphoses
into the rocks and gushing water around it. Everything is in
constant flux—even the statues, and the rocks, and all is very
"antitectonic" and absurd as far as architecture goes, but it is in
keeping with the fantastic. There must be magic in the Fontana
di Trevi, for the small square is always thronged with people—
even natives.

Lastly, we may consider the *Via Appia* and the **Catacombs,** although these are touristic, rather than artistic attractions. Not so
Tivoli, however, where nature and art collaborated to give their
best. Here a river leaves the mountains, forming many waterfalls
as it descends to the Roman Campagna, and these have been
utilized to provide the *Villa d'Este* (once a Benedictine abbey)
with spectacular waterworks and fountains—1500 of them. The
park, built on many terraces, is Baroque, and Bernini's genius is
evident in its design. Can a terraced park be considered a work of
art? I believe so, for it harbors art's most precious ingredient:
imagination.

Naples

Having now traveled as far as Rome, we might ask ourselves
whether, in quest of art, we should proceed to Naples. In case we
plan to visit Sicily, Naples would be conveniently on our list.
Before extending the itinerary, one should be aware of what art
treasures the city offers, for having covered so much territory,
one's taste might be—if not jaded—more demanding.

To say that Naples is picturesque is a truism as well as an
understatement. And it is not only nature that conspired to
make it so, but history as well. From the 12th century on, the

Street Scene (Naples)

Castel Nuovo (Naples)

Hohenstaufen princes—and later the Angevin kings, the Span-
iards, and the French—ruled the city, leaving their imprints and
making it unlike any other place in Italy. Naples is Baroque; it
is also full of slums, and I do not sentimentalize or romanticize by
saying that they lack the aspect of sordidness so characteristic
of depressed areas in other cities. Here many slum dwellings have
palatial portals, royally proportioned staircases and arcaded
courtyards—all in decayed condition, of course. Poverty here
appears to be theatrical rather than pitiful—and very, very
colorful.

Museums, Churches, and Edifices

Two famous museums will occupy our attention. The first is
the **Museo Nazionale** which contains sculptures and archeological
finds of great importance. The murals from Pompeii and Herculaneum are the only evidence to give us a comprehensive idea
about Roman painting which was varied in style, and shows a
wide range of talent. Sophisticated, refined taste distinguishes
these decorations, making it evident that their owners were "accustomed to the best." Interesting also, are the bronze figures of
men and animals. These were covered by hot volcanic ash and
oxidized to a deep black; only the enamel of the whites of the
eyes appears in the original color, giving an odd look to the
statues. A large mosaic of the 2nd century B.C., representing
the battle of Alexander and Darius, has also been retrieved from
the ruins.

The collection of Roman statuary is of no less importance. In
fact it is not inferior to that of the Museo Terme in Rome. The
majority of the sculptures are copies after Greek originals, and
many are of Hellenistic origin—among them the famed—and

Venus Callypigos. Hellenistic

Bronze Horse. Greek

much restored—*Venus Callypigos*. The collection is very large and includes Etruscan terra cotta works, vases, objects of decorative art, and utilitarian implements.

Museo Capodimonte, newly installed in the former Royal Palace, does not have a collection of first order judged by international standards, but it possesses a number of great works and is particularly rich in those by 17th- and 18th-century Neapolitan painters. As usual, in the entrance halls are gathered Gothic masters of the 13th and 14th centuries—always charming. There is also a sprinkling of illustrious names: Simone Martini, Bernardo Daddi, Masolino, Masaccio. Of the Renaissance masters there is a great portrait of *Pope Leo X* by Raphael, a hard-edged Mantegna, an Antonio Vivarini, and one of Bellini's finest early paintings, the *Transfiguration.* If Titian had only followed his

Alexander's Battle. Pompeian Mosaic

Pompeian Mural

master Bellini's technical precepts! Alas, the method he began to employ in the middle of his career was not conducive to permanence, and the climate of Venice contributed to further decay. Several of his works, particularly the portrait of *Paul III with his Nephews* and *Danae*, are in very poor condition.

The Flemish school is represented by Brueghel's extraordinary *Blind Leading the Blind*, a tempera painting on a thin fabric, the only one in existence executed in this technique, and the *Misanthrope*, which demonstrates that this painter did not have genius merely in his fingers, but that his intellectual depth paralleled his artistic potential. Other outstanding Flemish paintings are those by Herri met de Bles; these are landscapes such as only a Flemish master could have visualized. Among the Baroque painters, Salvator Rosa and Luca Giordano are the strongest, and Ribera, the Spaniard who ended his life as a Neapolitan, is poorly represented. Two Goya portraits, exquisite as always, hang in the last room of the gallery.

The tasteless royal rooms on the floor below are decorated by equally tasteless—and pretentious paintings—all of them from the 19th century.

The Duomo, Naples' finest church, is Romanesque-Gothic and dates from the 13th century, but its interior is in sumptuous Renaissance style. In one of its chapels, the Capella del Tesorio, devoted to San Gennaro the patron Saint of Naples, is a unique collection of statues of saints wrought in silver; masterpieces of Baroque art. *San Paolo Maggiore* has a splendid Renaissance ceiling, and *Gesù Nuovo*, the front of which is faced with curiously faceted stones such as are found on some 15th-century Italian palaces, has an ornate 16th- and 17th-century interior. The Gothic church of *San Lorenzo* was a'most destroyed, as was *San Chiaro;*

San Gesù Nuovo (Naples)   Silver Statue (Duomo)

but the latter is now completely rebuilt in a modernistic "Gothic" style.

The *Piazza Plebiscita* is formed by imposing edifices, among them the *Palazzo Reale*, and the vast *Piazza Municipio* dominated by the 13th-century fortress, *Castelnuovo*. It is surrounded by a wide moat, and wedged between its bleak, crenelated towers is a triumphal arch of glistening marble—a masterpiece of Renaissance sculpture by Francesco Laurana. These are the city's emblem. The interior of the fortress, now housing municipal offices, was repeatedly reconstructed and hence is now of little interest.

The Countryside

To view the Bay of Naples on a clear day, one should ride to the top of Mount Vesuvius. In the light of the setting sun, the sight is all that the travel folders promise.

Pompeii—Amalfi—Ravello—Positano—Sorrento. Pompeian art can be seen in the *Museo Nazionale* in Naples; very few objects have been left in their original places. The city was a luxury resort until the year 79 A.D., when it was covered by ashes and lava from the erupting Vesuvius. To this catastrophe we owe the preservation—even if a fragmentary one—of a complete Roman city.

Famous as the site is, it is also disappointing, and our curiosity and esthetic sense are hardly gratified by the lecture of the guide,

Pompeii   Amalfi Cathedral

who will point out various houses, villas, and the names of the former occupants—facts to be forgotten as soon as we visit another ruin.

Leaving the eerie silence of the dead city and turning toward the sea, we come upon one of the most scenic coastlines in Europe. It is dotted with enchanting places; **AMALFI** is the first. Powerful in the Middle Ages, it is now only a small fishing village, for in the course of time it suffered intermittent landslides and tidal waves. Not only is the location of the village and its main square incredibly picturesque, but it is also graced by an exotic *cathedral.* At the summit of a long and very steep stairway, this astounding structure combines Romanesque, Moorish, Sicilian, and Hohenstaufen features with rare felicity. Its façade is polychromed; the *campanile,* topped with polychromed turrets, is reminiscent of the Giralda in Seville; the arches are typical'y Moorish. The interior is equally fantastic, incorporating many Grecian and Roman relics.

Continuing on the loop back toward Naples, **RAVELLO,** nestling on the slope of Monte Lattari, is the next stop. There never has been a more bewitching place, and the same can be said of **POSITANO** and **SORRENTO.** Should one wish to turn from the beauty of the landscape to man-made objects, a visit to the Romanesque *Duomo of Ravello* and the 11th-century *Palazzo Ruffo,* with its fantastic gardens, will reward the effort.

SICILY

The short distance between Naples (or Rome) and Sicily is not sufficient reason to visit the island; and what can the traveler who has "taken in all of Italy"—or nearly all—expect to find there? The answer is that it has much to offer. First, Sicily is not quite Italy, and it is not Africa, although the tropical fecundity and lush vegetation of its southern part are reminiscent of the hot continent. It is more Greek than Roman; in fact, Greek mythology is almost as alive in some sections as it is in Greece, and Classic remains are more plentiful than anywhere outside Athens.

The Greeks settled here around the year 800 B.C. and had to battle the Phoenicians and the Carthaginians, also not the original inhabitants of the island. Eventually Sicily became the most prosperous of the Greek colonies, and its main city, Syracuse, was as large as Athens itself. In Agrigento, the second city of importance, called by the Greek poet, Pindar "the most beautiful one of mortal man," only ruins remain, some better preserved than those in Greece. Other antique sites are in Segesta and Selinunte. There are also edifices left by later conquerors—the Romans,

Saracens, Normans, Arabs, and lastly, the Spanish and French.
Hence the art of Sicily is variously Greek, Roman, Arabic, Byzantine, and Baroque. But the most renowned are the Byzantine
structures and their mosaic decorations.

Palermo

The visitor to the island of Sicily will do well to start with its
principal city. Since it was founded by the Roman Emperor,
Augustus, the great patron of arts, there have been many
Palermos; the city was perhaps most powerful under the rule
of the Moslems. A thousand years ago, there were more than
300 mosques, only two of which remain today. Palermo was also
Norman, and later Gothic. However, traces of these cultures were
largely eliminated by the wild exuberance of the Baroquists, who
converted everything they could into their "modern" style, which
luckily favored the art of architecture. For us, however, the most
recent vicissitude has been the most serious one, for it transpired
in our own time; the damage suffered during World War II was
very extensive, and many of the ancient buildings were either
totally destroyed or permanently disfigured.

In what way does Palermo differ from other southern cities?
It is difficult, indeed, to pin down its elusive charm. For it is
unlike any other European city, although its Baroque aspects are
closely related to those of southern Italian towns.

Museums and Edifices

It would seem natural to expect that in Sicily, once the most
important colony of Greece, we might find important repositories
of fine art. However, this is not the case. The *Museo Archeologico
Nazionale,* housed in a Baroque palace distinguished by an exquisite courtyard, is rather unimpressive. The statuary, whether
of Greek, Asiatic, or Roman origin, is, for the most part, crude.
Moreover, the remains are so fragmentary that one is hard put
to divine their original appearance. But the exhibit is rich in
beautifully carved sarcophagi and urns, 6th- and 5th-century
pottery, terra cotta work, and Tanagra figurines.

The *Galleria Nazionale di Sicilia,* in the *Palazzo Abbatellis,* is
located in the waterfront slums. Originally of Norman construction, it was almost completely destroyed during World War II,
but its fragments have been incorporated with great taste and
ingenuity into a modern building. Paintings by early Sicilian
masters as well as beautiful Renaissance statuary are displayed.

Near-by are two striking edifices, the **Porta Felice** and the **Palazzo Chiaromonte o Steri.**

There is another cluster of picturesque buildings in the center of the city, where Via Maqueda and the Corso Vittorio Emmanuele cross. The Piazza at the crossing, known as *Quattro Canti di Città*, is flanked by four extravagantly Baroque façades with built-in fountains, a fantastic sight.

La Martorana near-by, dates from the 9th century and is one of the two remaining mosques in the city. It combines several styles that, although quite contradictory, do not invalidate the harmony of the whole. Next to a noble Baroque façade of very restrained design, stands a Saracen tower, and inside, 12th-century mosaics vie for the viewer's attention with a fussy Baroque altar, a Cosmatic floor, and Renaissance ornaments. The **San Cataldo Chapel,** next to the church is wholly Arabic in structure. Under the Normans it was converted into a church, but is now just an empty shell. The second mosque is **San Giovanni degli Eremiti,** which also dates from the 9th century. It has a fairytale arcaded courtyard lush with vegetation.

Adjacent to La Martorana, on the *Piazza e Fontana Pretoria*, stands a fountain surrounded by a host of Baroque statuary. Arranged in a wide circle, three deep, these figures diminish in size as they approach the fountain—a trick of perspective to make the space appear larger. On the *Piazzetta San Giuseppe* (also next to the Quattro Canti), stands the church of **San Giuseppe;** here we see Baroque ornamentation at its most untamed. Nowhere have marble inlays been used with greater intricacy; indeed, here they proliferate almost obsessively. Farther up the Corso is the *Piazza Bologna* with a fine 17th-century bronze statue.

The **Duomo** was built in 1185 in Norman and Gothic style, with

San Giovanni degli Eremiti
(Palermo)

The Cathedral

Byzantine and Arabic overtones. It stands on a spacious square, flanked by 18th-century statuary—a strange sight, more exotic than beautiful. Inside, a complete and unimaginative restoration during the 18th century ruthlessly destroyed its original appearance. In fact, of the ancient relics only the sarcophagi of the early rulers are preserved. It is worth-while to employ the services of an attendant (always present) who will guide the visitor to the sacristy chambers where ornately decorated vestments are preserved—works of art, all fashioned by nameless nuns.

The *Palatine Chapel* is housed in the former Norman *Palazzo Reale* or Palazzo Normanni; now totally Baroque, it is occupied by government agencies. The chapel's 11th- to 15th-century mosaics belong with the finest—the walls glisten with gold and other luminous colors, the polychrome marbles are woven like precious fabrics, and the Moorish ceiling, very much like that of the Alhambra in Granada, is filled with heavenly stalactites. This edifice alone would justify a trip to Palermo. Just outside, on the walls of the chapel, the 18th-century mosaics eloquently demonstrate that if realistically conceived, representations in this medium lose their appeal.

Monreale Abbey, a few miles outside the city, was built from 1164 to 1182; it combines Saracen, Byzantine, and Norman elements, and together they produce a style of greatest picturesque-

Palatine Chapel, Interior Details (Palermo)

The Duomo (Monreale, Sicily)

Motifs, Courtyard of the Abbey
(Monreale)

ness and preciousness. The abbey church is a basilica of considerable size, and its interior and floor are entirely encrusted with
mosaics and marble paneling. Though of the Cosmati type, they
are earlier and derive from Oriental and Greek sources. As if
these ornaments did not lend enough brilliance to the interior, the
entire upper part of the walls is covered by Byzantine mosaics
representing great events from the Old and New Testament. Unfortunately, these are placed high on the wall, which makes close
observation of the details rather difficult. In the semidome of the
apse rises a colossal bust mosaic of *Cristos Pantocratos*—a
standard decoration in most Byzantine churches—and the space
all around is filled with mosaics, works of Greek masters, and

Motifs, Courtyard of the Abbey (Monreale)

also some of their local followers. The inlaid marble floor and the timbered, gilded, and carved ceiling add to the extraordinary colorfulness of the interior. To withstand the thrust of the ceiling the walls are held by richly sculptured tie rods, a common feature in Italian basilica-type structures. Also interesting are the bronze doors to the west and north, wrought at the end of the 12th century.

Adjoining the church is the cloister. Its Saracen arches rest on Romanesque columns, carved and inlaid, and graced by capitals such as only that age produced; they are incomparable. (To concentrate fully on the marvelous details of this edifice instead of on the guide, it is best, on this occasion, to dispense with his services.)

The Country

I spoke of a tour around the island and of the ruins of Greek temples at **SEGESTA, SELINUNTE,** and **AGRIGENTO.** Of these, the remains at Agrigento are the most important. Actually, the most outstanding reason for this tour is the landscape, or more precisely, landscape "enlivened" by ruins. As for **SYRACUSE,** half a million people are said to have inhabited this Greek colonial city, second only to Athens in size; today the population is less than one-tenth of what it was. There is a well-preserved amphitheater, and in the local museum is the famous *Venus of Syracuse.*

Like Syracuse, **CATANIA** is largely Baroque. Its most remarkable feature is the *Duomo* and, in front of it, the monument of an elephant carrying an obelisk on its back—a favorite Baroque decoration.

TAORMINA seems to have one purpose: pleasure. It is on all counts one of the most delightful resorts in Europe, for it possesses an unmatched natural setting: rising in terraces above the bay, its rocks form fantastic promontories with a view over the sea and with snow-capped Mount Etna to the southwest. Its

The Fallen Giant (Agrigento)

The Temple (Segesta)

Venus of Syracuse

Catania Duomo

ruined Greek theatre is like a gay stage setting, and above, following a steep, winding road to the highest plateau and the village of Castel Mola on top of Monte Tauro, a panorama of unbelievable beauty unfolds itself. In places like Taormina, man-made art such as the Baroque *Duomo, Palazzo Santo Stefano* (14th century), and *Palazzo Corvaja* (15th century) seems to take second place.

The last edifice to be visited on our journey is the great Norman *cathedral* of **CEFALU**; started in 1132, it is typically Sicilian— that is, Byzantine and Saracen influences predominate. Replete with mosaics, its interior is reminiscent of the Capella Palatina, except for its ogival vaults over the choir. And in the apse, the enormous mosaic representation of the *Pantocrator* is the most majestic and radiant of its kind.

Greek Amphitheatre (Taormina)

Section 8 / Greece

INTRODUCTION TO THE ART OF GREECE

It is said that in London, rather than in Athens, Greek art can be seen in its greatest splendor. Theoretically, this is true; however, there is a vast difference in the way this art is viewed. The *Elgin Marbles* in the British Museum are unequalled, but are certain of the objects in Greece—and not necessarily Praxiteles' *Hermes* in Olympia but the many less celebrated sculptures in Athens and elsewhere—not also inspiring? Seen at the point of origin under Greek skies, a sculpture, even a mere artifact, takes on a different complexion and impresses one differently than do pieces in museums outside the country. In other words, when traveling in Greece, esthetic contemplation is instinct with sentiment.

As to sculpture, another aspect should be considered. Created under the influence of a good style, "minor" and "major" works are infinitely closer in artistry than are paintings.

A thought not easily acceptable to us is that Greek statuary once looked entirely different than it does today, for it aimed at verisimilitude. The flesh portions of the figures were colored with pigmented wax (not paint, as is commonly held), the hair, eyes, and other details were polychromed and garments were often gilded. Should the ancient Greeks see their sculptures in their present fragmented condition, they would not consider them works of art.

I have briefly discussed the history of Greek styles in Section I, but perhaps it would be worth-while to repeat certain historical facts. The earliest objects we see in the National Museum of Athens are from the Cyclades (a chain of islands in the Aegean Sea). These date from about 3000 B.C. and are held as belonging to the Neolithic-Cycladic transition period. Next appeared the art of Crete (about 2000–1500 B.C.), preserved in small statuary, fragments of wall painting, household goods, and objects of décor. These show an extraordinary refinement and sophistication. They can be seen in considerable quantity in Heraklion on Crete and also in the National Museum in Athens.

The civilization of Crete, referred to as "Minoan," appeared and vanished leaving few clues to its origins or to the reason for its extinction. Next came the Mycenaean civilization on the Greek mainland, influenced by the Minoans, but more primitive. Architectural remains, ornaments, and pottery are preserved from that period which ended with the Trojan War, fought, it is now believed for commercial rather than for romantic reasons. From that period until the 8th century B.C., art on the mainland of Greece seems to have been limited to wooden temples and simple pottery. The earliest statuary, referred to as "Archaic," appeared during the 6th century. The figures are stiff and schematized, obviously influenced by Egyptian style, and their facial expression displays the typical, enigmatic smile. Among the best examples of this style in the National Museum is the statue of a youth almost seven feet tall. In the Museum of the Acropolis is the finest female figure, the *Koré of Athens*.

The Periclean, or Golden Age of Greek art, followed the liberation from the Persian invasion in the middle of the 5th century, at which time Athens became an imperialistic power. The Peloponnesian War, 100 years later, brought Athens defeat at the hands of Sparta, but until that time the Athenian style was widely imitated in southern Italy (the temple at Paestum was built in the 5th century), Sicily, and other parts of Greece not under the domination of Athens. During the era of Alexander the Great (356–323), Greek art appeared in many places in Asia Minor and Egypt and was, in turn, influenced by foreign styles. From the 3rd century on, we speak of "Hellenistic," not of "Greek" art. The older style is based on a design essentially static and geometric. Consequently it tends toward schematization; physiognomies remain unvaried, and body movements are relatively restricted. This art became the supreme example for generations of artists whose aim was to emulate the Classic ideal. Much of Hellenistic sculpture, freed from the restrictions of the rigorously Classic, aimed at dramatization and became progressively more realistic, more detailed and particularized. We can deduce from various contemporary accounts that Greek painting of the earlier era stood on a high level, but nothing of it has survived except for vase paintings. An enormous volume of pottery is preserved, for its manufacture constituted the main Greek industry. In it all of Greek painting is documented. Several basic shapes of pottery are represented by the characteristic *amphora,* identified by its slender neck and handles opposite one another; a wide-mouthed jar called *krater;* and a few more standard shapes. The jars were fashioned by potters but the designs were the work of painters.

From about the 12th to the 8th century these designs were simple geometric patterns and are classified as belonging to the *Geometric Period.* The *Geometric Figure* style dates from the 8th century; much later, oriental motifs were adopted. Late in the 7th century artists developed the *Black Figure* style which became enormously popular, and by the mid-6th century, red figures appeared on black backgrounds. Since these also relied on geometricity the pottery created in these styles was esthetically perfect. Because of their great commercial success, figural representations were used during the three following centuries, gradually employing more realistic means and thus acquiring the pat look of genre pictures. During the Empire period (beginning of the 19th century), the *amphora,* now neo-Classic and totally devitalized, became a favorite article of decoration.

Greek architecture was limited to a simple post-and-lintel construction. This method persisted until the domination of Rome in the middle of the 2nd century, whence came the arch and the dome—in turn Etruscan inventions. Because of their limitation the Greeks were able to develop the most perfect style of columnar architecture, to be adopted and cherished to this very day.

Greek Remains

Some years ago I wrote: "If you are fortunate enough to find a few stones in Greece still in their original position, they most likely have been placed by archeologists. . . ." This is somewhat of an exaggeration, but on the whole, despite extensive reconstructions, always most expertly carried out, the devastation that meets the eye at the sites of temples, stadiums, and cities is enormous. Whatever escaped destruction or was not carried away by a succession of foreign invaders—the Romans (great collectors of Greek art), Byzantines, Crusaders, Venetians, and the Turks who ruled Greece from 1450–1833)—fell victim to earthquakes. Nevertheless, excavations during the last 100 years have uncovered so many buried relics that today the National Museum in Athens—despite the expatriated Elgin Marbles—must be considered a very important repository of native art.

Athens

The *Acropolis* (High City) comes first. It occupies a steep rock plateau and was looked upon as the symbol of Greek civilization since it assumed its final shape during the age of Pericles. It was once the fortified seat of Greek rulers as well as a religious shrine and surrounded by a high wall, but it was destroyed by Persian invaders in 480 B.C. The Acropolis as we know it was built in the incredibly short span between 449 and 421. Yet by the middle of the 2nd century B.C., Greece had fallen under Roman domination and the Acropolis lost its standing as a religious center. At that time most of its movable statuary disappeared. Under the Turks, the plateau served as a bastion and many houses were built upon it. The Propylaea was used as an ammunition dump, and in 1656 during a siege by the Venetians it was hit by a shell, and the ensuing explosion destroyed much of the building. The Venetians entered for a short period, and with their retreat many more precious relics disappeared. Finally, in 1812, Lord Elgin bought from the Turkish government whatever statuary remained —the metopes, parts of the frieze and pediments, and one of the caryatids from the Erechtheum.

Reconstruction started in 1834 and is still going on; in order of size the buildings are the Parthenon, the Propylaea, the Erechtheum, and the tiny temple of Nike. No photographs can ever communicate the beauty and magic of the site; it must be seen against the mountain background, the sea, and the luminous Grecian sky.

The *Propylaea,* gateway to the Acropolis, was built after the erection of the Parthenon. Constructed on a steep slope of rock, it took five years to complete, at a cost of approximately $12,000,000, in gold. This figure makes us realize the enormous efforts made by the Greeks to beautify their city. The structure served as a passageway to the Parthenon (visible from the entrance) and was flanked by two patios, one of which served as a picture gallery.

Acropolis (Athens)

Metopes from the Parthenon

The small **Temple of Nike Apteros** (the wingless Goddess of Victory), built at the same time as the Propylaea, stands to its right at the edge of the steep rock. The small, graceful structure has two porticos, each with four Ionic columns 13 feet high. To one side, and over the architrave, runs what must have once been a magnificent frieze 85 feet in length. The temple was completely destroyed in 1687 to make room for a Turkish fortification; its pieces must have been lying in a heap for 125 years, when Lord Elgin picked four blocks from the rubble and brought them to the British Museum. The remains were reassembled in 1836 and the missing parts replaced by casts.

The **Parthenon.** The Athenians knew it as the "Great Temple." It was dedicated to the goddess Athena, the protectress of Athens, and a colossal statue of ivory and gold, made by Phidias (the material had come from the Persian loot), once stood in its cella. The Doric edifice with its metopes, and the frieze that ran around the upper edge of the cella, its pediments, and the statuary, must have been grandiose beyond imagination. Most of what remained of the fragments is dispersed in museums—the British, the Louvre, the Vatican; but some of it can still be seen in the museum on the Acropolis.

The physical dimensions of the Parthenon are as follows: the building measures 235 feet in length and 110 in width, from the lowest step of the platform. The average height of the columns is 33 feet, 9 inches; and their diameter is 6 feet, 6 inches. Eight of these stand on the gable side and 17 on the long side. These columns show an outward curve, the so-called entasis (if perfectly straight, from a distance they would appear to sag in the middle). Moreover, they are not quite vertical but lean inward; their distance from one another is not uniform, and on the outside the columns are thicker—otherwise, seen against the sky, they would appear attenuated. Nor is the platform straight, but curved. Yet all this is hardly obvious to the eye. It is responsible, however, for the incomparable aliveness, lightness, and elegance of the building, and it bears witness to the great mastery of its architects and their knowledge of optical phenomena. It is an indisputable fact that although much imitated in later centuries, the perfection of the Parthenon has never been duplicated.

The **Erechtheum,** to the left of the Parthenon, was an Ionian temple dedicated to the semi-mystical King Erechtheus and other deities. Under the Byzantines it became a church and under the Turks (in the 15th century) a harem for the garrison commander. Its style differs greatly from that of the Parthenon, being built on three different levels and hence irregular in construction. On the north and east sides it is flanked by graceful, slender Ionic

The Caryatid Porch from the Erechtheum

columns, and on the south stands the famous porch of the Korai—
the so-called *Porch of the Maidens*. Doctrine-minded Classicists
found that using human forms to support a roof is irreconcilable
with the spirit that guided Classic architecture. However, anyone
concerned less with architectural orthodoxies than with beauty
must concede that no porch of any age could be more perfect than
this one. The grave, solemn, and at the same time, lovely caryatids, dedicated with serious mien to holding up the weight of the
roof, are deeply moving. (The second figure from the left is a
copy of the original, now in the British Museum.) The figures
are almost 7 feet, 6 inches high, and stand on a base 8 feet,
5½ inches in height.

The *Acropolis Museum* is the last building behind the Parthenon. It is an unattractive modern structure, and in it are as-

The Calf Bearer (Acropolis Museum)   Archaic Kore (Acropolis Museum)

Grave Relief (National Archeological Museum)

Nike Untying Her Sandals (Acropolis Museum)

sembled all the fragments found among the debris at the site, and much of the Archaic statuary that was buried underground by the builders of the new Acropolis after the destruction of the old temples by the Persians. Strangely, the Greeks of the Periclean age did not think much of works produced in the older style— modernism was the cry of the day! The most attractive of these 6th-century statues are those of young girls, the Korai; in charm they surpass all later Greek sculpture. The surface treatment and concentration on details is reminiscent of ivory carving; obviously the sculptors relied on the older technique, later to be discarded. Most interesting also is the statue of the *Calf Bearer.* In this work the Archaic system helped to establish perfect formal relations in regard to geometricity, at the same time freeing itself from hierarchic rigidity. However, according to recent research, the attributed date of about 570 B.C. is considered to be rather too early.

The *Nike Untying Her Sandals,* in the Acropolis Museum is justly looked upon as the finest example of Greek relief sculpture. Dating from the 5th century, it was once on the balustrade of the Temple of Nike, which was literally "junked" by the Turks to make way for the erection of a bastion.

DESCENT FROM THE ACROPOLIS TO THE AGORA. There is no need for a conducted tour of the Acropolis. Ride up the rock in a taxi, descend on foot by the comfortable pathway that starts at the parking level and leads in a ten minute walk to the site of the Agora, northwest of the Acropolis. From there it takes about 20 minutes to reach the center of the city.

The Agora was the marketplace and civic center of the ancient Greeks. Excavations of this area were started 100 years ago, but not much was uncovered until the American School of Classic Studies began in the 1930's, to remove the large modern settlement built on top of it. Evidently the history of the site must have dated back to the remote past, for many objects dating from the Mycenaean era were unearthed in the excavations which continued until 1955. These objects are exhibited in the newly erected *Stoa of Attalus*. Among the buildings to be seen in this region and probably built right after the erection of the Parthenon is the rather clumsy but well-preserved structure, the *Temple of Hephaestus,* known as **Theseion.** It has a frieze above the inner colonnade over the entrance to the cella, representing the *Battle between the Lapiths and the Centaurs*. Like the Parthenon, the Theseion is built of Pentelic marble, the common but very fine building material obtained from the 3639 foot mountain in Pentelicus, near Athens.

A quarter of a mile away, to the east of the Agora, stands the octagonal *Tower of the Winds,* so-called because of the relief at the top representing the eight winds. This structure, dating from the 1st century B.C., is also known as *Horlogium,* for at one time it contained a water clock.

Other remains in the area of the Agora are a small, restored 11th-century Byzantine church, *Hadrian's Market,* and the *Roman Market*—in ruins, of course.

Athens as a city is lacking in character and has no particular beauty; its architectural aspects are, at best, indifferent. However, in a number of modern private dwellings one sees Classic elements employed with superb taste and ingenuity. Neo-Classic revivals in architecture have been carried out in many places with greater and lesser success but never in our time as in Athens.

National Archeological Museum. I have previously referred to Roman copies of Greek statuary and stated that a faithful copy in no way differs from the original, even in regard to the texture of the marble. This, of course, cannot be said of free interpretations of older examples, which quite often falsify the originals. We have seen the best copies in Rome and elsewhere, and the best originals in the British Museum. It would appear, therefore, that no surprises await us in the museum in Athens. Although no illustrious names are represented, and very few generally celebrated works are displayed, a visit to the place is still a great experience.

First there is the roomful of sculptures from the pediments

of the Temple of Asclepius and Artemis in Epidaurus, dating from approximately the first quarter of the 4th century. In my view these compare well with the great sculptures of the Parthenon. The small figures, none exceeding three feet in height, seem strangely related to the Classic style of the 5th century, in the same way that Baroque relates to Renaissance. In fact, one could consider them Baroque in their complex movements and animation and in their stress on thrust and recession. At the time of this writing no data was available on these works; even copying the labels on the various objects was not allowed.

Then, to realize the general high artistic level of Greek statuary one has but to study the gravestones, called "stele." Most of them are not the work of celebrated artists, but nevertheless many possess esthetic appeal in highest measure. These are preserved in the museum in great quantity and, instead of pointing out the "showpieces," it is best to move along from one object to another and to enjoy their exquisiteness. There are also a number of Archaic, full-length statues of *Kouroi* (youths), more or less crudely schematized. However, the few that have become sufficiently dematerialized through weathering because of their hieratic rigidity have attained an almost magic suggestiveness.

In the Mycenaean room, a large collection of objects uncovered in that area is assembled. These are small statuettes, weapons, jewelry, and household goods of great technical finesse, fashioned by artisans who, judging from their style, must have come from the island of Crete. The earliest of these objects dates from the 16th century B.C.; the most famous are the so-called *Mask of Agamemnon* made of beaten gold and the gold cups delicately chased and embossed. These are in the front hall facing the main entrance. To the right, in the adjoining hall, is Archaic statuary as well as Cycladic work. The latter, antedating our era by some four thousand years, could have been fashioned today, so "modern" are the images which are simplified almost beyond reference to natural appearance. Lastly, in the upstairs rooms, vases and all types of vessels are assembled in great quantity.

Byzantine Museum. The most important of its kind in Europe, it will delight anyone enamored of the style, so different from the Western yet not Oriental enough to appear alien—a style where the individuality of the artist never asserts itself sufficiently to stamp his work "original." Originality, a value so highly praised by our civilization, was entirely irrelevant to the Byzantines, whose art underwent no radical changes in 800 years. The largest collection is made up of icons. These are devotional paintings on panels ranging in size from a few inches square to about 20 by 30 inches. Their style is Byzantine, whether they date from the

St. John The Baptist.
Icon
(Byzantine Museum)

St. Michael. Icon
(Byzantine Museum)

Early Byzantine Capital
(Byzantine Museum)

6th or the 18th century, and the difference between the early and late panels rests in the degree of realism. Ancient craftsmen permitted no realistic references in their representations, whereas there are elements of Classic art in the work of the 17th and 18th centuries. Nevertheless, it is still quite difficult to detect a stylistic difference between an 8th- and a 12th-century panel.

The icons are anonymous, hence no great value has been put on them by those who influence the art market. Nevertheless, some of the early panels, by virtue of their dramatic expressiveness and sheer pictorial excellence, stand on a very high artistic level. The fact that these masters fashioned their images from exemplars rather than following their "creative impulses," as is expected of artists, should not make us look at their work as mere artifacts.

An intimation of the extraordinary splendor of Byzantine décor can be gained from the "common" objects of an architectural nature—columns, capitals, fragments of façades and interiors (the oldest dating back to the 5th century), carved chiefly in marble but also in wood. Perhaps the Oriental sumptuousness of this architecture has such great allure because ours has become a matter of mechanical engineering, standardization, and prefabrication.

Missing are objects of ivory—a favorite material with the early Christian craftsmen—works in enamel and cloisonné, objects of gold (some chased silver reliefs are displayed in an upstairs room); in short, whatever had great monetary value was either carried away by foreign invaders or by antiquarians.

The Country

Heroic and idyllic is the landscape of Greece. However, when traveling overland in search of art, we must make a distinc-

Motif from Delphi

Laughing Boy
(Delphi Museum)

tion between art and archeology, for many sites are only of historic, not artistic, importance. Thus, to fall into raptures when
beholding the famous *Lion Gate* at Mycenae, for example, would
indicate that not the object but the legend behind it, entrances us.
And the same applies to the sites of stadiums, amphitheaters, and
temples, now mere ruins; yet it must be conceded that for us ruins
have a romantic, nostalgic appeal, besides being intrinsically
picturesque.

DELPHI. Ancient Greece had two religious capitals; Olympia
and Delphi. The latter must have been the cult center during the
Minoan era, about 1500 B.C. But only in the 6th century did it
assume the eminence we associate with it and acquired a universal prestige among the Greek city states. Even hostile cities
contributed to its temples and competed to gain favor with its
priestess—Pythia of the "infallible" oracle. In fact, no important
state decision was made without first consulting the famous
oracle and sacrificing to Apollo, the god of Light, Beauty, Music,
and Prophecy to whose worship the shrine was dedicated. This
contributed, of course, to the acquisition of great wealth and with
it the building of temples, a theater, a stadium, and an entire
city serving that religious organization. Pausanias, who visited
the country in the 2nd century A.D., wrote in his *Description of
Greece* that more than 3000 statues, 590 of them Archaic, graced
the site. All is gone, mostly carried away by the Romans, and
what they left was destroyed by the Byzantines, who looked upon
Greek art as heathen, hence heretical. But luckily for us there
were earthquakes, too, and whatever fell was soon buried and
preserved for posterity.

The *museum* houses the unearthed material, largely in fragments. The most interesting are the few Archaic relics, especially
the 6th-century Caryatids, the very realistic *Laughing Boy* (3rd
century), and the popular *Charioteer of Delphi* (5th century),

A Caryatid (Delphi
Museum)

The Three Graces
(Delphi Museum)

Charioteer of Delphi.
Bronze

made of bronze, hence very rare among Greek remains. Minus
the horses and chariot (which were never found), this statue
seems overrated, but like the bronze *Boy Jockey* in the National
Museum of Athens, without the missing components the total
effect cannot very well be assessed. The fragmentary frieze of
the Treasury is an outstanding work in Archaic style inasmuch
as the rendering, although employing somewhat rigid attitudes,
is thoroughly imbued with vitality. The low point of the collection
is the statue of Emperor Hadrian's protegé, Antinoüs. This work
from the 2nd century A.D. well illustrates the travesty of an
ill-conceived imitation of the grand Classic style.

Leaving the museum, one is tempted to say that of greatest interest to us might be the area about Delphi for it offers a spectacular scene—nature at its most dramatic. Rising in a semicircle
on terraces over sheer precipices; situated amid a wildly romantic
mountain landscape 1700 feet high, with an 800-foot cliff rising at
its back and, hidden from sight but plainly visible from a distance, the 8000-foot peak of Mount Parnassus, Apollo's own domain—the panorama with its interspersed ruins is truly awe-
inspiring. As if to add greater emphasis to this majestic sight,
proud eagles glide silently on widespread wings amid the fog-
shrouded peaks.

Instead of returning to Athens from Delphi (usually done with
a stop at **DAPHNI** where fragments of 11th century mosaics are
preserved in the Byzantine church), it is best to continue to
Olympia, rounding up a two-day tour.

OLYMPIA. Olympia is set in totally different environs than
Delphi. The landscape is idyllic, the hills serene, and the river
bed rarely filled with water. The bridge leading to the site is
incredibly ugly. This was a cult area long before it became the
arena of the Olympic Games, to which people from Greece's dis-

Hermes of Praxiteles
(Olympia Museum)

Pediment of the Temple of Zeus (Olympia Museum)

tant colonies—Sicily, Italy, North Africa, and Asia Minor—would travel to attend the religious festivals. Only a part of these were the athletic games in honor of Zeus. His temple stood in the middle of the site, and his statue, which was made by Phidias about 432 B.C. after he finished work on the Parthenon (42 feet high and plated with gold and ivory), glistened from afar, dominating the region. It was considered one of the Seven Wonders of the World, the materialization of the god himself and an object of great veneration. This work perished without a trace or clue, but we know that it was still in existence during the time of Caligula (1st century A.D.), who, according to an ancient chronicle, planned to transport it to Rome and replace its head with his own image!

The first Olympic Games were recorded in 776 and the last, 1169 years later when they were finally stopped by the Christian Emperor Theodosius I in 393 A.D., and his successor Theodosius II ordered the destruction of the pagan shrines. Pillaged by various invaders, mainly by Goths under Alaric, ravaged by flood, earthquake, and inclement climate, the site is in ruins.

When we consider how closely Greek art follows athletic dis-

Pediment of the Temple of Zeus
(Olympia Museum)

The Palaestra (Olympia)

plays, we know that athletic contests must have been an esthetic experience. If only we could see the area of the Altis (the site of the games)—how many exquisite statues must have adorned it! Today, the locations of all of the ancient edifices have been established, so that the guide may point out: Here stood the temple of Hera, here the one of Zeus, the Gymnasium, the Palaestra, there the priests used to take their meals; even the workshop of Phidias is singled out. Unhappily, all the broken shafts of the columns, minus their capitals, have been pieced together by the archeologists; only the inarticulate foundation stones remain in their original positions.

In the *museum*, Roman statuary predominates, most of it mediocre. But the 5th-century sculptures from the pediments of the Temple of Zeus teach us a lesson—namely, to resist the compulsion to use clichés. Not all that is Archaic must be, *ipso facto,* retrograde, and not everything that has been created in the progressive spirit of the age represents an advancement. The stiff and rigid figurations to the left as one enters the hall appear more appropriate to the occasion than the more lifelike sculptures on the right. In considering lifelike appearance we should remember that these sculptures were once polychromed with wax and pigment, and, indicated by the small round holes in the marble, bronze objects such as helmets and shields had been attached to them. Such treatment of sculpture would hardly satisfy our esthetic predilections. In all, the fragmentary condition of the pediments and metope figures does not fail to activate the imagination, which forever attempts to recreate what is missing and to conjure up the complete scene: the battle between the Lapiths and the Centaurs—the eternal fight between the blind forces of nature and human reason; the struggle between the civilized (always the Greek) and the barbarian (all foreigners). This Aristotelian assumption sounds a bit strange when we consider, for example, that Pericles himself ordered the amputation of the thumbs of all men exiled from the conquered island of Aegina since "even in exile they could use their spears and bows against the Athenians."

Among the best-known statues in the museum is the *Nike of Paeonios,* the particular merit of which escapes me, and *Hermes with the Child Dionysus* by Praxiteles, from about 343 B.C. Here is a masterpiece of the first order, and when the guide points out a triviality such as "one side of Hermes face is smiling and the other profile appears sad," or when the professor at college refers to the daring asymmetry of the figure and attempts to give a pat explanation of its balance and so forth, none of the charms of this work are thereby elucidated. The fact remains that the poetic sensibilities in the figure, the rhythmic sequence of the body movements, cannot be assayed in words; none of the many statues that follow similar esthetic precepts stand as high, artistically. It must be understood that difficult as it is to distort convincingly, to make a distortion "function," it is equally difficult not to make an idealization sentimental and trivial.

As I intimated, a distinction should be made between art and archeology. Hence a visit to any famous site other than those mentioned will not be in quest of art. And when thinking of famous sites, the first that comes to mind is Mycenae.

MYCENAE. The grim character of this citadel instantly evokes the ferocious stories of its legendary past. This was the stage populated by the pre-Hellenic warriors, 5000 years before our time. In the years 2000 to 1600 B.C. it fell to people belonging to the Greek race who controlled the trade routes from the Gulf of Argos to Corinth and the north. These people built the spectacular beehive graves (the largest belonging to King Agamemnon, a hero of the Trojan War) and the famous Lion Gate, the only remaining monument of that age. It was uncovered in 1876 by the German archaeologist Schliemann, who is chiefly responsible for the excavations at the site. Mycenae was the home of the incredibly sanguinary warriors of the Homeric tale who went out to battle Troy in 1240 B.C.; the citadel is all archeological remains, and whatever artifacts were unearthed by Schliemann are now gathered in the National Museum in Athens. This sombre place, built like a fortress, high on a rocky plateau does not invite us to linger.

Lion's Gate (Mycenae)

The Islands

It would seem that after Athens, Delphi, and Olympia the impressions gained from a tour of Greece would be adequate. Although the exploit in the field of art or even archeology will hardly be deepened by a visit to the islands, they do offer a different aspect of the Greek scene. Besides being strangely picturesque in their own way, each has a museum in which local finds are collected, and, although there is no Phidias among them, the collections are by no means negligible. There is something about Greek fragments—something more than conventional admiration bestowed on an old and rare object—that makes them appear precious: the intrinsic beauty of their style.

Of the numerous islands in the Aegean Sea, only a few on the regular ship routes will be discussed.

DELOS. The island, one of the Cycladic chain, is nearest to the mainland. It is barren and uninhabited; covered with debris, it was an archeologist's delight, for under its not so ancient rubble, Greek and Roman dwellings emerged—in ruins, of course, but with their mosaicked patios well preserved. However, these are not the reason for having made the journey—it is the group of marble lions along the Sacred Lake. If ever the much-worn word "magic" were justly applied, these strange, Archaic monuments would deserve it. Somehow the soul of the place seems to dwell in them; silhouetted against the brilliant sky, silently they seem to proclaim the fulfillment of a prophecy.

A few facts might be briefly recalled about the history of Delos: In the 7th century the island was the center of a cult of Apollo, who according to legend was born here. Thus it became a place of pilgrimage and later developed into an important trade center and the seat of the Delian League, a maritime confederacy. Still later, it was declared by Athens a sacred place where no one was to die or be born—for this would have constituted "pollution" of the shrine. With this measure the Athenians succeeded tempo-

Ancient Theater, Island of Delos

Mosaic Floor (Delos)

Motif of Delos

rarily in "purifying" the island of most of its inhabitants. Under the Romans, one sack followed another, finishing Delos as a populated domain.

The small museum contains examples of Archaic art, 5th-century sculpture, burial steles, and vases.

MYKONOS. The island, 40 minutes by boat from the city of Delos, belongs not only with the most enchanting places in Europe but is also endowed with a very special atmosphere of *joie de vivre*. The picture post card harbor is busy with all manner of activity, none too serious; the bistros on the waterfront invite one to relax, the shops are very touristy, the houses gleam with fresh whitewash, and the numerous windmills pretend to be engaged in some kind of work.

SANTORINI. Of all the rocky islands the seasoned traveler may have visited, this one is the most dramatic, especially when seen from aboard ship and approaching the harbor. In fact, the whole island is the crater of a great volcano that exploded in a very distant past, leaving the fantastic out-of-this-world look. The ascent of 1000 feet to the plateau is made by mule, and of course, the local museum has some beautiful marbles.

CRETE. The largest of the islands, Crete had a glorious past: a highly developed culture, a sophisticated, easy way of life, ele-

Lions of The Sacred Way (Delos)

Isle of Santorini

The Snake Goddess. Terra cotta
(Herakleion, Crete)

The Prince of Lilies
(Minoan Palace, Knossos)

gance, and refinement. Where this culture originated is uncertain, and the reasons for the sudden disappearance from the entire island of its many cities and villages, have never been sufficiently explained, but the date of this occurrence has been accurately established to be around 1400 B.C. Cretan culture is called "Minoan" (the name given by Sir Arthur Evans, the discoverer of Knossos) ; it flourished under King Minos of whom Homer spoke in his *Odyssey* as the one who "ruled in the great City of Knossos." Judging from its art and architecture, Egyptian and Asiatic influences prevailed, yet the style of Minoan art cannot be identified with either of these. Moreover, their way of living, very much like our own (down to plumbing with running water and a sewer system), was entirely different from that of Egypt and Asia.

The palace was partially reconstructed by Sir Arthur, and although he used a great deal of his own imagination in rebuilding the site, the picture that he left us of the place is vivid and intriguing. In its intricate arrangement of courts, chambers, shops, storerooms, and so on, the structure might well be identified with the legendary labyrinth built by Daedalus of the fateful fable.

In the museum of Herakleion is assembled the largest existing collection of Cretan relics, much of it of archeological interest, and of the kind that impresses us as very modern, especially the fashion items—the fineries of the Cretan ladies could have been designed by one of the most sophisticated of couturiers! Besides murals and stucco work of a stylized, decorative character, there are small figurines, pottery, ornaments, and household implements. Herakleion, a village near Knossos, is a dusty little place of small interest, as is the landscape around it. However, about 40 miles farther inland the country is mountainous, furrowed by deep gorges, and dotted with caves.

RHODES. The farthermost and last island on our return trip to Athens is practically the only one without Greek remains. Because of its particular past, this one-time independent, maritime power, later a thriving Greek colony and still later a Roman colony, was captured by the French order of the Knights of St. John in 1309 and used as a citadel against the Turks. Until their expulsion by the Turks more than two centuries later, the Knights succeeded in erasing all the antique features and transformed the capital of the island into a medieval fortress. The Turks ruled until 1912 and the Italians until 1945. Thus, what we see today (aside from the very few antiquities) are the severe restorations of the Italians—thus these French medieval edifices, the ramparts around the harbor, the Hospital (now a museum), the Palace of the Grand Master, and the Street of the Knights, although authentic in style, appear to have been built yesterday. Nevertheless, Rhodes has a strange, remote look—in fact, we almost expect to see its 120-foot-high statue of the Sun God, the "Colossus of Rhodes," to be standing as it once did, in the harbor area. Alas, it fell during an earthquake in 227 B.C., and its remains were melted down for armor.

The island has great natural beauty, and the ride along the seashore to the little harbor town of **LINDOS** 35 miles away, is delightful. Here, atop a 1000-foot-high promontory, are remnants of a medieval church, and right on the edge of the precipice are the ruins of a small Doric temple. But even these do not look quite authentic—have they been made to order? Not so the view of the coastline—here the ordered hand of nature has created its best.

Section 9 / The Scandinavian Countries

DENMARK

Of all the Scandinavian countries, *Denmark* possesses the richest art collections. The **State Art Museum** (Statens Museum for Kunst) in Copenhagen although modest in scope, has some fine old masters, among them a first rate Mantegna, *Christ with Angels,* with a background and sky of great beauty such as only he and Bellini in his early work, were capable of producing. A large group of paintings by Lucas Cranach the Elder are, as usual, charming. Who else could look at Greek mythology with the delightful naïveté of a German provincial? Other paintings are *Christ Driving the Money Changers From the Temple,* attributed to Brueghel, an ingenious composition worthy of his name; two Rubens on a modest scale but of great technical excellence— an important lesson to the professional painter on how an *alla prima* painting can best be handled; a Barroccio portrait in his highest Mannerist form; Luini's *St. Catherine of Alexandria* in the best Leonardo manner; a Frans Hals—and who knew how to elicit richer nuances out of black paint? Philips Koninck's landscape of 1654, which presages Constable and Courbet; a fine Magnasco; a Guardi; and finally 19th- and 20th-century French run-of-the-mill paintings are also to be seen here.

The **Carlsberg Glyptotek** is, as its name indicates, primarily a sculpture museum. (Those interested in studying the difference between what we may call run-of-the-mill Hellenistic and Roman statuary and that of Thorwaldsen, the renowned neo-Classic sculptor, may visit the museum carrying his name. The comparison will show that all 19th century imitation of the Classic, is always feeble and devitalized.) Upon first entering the Glyptotek, the impression is quite shocking, for the lower regions of the

Judgment of Paris.
Lucas Cranach
(State Museum of Art,
Copenhagen)

Christ and the Angels.
Mantegna

The Abbot. Rubens

museum are filled with late 19th-century statuary in unbelievably
poor taste. Nor is Rodin an exception to the rule, although a few
of his works belong to an entirely different category such as the
Burghers of Calais, St. John, and, upstairs, the portrait busts.
These are authentic masterpieces, created in the best Classic tradition, not merely pastiches of the Classic or sentimental inanities.

As for the department of antiques, it is perhaps the largest
and most impressive on the northern Continent. Should one have
ever entertained a doubt as to the superiority of Roman portraiture, such doubts should be dispelled by the row upon row of
heads covering a period of five centuries. No matter how many

Faustina, Hellenistic
(Carlsberg Glyptotek)

Etruscan (Detail. Carlsberg Glyptotek)

Greek Statue
(Carlsberg Glyptotek)

Roman Sarcophagus (Carlsberg Glyptotek)

Burghers of Calais. Rodin (Carlsberg Glyptotek)

Thorwaldsen Mercury
(Thorwaldsen Museum)

of these pass our scrutiny, the temptation to read their features remains alive. The Impressionists upstairs, many Gauguins, and a complete collection of Degas' small bronzes make a weak showing. Can one successfully realize a snapshot idea in bronze? It appears that even an artist of Degas' stature could not.

Copenhagen and its Edifices

In spite of its romantic reputation, this friendly and lively city is predominantly modern. There are very few historic sites in evidence, and even these are not of earlier date than the 17th century. The history of the cathedral is typical of Copenhagen's vicissitudes. The 12th-century structure burned down in 1728,

The Organ, Frelsers Kirke
(Copenhagen)

Fredriks Kirke (Copenhagen)

was reconstructed ten years later, once more destroyed by fire in 1807 during the English bombardment, and again rebuilt in 1829. A few 17th-century edifices are still preserved. These represent the peculiar northern Baroque—solemn, weighty, and selfpossessed—and owe their existence to King Christian IV and the good fate that saved them from destruction. The most interesting among these buildings is the Stock Exchange (*Borsen*) an early 17th-century structure, patterned after Dutch Baroque, as is the Church of the Redeemer (*Frelsers Kirke*) with the strange external spiral staircase that forms its steeple. The most noteworthy object in the interior is a splendid Baroque organ and high altar. The domed *Fredriks Kirke* dates from the middle of the 17th century but was not completed until two hundred years later. The design of the lantern-crowned dome and the drum, obviously derived from St. Peter's in the Vatican, is impressive, but, resting directly on a low structure fronting a Pantheon-like columnar porch, it is too heavy. Near-by, the *Amalienborg Palace* is the residence of the royal family, and it looks "royal," as do the other places, the *Christianborg* (the seat of the Parliament) and the *Rosenborg Castle,* in which the crown jewels, tapestries, furniture, silver, and porcelains are displayed. But to enjoy the intimate beauty of simple things one should walk along *Nyhavn Canal* lined with unpretentious, small, 18th-century dwellings. These relieve us from the compulsive obligation to walk on tiptoe, as it were.

Christianborg Palace Gateway
(Copenhagen)

Kronborg Castle (Elsinore)

The Country

There are a few very interesting sites not too far away from the city. At a distance of 17 miles to the west lies the ancient former capital of Denmark, *Roskilde*, with its cathedral. Started in 1170, it is built of red brick in Romanesque-Gothic style (except for its odd, needlelike 17th-century spires) and is the burial place of Danish kings. Its outstanding feature is the high altar, a large polyptich carved in high relief, gilded and polychromed, a 16th-century masterpiece of Dutch origin.

The tour north from Copenhagen (a round trip of a few hours) touches on the following sites: the *Fredensborg, Kronberg,* and *Frederiksborg*—proud castles, French Renaissance in design but Nordic in décor.

SWEDEN

STOCKHOLM. The city's natural location is such that even the sober, functional buildings cannot mar its beauty—if we do not allow their irredeemable prosaicism to register. However, the compact, large compound of the old city is utterly charming and heartwarming. Here one finds the ancient houses with their stepped gables, some adorned with the graceful volutes so characteristic of the northern countries. Some display fine sculptured doorways and window enframements, but simple or palatial (the latter date from the 17th and 18th centuries), these houses are always a welcome sight. There is, too, the ever-present nearness of the harbor and the waterways, ubiquitously felt in the city.

Of the churches, there is the 16th-century *St. Klara,* the 17th-century *St. James,* and the domed *St. Katarina.* But the most remarkable of the ancient relics is the St. George group in the *St. Nicholas Church,* its largest Gothic edifice. As we have so often repeated, Gothic churches cannot go wrong; however, in Protestant countries they are often "purified" to the point where

Detail. St. George Group
(St. Nicholas Church, Stockholm)

Interior, St. Nicholas Church

their interiors are as aseptic-looking as hospital halls. But not the polychromed St. George statue; this figure made of wood in 1489 is High Gothic in an original—one is almost tempted to say exotic—conception.

Paintings, of course, can be seen in the *National Museum.* These are chiefly from the Royal Collection, established in the 18th century by a francophile king who acquired them in France at a time when they were considered modern art. Alas, 18th-century French modernism expressed itself in the shallow frivolities of the champions of the Rococo—Fragonard and Boucher. More talent and artistic sensibility, however, are evident in the works of Watteau; nor can we have any quarrel with the many Chardins, for he is numbered among the best of the still life painters. It is surprising, indeed, that this was recognized by his contemporaries,

Detail. St. George Group
(St. Nicholas Church)

Claudius Civilis. Rembrandt
(National Museum, Stockholm)

who bought these works directly from his studio. But the *pièce de résistance* of the museum is Rembrandt's large canvas, the *Oath of the Batavians* (also known as *Claudius Civilis*). Painted for the Town Hall in Amsterdam, it was, for reasons unknown, rejected and returned to the artist, who promptly reduced its original size to half (it is now 71 by 110 inches), and then overpainted it completely. Because of its bold technique it is a very interesting painting.

NORWAY

At the beginning of the guide I mentioned the need for a clear objective before setting out on a European journey. Norway is the last country to be discussed, although it might have been the first, since the direction of travel has been planned to proceed from north to south. But it is art in all its manifestations with which we are concerned, and Norway is not as well endowed as others in this respect. We could even say that it is, in a large measure, devoid of real artistic heritage. That this country had no great painter, sculptor, or architect is not surprising; several of the civilized European countries have not produced significant art. As for art collections, because of Norway's particular political history, these are very modest in scope. The *National Gallery* in Oslo has some good old masters and many works from the 19th century, in addition to a large collection of paintings by Edvard Munch (1863–1944). In the *Historisk Museum* in **BERGEN**, small panels removed from ancient churches show a curious similarity with Byzantine icons and illuminated manuscripts from the Romanesque-Gothic period in France.

It is strange that even the architectural relics (with few exceptions, such as the cathedral in Trondheim, built in the late 11th century but much restored and rebuilt), are of no great account. During the 12th and 13th centuries "everybody" built (more or less) splendid cathedrals, and one would think that the Vikings, with their far-flung maritime exploits, might have left great monuments. However, this is not the case. Only a very few ecclesiastic edifices are left, and the Reformation and subsequent depredations have done away with most of their ornamentation. What characteristic marks did the great race of warriors and explorers leave behind? Stave churches, a few ships, log cabins, and wood carvings. The churches are small, their interiors accommodating in most instances some fifty closely packed standees. Only 30 of the original 300 log structures are left, and they appear much more like pagan shrines than churches. Their construction points to the fact that the Vikings were skillful boat-builders. Atop the gables, the dragon heads with their long outstretched necks echo the prow designs of the Viking ships. The most attractive feature of the churches is the steep, many-gabled, superposed roofs covered by imbrication of curiously cut heavy shingles, and the open columnar porticos that run around the structures at ground level. These have a distinct Romanesque look. The interiors of the churches are very dark, and although at one time they were decorated by carvings and some painting, they are today without adornment of any kind.

Why is it that in a country where rocks can be found everywhere, only log cabins are in evidence? Those of the 13th to the 17th centuries are massively built, windowless, and starkly primitive. The interiors of the 16th- and 17th-century cabins are less grim, and the painted and carved decorations are very attractive —as ancient folk art has always been. Traveling through the countryside, however, one finds the tasteless 19th- and 20th-century architecture quite disturbing; small or large, these structures show an unrelieved lack of charm. The same can be said of the cities, modern throughout except for the very few ancient dwellings that escaped the various fires which have devastated the clapboard dwellings over the centuries.

The Norwegian landscape is another story. The fjords, the thickly wooded and rocky mountains, the often grandiose waterfalls and seemingly never-ending chains of lakes are as enticing as the travel pamphlets depict them to be. Although there is a certain sameness in the recurrent rhythm of rock and water, nature's own handiwork, Norwegian style, is a refreshing experience after the man-made art of other European countries. It is best to start the tour in Bergen and travel by tourist bus to **OSLO**, or vice versa. En route, in Bergund, is one of the best-

Stave Kirke
(Folk Museum, Oslo)

Log Cabin (Folk Museum, Oslo)

preserved stave churches. There is another near Bergen. In the
Folk Museum in Bygdoy, a suburb of Oslo, an entire village of
ancient log cabins has been assembled, including an overrestored
stave church.

There remains to be seen the rediscovered Viking ships (also
in Bygdoy) and the wood carvings. These somehow "barbaric"-
appearing artifacts—or rather objects of art, as they can be justly
termed—are among the few relics of ancient Norwegian art that
have been preserved.

Glossary

Abbey—monastery or convent.
Agora—Greek place of public assembly.
Aisle—corridor on both sides of the nave.
Alcazar—a castle (Spanish-Arabic)
Alla prima—finishing a painting in one operation while painting wet-in-wet.
Ambulatory—side aisle surrounding the choir.
Apse—semicircular projection behind the choir.
Arcade—arched gallery.
Architrave—lowest division of an entablature resting directly on the columns.
Archivolt—band of ornaments above an arched opening.
Baluster—single shaft supporting a railing.
Baroque—style following the Renaissance (16th-18th century).
Barrel vault—simplest form of a vault continued from wall to wall.
Basilica—oblong rectangular (originally Roman) church with a clerestory.
Battlement—indented (crenelated) upper wall.
Belfry—bell tower.
Blind arcade—decorative arrangement of arches set against a wall.
Boss—block ornament covering the crossing point of ribs in a groin vault.
Buttress—structure built against a wall as its support or prop.
Byzantine—style originating in Byzantium (now Istanbul) in the 5th century and prevailing for the following six centuries.
Campanile—bell tower usually built separate from a church.
Cantilever—beam projecting from a structure to support a weight.
Carillon—set of stationary bells hung in a tower and operated with a keyboard.
Cella—inner enclosed space in a Grecian or Roman temple.
Chapter house—room or building connected with the church and serving as a meeting place for the clergy.
Choir—section of the nave between the transepts and the main altar.
Churriguerresque—overornamental Spanish style, corresponding to the Baroque (17th and 18th centuries). Named after the architect Churriguerra.
Cinquefoil—opening—arch or window—forming five radiating leaves.

265

Clerestory—upper section of a church wall with windows.

Close—church ground (English) completely surrounded by buildings.

Colonnade—series of columns spaced in regular intervals supporting a roof, arches, or architraves.

Console—ornamental bracket used to support a cornice.

Corbel—projection on the face of a wall to support a weight.

Corinthian—order of Grecian style characterized by bell-shaped capitals decorated with acanthus leaves and a continuous frieze.

Cornice—horizontal projection of the roof over the walls.

Crenel—battlement opening.

Crocket—Gothic ornament usually in the form of a leaf on slope of a pinnacle.

Crypt—portion of a church located underground.

Decorated—Late Gothic (England) 14th century.

Diptych—two painted panels hinged together.

Doric—simplest of the Greek orders, characterized by columns without base, saucer-shaped capitals, and a frieze divided into metopes and triglyphs.

Drum—cylindrical structure upon which the dome rests.

Embrasure—recess enlargement of an aperture of a door or window.

Engaged columns—columns attached to a wall.

Entablature—part of a Classic roof that rests above the columns.

Entasis—outward curve of a column. First used by the Greeks to make the column appear straight, not concave, when viewed from a distance.

Façade—face of a building.

Fan vaulting—decorative arrangement of ribs in English churches.

Fenestration—over-all design of window arrangement.

Flamboyant—ornate curved window tracery (French Gothic).

Fluting—perpendicular grooves on a column.

Flying buttress—support of a wall in the shape of an arch segment.

Font—basin for holy water in churches.

Fresco buono—painting on wet plaster with pigments dispersed in water. Fresco secco—painting on a dry plaster. Both expressions are referred to as "mural painting."

Frieze—ornamented part of the entablature above the architrave.

Furbelow, flounce—frilly design.

Gable—triangular portion of a pitched roof.

Genre painting—painting using themes of everyday life.

Georgian—neo-Classic (English) style (18th–beginning of 19th century).

Gothic—style following the Romanesque (12th–14th century, but appearing in certain countries as late as the 16th century).

Greek art—art in Greece up to the 5th century B.C. and prior to Hellenistic art; the latter embracing all styles of the Greek mainland and colonies after the time of Alexander the Great.

Greek cross—cross whose arms are of equal length.

Groined vault—intersection of two barrel vaults.

Half-timbered construction—timber framework exposed and filled with masonry.

Hammer-beam roof—arrangement of beams and trusses (left open) to support a roof.

Helicoidal—spiral.

Hellenistic art—Greek art after the age of Alexander the Great.

Hemicycle—semicircular construction, usually of chapels.

Iconography—classification of subjects and symbols in a painting.
Ionic order—Greek style characterized by capital columns adorned with scrolls and possessing a continuous frieze.
Imbrication—overlapping, as of tiles or shingles.
Incunabula—books produced prior to 1500 from movable type.
Lantern—small cylindrical structure with windows forming the crown of a dome.
Lierne vaulting—subsidiary ribs in English fan vaulting.
Lintel—horizontal beam above window or door, resting on vertical supports.
Lunette—semicircular opening or mural above a wall, within a vault.
Mannerism—post-Renaissance and pre-Baroque style in art.
Manueline—Portuguese style (16th–17th century), based on Renaissance architecture but distinguished by profuse ornamentation.
Metope—rectangular part of a frieze between the triglyphs, usually adorned with statuary.
Mudejar—style combining Moorish and Christian decorative form elements.
Mullion—vertical bars separating segments of a window.
Nave—main section of a church set at right angles to the transepts.
Neo-Classic—style adopting classicistic features.
Norman—English version of Romanesque style.
Obelisk—square shaft tapering as it rises.
Ogee arch—arch made of two juxtaposed concave and convex curves meeting at a point at the top.
Ogive—pointed (Gothic) arch. (ō'jīve)
Oriel—bay window in an upper story found in late Gothic secular architecture.
Palimpsest—a parchment from which the original text has been erased to make room for another text. Usually traces of the old text reappear in time. This creates a kind of double image.
Pediment—low triangular gable crowned with a projecting cornice in Classic architecture.
Pentagonal—polygon having five angles and five sides.
Peristyle—range of columns surrounding a court or a building.
Perpendicular—last phase of English Gothic style.
Pilaster—column attached to a wall.
Pinnacle—spirelike structure above the piers of a building.
Plateresque—(from *platero*, silversmith) name for the Spanish style, corresponding to Italian Renaissance and characterized by rich surface ornamentation and attention to minute details, often Gothic in nature.
Plinth—lower base of a column; a pedestal.
Polychromy—use of many colors.
Polygon—figure (or plane) having many angles and sides.
Polyptich—panels unfolding to more than three sections.
Predella—base of an altar.
Presbytery—part of a church reserved for officiating clergy.
Quatrefoil—opening or window forming four radiating leaves.
Quoin—external solid corner of a wall.
Rayonnant—More advanced and ornate form of French Gothic.
Refectory—dining hall in a cloister.
Regency—period (1811–1820) during which George, Prince of Wales, was regent.

Renaissance—style originating in Italy (15th–16th century), relying on Classic precepts.

Reredos—screen or decorated wall behind the altar.

Retable—raised ledge above an altar to hold objects.

Ribbed vault—Romanesque structure of crossing arches of groined vault.

Rococo—style evolved from Baroque, employing a profusion of delicate ornamentations, used chiefly in interiors (18th century).

Romanesque—style preceding the Gothic (11th–12th century), developed from earlier Medieval and Near-Eastern types.

Rose window—circular window with tracery or radiating mullions.

Rustication—use of rough-hewn stone masonry for façades.

Saxon—Early Romanesque (England).

Spandrel—triangular wall space formed between two adjoining arches when the outer arch is rectangular, and the inner one curved.

Splay—oblique angle of a wall surface forming a door or window opening.

Stepped gables—typical of gables in north European (17th–18th century) houses.

Stringcourse—horizontal course of stone dividing the stories.

Tabernacle—ornamental receptacle on the high altar.

Tempera—type of painting in which dry pigments are mixed with an emulsion such as egg or oil and water in the presence of an emulsifying agent (egg, glue). Tempera technique was used chiefly in the Middle Ages, also in antiquity.

Tondi oro—the early Medieval paintings with gold backgrounds.

Tracery—ornamental work consisting of ramified bars and ribs on the upper part of a window; network of carvings.

Transept—arms extending at right angles to the nave of a cruciform church.

Trefoil—opening or window forming three radiating leaves.

Triforium—central section of the nave wall (below the clerestory).

Triglyphs—divisions between the metopes.

Tripartite—divided into or consisting of three parts.

Tympanum—semicircular space above a door or a window.

Vault—arched roof structure.

Volute—scroll-like ornamentation of an Ionic capital.

Index of Artists and Architects

PART II

Travel Section

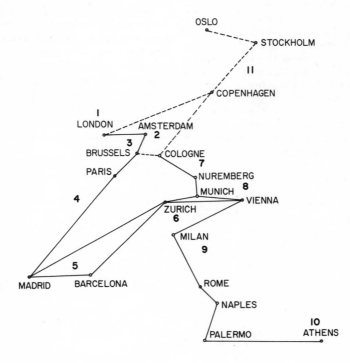

GENERAL SUGGESTIONS

When visiting art museums, the presence of a guide is—as most tourists must have felt—not desirable. Too often attention is directed to irrelevant objects, or, as the case may be, irrelevancies are propounded with an air of connoisseurship that is quite disturbing. This is not the case where architecture is concerned. The complexities of a building, its many not readily detectable or accessible parts, and especially the fact that attendants in charge of such buildings do not, as a rule, speak English, necessitates a conducted tour.

Further, one should keep in mind that even the most experienced traveler will quickly become saturated by too many new sights, and hence the objective of his travel—to retain the experience in his memory—will not be achieved. It must be understood that for it to be worth-while and enjoyable, a visit to a large museum should not last more than two hours at a time, even less.

In the country, where no adequate transportation exists, it is necessary to travel by automobile. But one should consider that the traffic in and around the big cities is so forbidding it makes driving a frustrating experience. Hence in many cases it is more prudent to avail oneself of train and bus travel, or in others to take a conducted tour.

The time suggested for the different visits must be considered a bare minimum, for the author's aim has been to include as many countries as possible in a single trip. Thus, in most instances, the schedules indicated do not leave much time for relaxation; hence it will be up to the traveler to make whatever adjustments he wishes.

ENGLAND (4–14 DAYS)

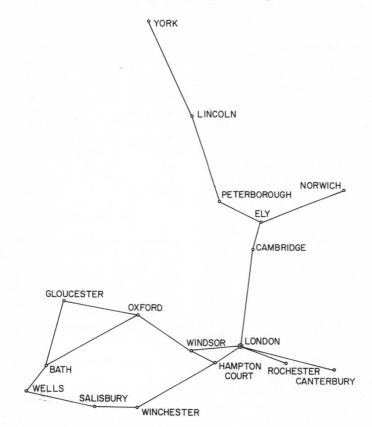

In London, neither a street map nor an Underground (subway) map would be of any practical value. However, a conducted tour will help you to gain a general picture of the city. The art collections alone will require four days. An interesting trip is to Hampton Court and Windsor Castle (a one-day conducted tour); an additional day will be required for a visit to Canterbury Cathedral (55 miles from London). Thus in a week of intensive application a fair impression of the city and a portion of the countryside can be gained. When planning to visit Windsor Castle (a round trip of 60 miles), however, one must realize the possibility of not being admitted to the state rooms where the art treasures are displayed; this will depend on the presence or absence of the royal family.

There are not many art collections of great importance outside London. Only the one in the Ashmolean Museum in Oxford appears on our schedule. The round trip to Oxford can be made in one day, and it is also our first stop on the three-day trip to the sites of cathedrals within easy reach of London.

This trip (see map) will proceed as follows: Oxford (54 miles), Gloucester (102 miles), Bath (106 miles), Wells (125 miles), Salisbury (81 miles), Winchester (63 miles). All mileage is calculated from London; hence Wells will be our farthermost point, and the entire journey can be made in the following way: Leave for Oxford (1½ hours by train) and plan to stay there overnight. Next morning, on to Gloucester (2 hours, changing trains in Didcot). Leave for Bath (2 hour ride, changing trains in Bristol) in the afternoon. Remain overnight in Bath and continue by rented car or bus to Wells, then to Salisbury and Winchester, a distance of about 80 miles. It takes about two hours to return by train from Winchester to London.

Should there be more time available, a number of magnificent cathedrals north of London (see map) could be visited. These can be reached in the following sequence (all distances are measured from London) : Ely (Cambridgeshire, 68 miles) ; Peterborough (Northhamptonshire, 80 miles) ; Norwich (Norfolk, 110 miles) ; Lincoln (Lincolnshire, 135 miles) ; York (Yorkshire, 196 miles). This tour can be planned in the following way: Make your first stop in Oxford, the second in Cambridge; continue to Ely and stay overnight in Norwich. Next day, visit Peterborough and Lin-

coln, remaining overnight in Lincoln. Continue to York (40 miles).

York lies midway between London and Edinburgh; the latter is located on both sides of a ravine, and is the most interesting city in Scotland. Its National Gallery has a fine collection of old masters, although the highly publicized "glamour" works are not among them. When in Edinburgh, it is worth-while to take a guided one-day bus trip to the Loch Lomond region. The traveler should not expect to see any sea monsters on this occasion, but many a ruined castle will be in evidence.

List of Sites in London

Museums: N a t i o n a l Gallery (paintings) ; British Museum (sculptures, illuminated manuscripts, Far Eastern, African, Egyptian art) ; Victoria and Albert Museum (statuary, artifacts, architecture) ; Wallace Collection (paintings) ; Courtauld Institute (paintings) ; Tate Gallery (paintings).
Cathedrals: Westminster Abbey, St. Paul's.
Edifices: The Tower of London, Whitehall, Parliament. Lambeth Palace, Kensington Palace, Fulham Palace, Cumberland Terrace, Chester Terrace, Park Crescent.

List of Sites in the Country

Hampton Court, Windsor Castle.
Oxford: Ashmolean Museum (paintings, sculpture, archeological finds, artifacts) ; Merton, New Magdalen College, and Christ Church, Divinity School; All Souls College Chapel; Bodleian Library.
Cathedrals: Canterbury, Gloucester, Bath, Wells, Salisbury, Winchester.

BELGIUM AND HOLLAND (6 DAYS)

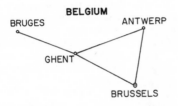

In no place else in Europe can so much art be seen in such a short time and in so many museums as in these two countries. For in Belgium as well as in Holland, a two hour train ride takes the traveler across the entire country. From Brussels in 30 minutes one reaches Ghent; from there it is 65 minutes to Bruges; and in 40 minutes more we arrive in Antwerp. In Holland the distances are still shorter.

Brussels. There is one museum, Musée d'art Ancien (Rue de la Régence); two Gothic churches, Cathédral St. Michèle and Church du Sablon; and a Civic Center, the Grand Place, with the Town Hall and Guild Halls (15th-18th centuries). A guided tour of the city is not indicated.

Ghent. Because of their prox-imity to one another, the points of interest can be surveyed on a leisurely two-hour walk. Hence the city tour will proceed as follows: Starting from the Cathedral of St. Bavon; St. James Church, the medieval Castle of the Count (a view from the outside should be sufficient); past St. Michael's Church, then along the Guild Halls past St. Nicholas' church; over the St. Nicholas Bridge (excellent view of the complex of the old houses); past the belfry and the Cloth Hall—back to St. Bavon.

The Museum voor Schone Kunsten (the art museum), however, is located in the modern section of the town, a taxi ride of about 15 minutes.

Bruges (Brugge). This is one of the few places where the tra-

277

veler does not require a conveyance to reach the center of the town from the railway station. Passing the Beguinage (a 13th-century monastery), and then on to the Memling Museum (in the St. John Hospital) one reaches the marketplace, with its Church of Our Lady (Notre Dame) and, a short distance away, the cathedral. The Belfry is two blocks away.

Next we proceed to Burg Square with its fabulous group of buildings: the Court of Justice; Recorders' House; Town Hall; and the Basilica of the Holy Blood. On the way back to the railroad station one can visit the Groeninge Museum, thus completing the circuit in a half-day's time.

Antwerp. It is neither easy nor pleasurable to get around in this sprawling city. Hence it is recommended to take a taxi to the Royal Gallery of Fine Arts (Leopold de Wael Plaats), quite a distance from the center of the town. Then return to the cathedral and make the rounds as follows: Town Hall; Grote Markt (the marketplace), old Butchers' Hall, and the surrounding area. Next take a taxi to the Mayer van den Bergh Museum (Lange Gasthuis Straat 19—little known, hence the address is important).

The Rubens House is 20 minutes away.

List of Sites

Brussels: Museum of Ancient Art (paintings); St. Michèle Cathedral; Grand Place.
Ghent: Museum voor Schone Kunsten (paintings); St. Bavon Cathedral (Van Eyck altar); Town Hall; Belfry; Castle of the Count; Guild Houses.
Bruges: Memling Museum (paintings); Groeninge Museum (paintings); Cathedral; Notre Dame Church; Burg Place; Court of Justice; Old Recorder's House; Town Hall; Basilica of the Holy Blood; Beguinage.
Antwerp: Royal Gallery of Fine Arts (paintings); Mayer van den Bergh Museum (paintings, statuary); Cathedral; Grote Markt; Town Hall; Guild Houses; Rubens House.

As in Belgium, guided tours are pointless here. In Amsterdam half a day will suffice for the Rijksmuseum and the Rembrandt House; this plus a boatride through the canals, will add up to one day's stay.

Haarlem and **The Hague** (Frans Hals Museum on the first and Mauritshuis on the second) can each be easily managed in one day, and the better part of a day will be necessary for Rotterdam.

FRANCE (PARIS 5, THE COUNTRY 14 DAYS)

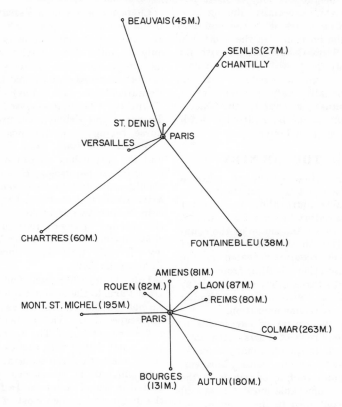

For paintings and sculptures, Paris offers everything, and the provincial museums are with few exceptions such as the Grünewald Altar in Colmar, and the Chantilly Museum, just —"provincial."

When we consider architecture, however, the opposite is true. In Paris, because of what is referred to as "dynamic progress," frequent political upheavals, and concommitant vandalism, few architectural relics remain; unhappily, these are lost in a sea of cement. Hence the traveler interested in ecclesiastic or secular architecture will, with few exceptions, be obliged to seek it outside Paris.

Our five-day tour could proceed as follows: **First day,** the city tour. **Second day,** the Louvre, Musée de Jeu de Paume, and the squares near by, Place de la Concorde, Place Vendôme, Place de l'Opéra, the adjoining boulevards. **Third day,** Notre Dame, Saint Chapelle, and the adjoining region on both sides of the Seine, Musée de Cluny. **Fourth day,** the Eiffel Tower. Is the last a touristy attraction? There is no doubt about it, but it is a marvel, the symbol of Paris, and to ascend it is quite an experience. Seen from this height the city is most impressive, especially during the evening hours with the sun low on the horizon. On the same day the Sacré-Coeur district with its picture-post-card streets and corners might be visited. (An exceptionally ugly pastiche of a Romanesque church, the Sacré-Coeur, could be omitted.) **Fifth day**, again a Louvre day.

THE COUNTRY

Traveling in France poses a problem not found in Italy where circular tours allow us to cover the territory "from stem to stern." In France, the shape of the country is such that visiting sites of interest requires repeated trips in all directions, lasting from half a day to three days, with Paris as the focal point—a time-consuming and wearisome operation.

In the course of excursions to the environs of Paris, with daily returns to the city, many remarkable sites can be visited; however, we shall confine ourselves to the most memorable ones. These will be mentioned in the order of importance, or, as the case may be, in order of proximity.

Ecclesiastic Buildings. Of these, Chartres (60 miles) should be mentioned first. It is always on the list of guided tours. On the outskirts of Paris (7 miles) is St. Denis. Today it has more historic than artistic importance. Next, and nearest to Paris, are Senlis (27 miles) and Beauvais (45 miles) ; both have significant edifices.

Sites rivaling those of Notre Dame in Paris and Chartes are Rheims and Amiens (both 80 miles

from Paris). All these can be reached by train in half-day excursions.

Châteaux near Paris. Versailles is the first one that comes to mind, because it is the most famous and only 13 miles from Paris; Malmaison is 10 miles. Both visits can be combined on a guided tour. Fontainebleau (38 miles) and Chantilly (25 miles—closed on Tuesdays and Fridays because of horse racing) are the most interesting châteaux near Paris, and the latter has an important collection of paintings. However, should only limited time remain after a visit to Versailles, I would skip the last two and take instead the two-day (guided) tour to the château country in the Loire Valley. Usually these trips include Chartres as well.

Loire Valley Châteaux. The trip from Paris to the château country cannot be called scenic, as the landscape of the valley itself is rather monotonous. The countryside is not dotted with castles and other romantic architectural attractions, as is sometimes suggested in travel accounts. In fact, the distances between most of the sites are relatively long, and there is not much along the routes to engage our attention. But one should also remember that intimate contact, even with an undramatic landscape, will reveal hidden charms which remain unobserved by the hasty traveler. In all, although there are dozens of châteaux in the valley, these five are all the nonspecialist need take in. They can be surveyed in two busy days.

As I have mentioned, guided tours are only indicated when traveling to architectural sites, because these cannot be properly inspected otherwise. Of course guides are in attendance at every site, but one should consider that in France, as a rule, none of them has a good command of English. Should we extend our trips to three days each, Colmar, Autun, and Mont-Saint-Michel may be visited. Colmar can be reached by train from Basel (Switzerland) in about three hours, but the trip from Paris takes a full day, and the same applies to Autun and Mont-Saint-Michel. There are no direct train connections to these places, and changing trains with the usual unavoidable delays is the rule. Neither in Colmar nor in Autun will the services of a guide be required, but the cloister of Mont-Saint-Michel can be visited only on a guided tour. These are conducted from the office of the abbey.

When moving our headquarters south to Nice, Aix-en-Provence, Nimes, and Avignon can be covered on a two-day guided tour.

List of Sites in Paris

Museums: The Louvre (Métro Palais Royal or Louvre, paintings and sculpture); Musée de Jeu de Paume (Métro Concorde, 19th-century paintings); Musée de Cluny (Métro Cluny or Odéon, ecclesiastic statuary); all museums in Paris are closed on Tuesdays.

Edifices: Notre Dame; Sainte Chapelle (both Métro Cité); Opéra (Métro Opéra); Tour Eiffel (Métro Bir Hakeim); Sacré Coeur (Métro Abesses).

List of Sites in the Country

Museums: Colmar (Matthias Grünewald), Chantilly Museum (paintings).

Cathedrals: St. Denis; Chartres, Senlis, Beauvais, Rheims, Amiens, Rouen; Mont-Saint-Michel. Autun (Gislebertus sculptures).

Edifices: Malmaison, Versailles, Fontainebleau, Chambord, Blois, Cheverny, Chenonceaux, Amboise.

SPAIN (3 TO 16 DAYS)

OPORTO

SPAIN

COIMBRA

BATALHA
TOMAR
ALCOBAÇA

BURGOS

VALLADOLID

SALAMANCA

SEGOVIA

AVILA
ESCORIAL

MADRID

LISBON

BEJA

Sevilla

TOLEDO

PORTUGAL

CORDOBA

SEVILLA

GRANADA

CADIZ

MÁLAGA

GIBRALTAR

Three days will suffice for Madrid and Toledo; two days for Madrid—or more accurately, the Prado (as a city Madrid is not of special interest)—and one day for a conducted tour to Toledo. Madrid-Toledo-the Escorial—one day for each—also seems an adequate plan for a short visit. (It is 55 miles from Madrid to Toledo, 30 miles to the Escorial.)

Six additional days will be required for a round trip (by excursion bus or car) from Madrid - Seville - Cádiz - Málaga - Granada-Cordova-Madrid, including a two-day stay in Seville and an over-night stay in Málaga, Granada, and Cordova. Toledo can be included on the return trip, but this would mean staying overnight in that city. The entire trip can be shortened by flying from Madrid to Seville and starting by car from the latter.

For a round trip (about 450

miles) from Madrid north to Segovia - Avila - Salamanca - Vallado-
lid-Burgos-Madrid, three more
days will be required.

Salamanca is one of the most
charming old Spanish towns with
a Romanesque-Gothic cathedral of
great beauty. The largest and finest collection of statuary in the
country is housed in the Museo
San Gregorio in Valladolid; and
the interior of the cathedral in
Burgos is undoubtedly the most
precious in all of Spain.

Since Barcelona is not on either
one of these routes, it is best to
visit this city separately or to
start from there and continue to
Madrid by air, a flight of less than
two hours. Majorca can easily be
reached by air (one hour flight)
from Barcelona; it is a charming
place with a remarkable Gothic
cathedral.

Madrid Museums

Madrid: Prado museum (paintings and a small collection of antique sculptures); Academia de
San Fernando (Calle de Alcalà
70, paintings.)

List of Sites in the Country

Escorial: Castle.
Toledo: Cathedral, Palace de
Tavera, San Tomé, and San Juan
de Los Reyes, Transito Syna-
gogue, Santa Maria la Blanca, El
Greco House.
Seville: Cathedral, Alcázar and
the park.
Cádiz: Cathedral.
Málaga: Cathedral.
Granada: Alhambra, Generalife,
Cathedral, Cartuja monastery.
Cordoba: Mezquita (the Mosque).
Barcelona: Museum of Catalonian
Art (in Montjuich Park), Cathe-
dral, Gothic quarter.

When traveling by car, one will
find the roads well marked, uncluttered (except near the bigger
towns), and generally in good condition. Guides or guided tours
(except to Toledo and the Escorial) are not essential, but if one
wishes to secure the services of
a guide, they are generally to be
found in front of the tourist attractions; guides speak English
and their fees are moderate. The
best time for travel is autumn,
when the skies are cloudless and
temperatures ideal.

PORTUGAL (2–4 DAYS)

Those unfamiliar with Lisbon
should take a conducted city tour
which covers the few sites of interest and the suburb of Belem,
with the Tower of Belem and the
Jeronimos monastery. Instead of
a visit to the rather unimportant
Museum of Ancient Art (Rua des
Jeneles Verdes) in a remote district of the town, it is more reasonable to take a half-day tour to
Sintra.

A one-day round trip by car will
cover the following places: Alcobaça, Nazaré (a picturesque
fishing village), Batalha, Tomar.
A motor trip to Oporto can be
managed in one day via the towns
mentioned with the addition of
Coimbra. From Coimbra, it takes
two hours to cover the 60 miles
to Oporto. The return to Lisbon
is best made the next morning by
plane. The flight takes one hour,
and there is a connecting flight
from Lisbon to Madrid. Thus, in
four days, the most noteworthy
sites can be adequately surveyed.

Motoring through Portugal is
easy, for there is not much traffic

and the roads are well-marked and, by European standards, quite good. The landscape, hilly with occasional distant vistas, is unspectacular and lacks distinctive character—at least on the route just discussed. The country houses are also indifferent and do not harmonize with the landscape as do the old farm dwellings in some other countries of Europe. Evidently they are of modern construction or have been remodeled over the years. For those motoring to Spain, Seville can be reached in a one-day drive from Lisbon. Less than halfway to Seville is the little town of Beja, with its former convent, now a museum.

List of Sites

Lisbon: Museum of Ancient Art (paintings, statuary), Tower of Belem, Jeronimos monastery.

List of Sites in the Country

Monasteries, cathedrals: Alcobaça; Batalha; Tomar; Coimbra, Museum Machado de Castro (statuary).
Sintra: Palace.
Oporto: Cathedral, Church of San Francisco and Da Serra do Pilar.

SWITZERLAND (5–14 DAYS)

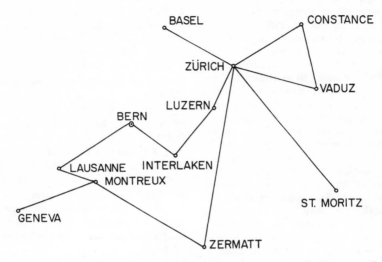

In Switzerland, certain regions should be considered for separate visits. To "sample" the country in only five days, for example, one would do well to start with Zürich. Spend one day there and take a train late the second day to Lucerne, one of the most delightful alpine towns (a ride of about one hour). From there one can make three spectacular excursions on consecutive days: Pilatus, Rigi, Bürgenstock. The trip can be extended by continuing from Lucerne to Interlaken and thence to the Jungfrau (two more days).

The area around Lake Geneva should be visited next. Take one day for Geneva and one for Lausanne; next, visit Chamonix via Montreux, returning to Montreux, Geneva, or Lausanne. This is one of the most dramatic alpine tours in Europe. On the fourth day you may return to Zürich by train, or, if more time is avail-able, you can reach Zermatt the same day from any place along Lake Geneva. Add two days for this trip.

To go to St. Moritz, one starts from Zürich and arrives in St. Moritz the same day. During the next two days, visit Pontresina, Bernina Hospitz, and Muottas Muragl, the landscape of which, it is said, suggested to Leonardo da Vinci the background for the Mona Lisa. The trip thus far will be made by excellent trains, cogwheel and cablecars.

If at this juncture you plan either a trip to Italy or to extend your stay in Switzerland, you will find that the route via Maloja, Chiavonna, and along Lake Como to Lugano offers unforgettable sights; this tour can be made by bus, and two days should be devoted to exploring Lugano and its environs. Milan can be reached in about two hours from Lugano.

A very interesting trip from Zürich can be made by car only, and it should be planned for three days (if necessary, it could be managed in two). It takes us to Lake Constance via the Rhein Falls, Schaffhausen, and to the medieval town of Stein am Rhein, one of the most picturesque in Switzerland. Next we go to Constance am Bodensee and across the lake by ferry to Meersburg, with the oldest and best-preserved castle in Germany (here we are in Germany; hence documents for car and tourists will be required).

Returning to Constance, we ride along the lake to Romanshorn, thence to St. Gallen. Here we will make our only visit to a "relic," in this instance an 8th-century abbey, today the bishop's residence with a library famous in all Europe for its extraordinary Baroque interior. The abbey is attached to the cathedral, also a beautiful structure. We continue to Teufen, Feldkirch, and then to Vaduz in the principality of Liechtenstein. In the Public Library of this picturesque ancient town, a part of the princely art collection of old masters' paintings can be seen.

To return to Zürich is a matter of less than three hours' drive, much of it along the Walensee and Zürichsee. Thus, the entire round trip covers not much more than 200 miles. Lastly, it should be mentioned that the best time for traveling in mountainous regions is during the summer months—June until the beginning of September.

GERMANY (7 TO 14 DAYS)

Depending on where one enters the country, we could start a trip through Germany from the north or south. Coming from the Low Countries, for example, one can take a train to Aachen from Brussels and thence to Cologne. A direct flight brings the traveler to Cologne from Brussels in less than one hour. Direct connections from Paris to Munich can be made in about two hours and in much less time from Zürich. It takes two and a half hours by train from Zürich to Freiburg. Travel throughout Germany is not as difficult as in France, for it is possible to follow a continuous route, though by no means a straight one.

Before undertaking the journey one must also clarify the objectives of the visit. The war took a heavy toll of historic edifices in the principal centers, although much rebuilding has been done. However, many isolated sections remain unscathed, but the casual visitor would hardly muster the energy, not to say the time, to reach these areas. In all, the plan devised here seems to conform with the objectives pursued in this guide.

In the first part of the guide to Germany, works related to the art of architecture were discussed— out of context, as it were, for they rarely appear in a homogeneous surrounding. It is another matter, however, in the Bavarian mountain region, for example, where nature provides art with a marvelous frame. The Bavarian and the Algäu Alps are not only wildly romantic, but their farmhouses and churches are one with the land; the former, although not always as old, rarely deviate in design from the traditional pattern. The churches are especially charming, each of them an accomplished work of art, and although their basic structure is Gothic, they are now graced by colorful Bavarian Baroque or Rococo elements.

Guided bus tours can be arranged from Munich, but it is decidedly preferable to travel by car. The distances are relatively short, the roads excellent, and the traffic no problem. From Munich the road leads first to Starenberg (15 miles), along the delightful Starenberg Lake to Weilheim, and then on to Garmisch-Partenkirchen (40 miles), an alpine mountain and lake region beyond compare. If possible, two days should be devoted to the exploration of this area and its 9000-foot-high peak, the Zugspitze.

Next we return to Garmisch and continue to Ettal, with its magnificent 14th-century Benedictine monastery, now in late Bavarian Baroque. Thence we go to Oberammergau (11 miles), Wies, Steingaden, and Rottenbuch. All these places are graced by exquisitely picturesque Baroque and Rococo churches (this will add another 20 miles to our trip). Returning to Steingaden, we continue to Schwangau over the "Romantic Road" to the center of another fantastic mountain range, with its famous Germanic fairytale castles, Neuschwanstein and Hohen Schwangau ("Wagnerian" 19th-century pastiches). Next door is the famous (authentic) medieval town of Füssen (20 miles), with its ancient castle and church. This tour totals about 110 miles, and the recommended time for a round trip from Munich is three days.

From Füssen it is about 80 miles to Lindau am Bodensee (through Immenstadt) and 30 miles more to Meersburg. Not only is the trip from Füssen through the Algäu Alps very scenic, but the region of the Bodensee (or Lake Constance, as it is known at the other end, where Meersburg and Constance face each other across a narrow strip of water) is also rich in medieval remains.

The trip from Freiburg by rail to Munich is rather wearisome and by far the longest on our journey, lasting about seven hours. Except for the few churches, Munich today lacks architectural interest. A stay of four days (this includes a visit to Nymphenburg) should be sufficient. From Munich a trip by car to Rothenburg leads through Augsburg, Donauwörth, Nördlingen, and Dünkelsbühl, a total of 125 miles. Nördlingen and Dünkelsbühl, the oldest towns in Franconia, have retained much of their late medieval appearance. The distance from Rothenburg to Creglingen and back is 13 miles and Nuremberg (through the ancient town of Ansbach) is another 45 miles. (This tour can also be made by train and bus from Nuremberg.)

The road from Nuremberg to Bamberg (34 miles) leads through Forschheim, where interesting half-timbered houses from the 16th and 17th centuries can be seen. To continue to Würzburg it is necessary to return to Forschheim (17 miles) and thence via Neuss to Würzburg (48 miles).

From Würzburg via Wertheim we reach Miltenberg (40 miles), a quaint little town with an authentic 15th-century marketplace, and continue through the scenic

Odenwald to Worms (46 miles) and Frankfort (55 miles). Mainz should be the next stop, for here the most interesting stretch of the Rhine journey begins. It leads to Coblenz through the many towns and hamlets of the famous wine region, dotted with ruined castles (as well as some in good repair) and ancient relics. This, as it were, is the soul of the Rhine journey. The trip can also be made from Mainz to Coblenz by boat which criss-crosses the river, offering the traveler an ever-changing panorama. The entire distance from Mainz to Cologne is 120 miles and takes one day. It is best to take a train from Cologne to Aachen and a plane to Berlin.

List of Sites by City

Museums

Munich: Alte Pinakothek (paintings), Glyptothek (sculptures), Prinz Carl Palais (sculptures), Bavarian National Museum (statuary, paintings).
Nuremberg: Germanisches National Museum (statuary, paintings).

Frankfort: Staedel Art Institute (paintings).
Mainz: Picture Gallery, Museum of Antiquities.
Cologne: Wallraf-Richartz Museum (paintings), Schnüttgen Museum (statuary).
Berlin: Dahlem Museum (paintings).

Cathedrals and Edifices by City

Freiburg: Cathedral.
Munich: Frauenkirche, Peterskirche, Asamkirche, Theatinerkirche, Die Residenz, Cuvilliés Theater, Nymphenburg Palace.
Rothenburg ob der Tauber: Jacobskirche (Riemenschneider).
Creglingen: Herrgottskirche (Riemenschneider).
Nuremberg: St. Sebalduskirche, St. Lorenzkirche, Frauenkirche, The Beautiful Fountain, Dürerhaus, Royal Castle.
Bamberg: Cathedral.
Würzburg: Cathedral, Die Residenz, Neumünster, St. Burkard, Franziskanerkirche, Marienkapelle, Mainfränkisches Museum. Here Riemenschneider's work can be seen.
Worms: Cathedral.
Mainz: Cathedral.
Cologne: Cathedral.
Aachen: Cathedral and the Sauermond Museum.

AUSTRIA (4–14 DAYS)

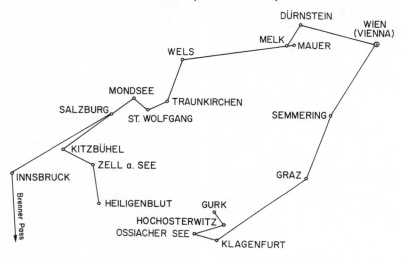

In practically every instance a visit to a country will start with its principal city, for generally all means of communication either initiate or terminate in the capital. The geographic location of Austria, however, will offer two alternate routes. Coming from Switzerland, Germany, or Italy, the first stop might be Innsbruck or Salzburg; one could then continue east to Vienna. From Vienna every major city in Europe can be reached by air, bus, or train. When motoring from Innsbruck over the Brenner Pass to Italy, one will encounter some of the most grandiose landscapes in all of Europe, in addition to rural medieval and Baroque architecture at every turn of the road.

A guided tour through Vienna is not necessary for the localities worth visiting can be surveyed on foot in a few hours. However, for its charming environs and the outlying districts—Klosterneu-burg (the abbey has an important relic, the so-called Verdun Altar, dating from the 12th century), Grinzing, Cobenzl, Heiligenstadt (much of it in Biedermeier style) —it is best to take a car or sight-seeing bus. There remains only the Palace of Schönbrunn, the former imperial residence outside the city proper. It can be reached by bus or taxi, and there are guided tours through some three dozen of the palace's 1400 rooms.

If we limit our journey to ten days (four in Vienna and six in the country), the tour to Salzburg and Innsbruck is the most interesting.

If possible, it should be made by car, for motoring in Austria is no problem. The entire trip covers less than 300 miles, and the roads are not congested. As for the scenery, it is an "exquisite work of art" throughout.

The next choice is to travel by excursion buses. If one takes the

290

train it is impossible to visit the important sights en route. During the summer months Salzburg and Innsbruck can also be reached by plane from Vienna.

THE COUNTRY

The distance from Vienna to Salzburg is about 175 miles. With the detour via Bad Ischl and St. Wolfgang, it is some 10 miles longer, and the road conditions are generally quite good. With stops in Dürnstein, Melk, Mauer, Bad Ischl, and St. Wolfgang, the trip should take about ten hours. However, I would recommend an overnight stop in St. Wolfgang (Gasthof Weisses Roessl—White Horse Inn—here again is one of my rare hotel suggestions, for this one is also part of the landscape), proceeding to Salzburg the following day, a ride of about one hour.

Salzburg should occupy us for at least three days, and we may as well start with its most spectacular site, the Hohensalzburg. When visiting the fortress, it is best to take the cogwheel car uphill, walk across the plateau, and descend by the elevator at the Winkler Restaurant. Half a day should be given to this; two more days to exploring the city, the churches and edifices; and half a day more for a visit to Schloss Hellbrunn (Hellbrunn Castle), which is located out of town and can be reached easily by an old-fashioned trolley.

FROM SALZBURG TO INNSBRUCK

If you are driving, there are three alternate roads from Salzburg to Innsbruck. The shortest leads through the Kaisergebirge via Wörgl (four hours). The next goes via Bischofshofen, Zell-am-See, Kitzbühel (the famous skiing resort), Wörgl, and Rattenberg (seven hours). The longest route is via the Grossglockner (a peak of 12,461 feet). This detour leads over a spectacular high alpine road to Heiligenblut. The small parish church in this remote mountain fastness contains a Gothic altar of great beauty.

The visit to Innsbruck will require two days, and it will not be complete without taking a cable car ride to the **Patcherkofel** and the **Hafelecar** heights, from which, on a clear day, the entire Tyrol can be seen in all its glory. These tours can be made on two consecutive days.

SUGGESTIONS

Considering our objectives, ten days should be spent on the trip: covering Vienna, Salzburg, and Innsbruck. Ten more days could be added without exhausting the repertoire of attractions that the Austrian landscape and architecture offer to the traveler. However, since our program is limited, and assuming that the tourist comes from the north and that he may continue on his route south, another approach to Italy (direction Venice) should be mentioned. Not quite as rich in visual attractions, it leads nonetheless through some very beautiful countryside. The following are highlights to be met along this route: Starting with Semmering (60 miles from Vienna), a dramatic alpine region, we continue through Graz, the capital of the province of Styria; and then to Klagenfurt, the capital of Carinthia (these are ancient towns with many historic relics, but our aim is to reach Wörthersee and the resort town of Velden the same day, a distance of about 175 miles). The next day will be devoted to exploring the lake region —Wörther and Ossiacher See— and the following, to a visit (via Klagenfurt) to Maria Saal, a bishop's seat from the 8th to the 10th centuries. The present parish church is of the 15th century (Gothic) and contains many relics. We then continue to the Castle of Hochosterwitz, built as a rampart against the Turks (16th century), and to the ancient village of Gurk, with its 12th-century cathedral and a collection of Gothic relics. This excursion will take the better part of a day.

Should one consider traveling over the high alpine region of the Grossglockner and the Brenner Pass, consider only the summer months to do it. Otherwise, the trips mentioned can be made in the spring or the fall, at which time one will avoid the heavy tourist traffic. During the summer months there are conducted tours by Europa Bus from Austria via the Tyrol to Italy.

List of Sites in Vienna

Museums: Kunsthistorisches Museum (Maria Theresien Platz, paintings, statuary and decorative objects), Akademie der Bildenden Künste (Schillerplatz, paintings), Osterreichisches Museum für Mittelalterliche Kunst (Rennweg, paintings and sculpture), Albertina (Augustinerstrasse I., graphic art). Historisches Museum der Stadt Wien.

Churches: Stefanskirche (cathedral, Stefansplatz), Karlskirche (Karlsplatz).

Edifices: Belvedere, Opera House, The Spanish Riding School, Redoutensaal, Hofburg, Schönbrunn.

Sites in the environs of Vienna: Grinzing, Heiligenstadt, Klosterneuburg.

List of Sites in the Country

On the road to Salzburg: Dürnstein (castle), Melk (abbey), Mauer (church), Enns, Gmunden, Bad Ischl, St. Wolfgang (church), Mondsee.

In Salzburg—Edifices: Hohensalzburg, Residenz, Hofmarstall and Hofmarstallschwemme, Schloss Mirabel, Hollbrunn, Mozarthaus.

Churches: Dreifaltigkeitskirche, Johannesspitalkirche, Ursulinenkirche, Der Dom (cathedral), Franciskanerkirche, Collegien Kirche.

On the road to Innsbruck: Kitzbühel, Wörgl. Or: Zell-am-See, Heiligenblut (church), Grossglockner.

In Innsbruck: Die Altstadt (the old city), Court Castle, Court Church, Silver Chapel, Museum für Volkskunde (Folk-Art Museum).

Outside the City: Patcherkofel, Hafelecar.

ITALY (2 to 5 WEEKS)

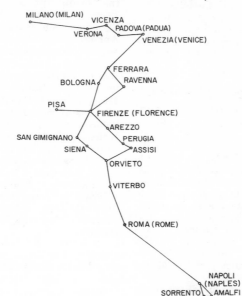

Because of the immense accumulation of art treasures in Italy only places which lie along our route will be considered, hence the following list includes only a selection of principal art objects and sites in easily accessible locations.

Styles of Paintings and Sculpture and Where to See Them

Etruscan Sculpture (6th-3rd century B.C.). Florence: Museo Archeologico. Rome: Museo Nazionale di Villa Giulia, Vatican.
Roman (Greco-Roman) Sculpture (3rd century B.C.-3rd century A.D.). Rome: Museo Terme, Vatican, Capitoline Museum. Naples: Museo Nazionale.
Pompeian Murals (3rd century B.C.-1st century A.D.). Naples: Museo Nazionale.
Byzantine Mosaics (6th-15th century). Ravenna: San Vitale, Sant' Apollinare Nuovo, Sant' Apollinare in Classe. Torcello: Cathedral. Palermo: Capella Palatina, La Mortarana. Monreale: Abbey.
Romanesque and Gothic Sculpture (12th-14th century). Milan: Castello Sforzesco, Museo del'Duomo. Venice: Museo Correr. Florence: Opera del'Duomo. Rome: Vatican (also in various churches dating from those periods).
Gothic Paintings (13th-14th century). Milan: Brera, Museo Poldi-Pezzoli. Venice: Museo dell'Accademia. Florence: Uffizi, Museo dell'Accademia. Rome: Vatican.
Renaissance Paintings (15th-16th century). Milan: Brera, Museo Poldi-Pezzoli. Venice: Museo dell' Accademia, Museo Correr. Florence: Uffizi, Palazzo Pitti, Museo dell'Accademia. Rome: Vatican, Museo Borghese, Museo Barberini. Naples: Museo Capodimonte

293

(also in various palaces and churches).

Renaissance Sculpture (15th-16th century). Milan: Castello Sforzesco. Florence: Bargello (and in various churches and edifices).

Baroque Paintings (16th-18th century). In every principal museum and in churches.

Edifices, Churches, Monuments

Milan: Duomo (Gothic), Sant' Ambrogio (Romanesque), Santa Maria delle Grazie (Renaissance), district around Via dei Mercanti.
Venice: St. Mark's (Byzantine), Palazzo Ducale (Gothic-Renaissance), Santa Maria Gloriosa dei Frari and Santi Giovanni e Paolo (Gothic), Santa Maria dei Miracoli (Early Renaissance), Ca' d'Oro (Venetian Gothic, as are many of the palaces along the Grand Canal), Verrocchio's Colleoni (Renaissance), Santa Maria della Salute (Baroque).
Florence: Baptistry (Byzantine-Romanesque), Duomo and the Giotto Tower (Gothic), San Miniato al Monte (Romanesque), Palazzo Vecchio (Gothic), Santa Croce (Gothic), San Lorenzo (Renaissance, Michelangelo sculptures), Santa Maria Novella (Gothic-Renaissance, 14th- and 15th-century frescoes), Or-San-Michele (Gothic and Renaissance sculptures), Medici-Riccardi Palace (Renaissance, Gozzoli Frescoes), Church of the Carmine (Renaissance, Masaccio Frescoes).
Rome: Forum Romanum (1st-4th century A.D.), Pantheon (1st century B.C.), Castel Sant' Angelo (2nd century A.D.), Campidoglio (Renaissance), St. Peter's and the Colonnades by Bernini (Renaissance and Baroque), Santa Maria Maggiore (Renaissance; Romanesque and Gothic features in the interior), San Pietro in Vincoli (Michelangelo's Moses), Santa Maria degli Angeli. Among the Baroque monuments the following should be noted: Il Gesù Church, Piazza Navona, Sant' Agnese and the Bernini fountains, Fontana di Trevi (Bernini), the Spanish Steps, the statuary on the Sant' Angelo Bridge.
Naples: Castelnuovo (Gothic), Triumphal Arch (Renaissance), Duomo (Romanesque and Gothic; interior Renaissance), San Paolo Maggiore and San Gesù Nuovo (Renaissance and Baroque).
Palermo: Cathedral (Saracen, Norman, Gothic, Byzantine, and Baroque), La Mortarana (Saracen, Byzantine, Gothic, Renaissance, Baroque), Capella Palatina (Byzantine), Monreale Abbey (Byzantine), and Quattro Conti di Città, San Giuseppe Church, Piazza e Fontana Pretoria—all Baroque.

PLAN FOR TRAVEL

After this brief catalogue it becomes apparent that a careful plan must be made before one sets out to explore the country. Moreover, from the preceding list one fact emerges: the city of Florence possesses a greater concentration and variety of art treasures than any other place in Europe. Hence Florence is of first importance on our map. Next in order are Rome and Venice. If we consider antiquities, Rome is the most beautiful metropolis in Europe, and Venice is beyond compare—the most improbable city ever built. Thus a 14-day trip might proceed as follows: Rome, four days; then to Florence via Viterbo, Orvieto, Siena, San Gimignano, or via Assisi, Perugia, and Arezzo; one day bus travel and four days in Florence (including Pisa); thence to Venice via Bologna, Ferrara, Padua, or via Ravenna, Ferrara,

Padua; one day travel by bus and four days in Venice.

If extending the tour to Naples and Pompeii (flight time less than one hour), three days should be added and at least four more days if Sicily is included (flight from Naples to Palermo takes one hour). On our return from Rome, any of the previously missed points (Assisi, Perugia, Arezzo, Orvieto, Siena, Bologna, Ferrara, or Ravenna) can be visited. Our final destination is Milan, via Venice, Padua, Vicenza, and Verona, thus rounding off four weeks of travel. Hence, besides the bigger centers—Milan, Venice, Florence, Rome, Naples and environs, Palermo—the following small towns, all possessing works of art and edifices of great interest, can be visited: Verona, Vicenza, Ferrara, Bologna, Ravenna, Arezzo, Siena, Perugia, Assisi, Orvieto, Viterbo, in addition to points in Sicily (see map).

In view of the allotted time, the program thus developed offers the most comprehensive and best survey of the country's art treasures. Of course, we could easily double the time for a more thorough and more leisurely visit without becoming bored, for the beauty of this land is inexhaustible.

OBSERVATIONS

Throughout the preceding text, little reference was made to the Italian landscape. Not that the landscape is negligible—it is simply superseded by man-made objects that will chiefly, if not exclusively, occupy the traveler's

attention. The countryside along our route is almost never dull or without interest, and some of it is of exceptional beauty and quite dramatic—for example, the southern Tyrol; the Lake Region; Umbria; Lombardy; Tuscany; the ride from Naples to Pompeii, Amalfi, Ravello, and Sorento (the entry port for Capri, a boat ride of less than two hours); the ride in Liguria along the Italian Riviera, beginning with the town of V e n t i m i g l i a (bordering on France) to Genoa, Portofino, Santa Margherita, and on to Pisa, with its airport (serving Florence) whence connections can be made for Rome. As for Sicily, it is scenic throughout.

Considering the means of travel between intermediate points, a self-driven car presents too many disadvantages that in the end restrict rather than facilitate transportation. Motoring in Italy today is a real hardship, hence, excellent, well-guided bus transportation can be used on the following routes: Milan-Venice, Venice-Florence, Florence-Rome. Buses stop for sight-seeing in all the localities enumerated in this guide. From Rome to Naples one can take a fast train or, better still, a plane. Palermo can be reached overnight by boat from Naples, or in one hour by plane. The best time for travel in Italy is the spring or fall, because the summer months are crowded and hot. But even out of season, it is often difficult to obtain the desired transportation by tourist bus without having secured a reservation well ahead of time.)

MILAN (3 DAYS)

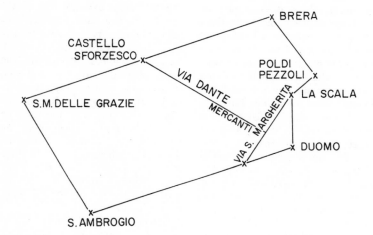

CASTELLO SFORZESCO x

BRERA x

POLDI PEZZOLI x

x S.M. DELLE GRAZIE

VIA DANTE MERCANTI

VIA MARGHERITA

x LA SCALA

VIA S.

x DUOMO

x S. AMBROGIO

This big city can be reached by plane directly from any part of Europe, or from New York. Thus whether one travels by plane or sightseeing bus, it is nearest to Venice, yet it need not be the first to be visited, for, as far as art is concerned, it has not as much to offer as Florence, Rome, or Venice. It may as well be the last on our itinerary.

Milan is a modern metropolis, and its industrial and mercantile aspect is ever-present; therefore our attention will be concentrated on the few points of artistic interest. In short, the city is too busy to put the traveler at ease. However, unlike Rome, the sites are not far apart; in fact, they can be surveyed in three days. There is also no need for a guided city tour, which is usually recommended when visiting most large cities for the first time. As can be seen on the map, almost the entire circuit, divided into

three separate daily tours, can be made leisurely on foot.

List of Sites

Museums: Brera (paintings), Museo Poldi-Pezzoli (paintings, armor, bric-à-brac), Biblioteca Ambrosiana, Museo del' Duomo (sculptures, architectural models, and ornaments).
Churches: Duomo, San Ambrogio, Santa Maria delle Grazie.
Edifices: Castello Sforzesco (sculptures, paintings, furnishings), the district near the Duomo (Via Mercanti).

MILAN—VERONA—VICENZA—PADUA—VENICE

The simplest way to travel this route is by sight-seeing bus, but it also limits one's visiting time to about one hour in each of the stops, for this is a one-day trip. When traveling by train, one could stay overnight in Verona, proceed to Vicenza by train or bus and thence to Padua (a very short ride), stay overnight in Padua, and continue the next day to Venice by bus or train. The trip to Venice could also be made the same evening. The entire distance from Milan is about 150 miles.

List of Sites

Verona: Amphitheater, Porta dei Borsari, San Zeno Maggiore and Santa Maria Antica, tombs of the Scaligare, Piazza dei Signori.
Vicenza: Villa Rotunda, Loggia del Capistrano, Olympic Theater (architect Palladio).
Padua: Arena Chapel (frescoes by Giotto), Donatello's Statue of Gattamelata, Basilica of San Antonio (cathedral).

VENICE

Whatever conveyance one takes to Venice, he will always arrive at the square of the railroad terminal. From here the newcomer should take a gondola to the spot nearest his particular hotel. This will give the novice his first good impression of Venice. The habitué will, of course, prefer fast motor transportation, and those not encumbered by luggage might as well avail themselves of the cheapest and very convenient transportation, the vaporetto.

Once in the city, all movement will start from the Piazza San Marco, and when not walking, only the vaporetto will be used.

List of Sites

Museums: Accademia (paintings), Museo Correr (paintings, statuary), Scuola San Rocco (Tintoretto paintings).
Museum-Palaces: Palazzo Ducale (paintings, furnishings), Palazzo Pesaro (Museo Orientale, armor, costumes, graphic art), Ca'd'Oro (paintings, furnishings), Rezzonico Palace (Museo del' Settecento Veneziano (Rococo décor).
Churches: St. Mark's, Santa Maria della Salute, Santa Maria dei Frari, Santi Giovanni e Paolo, Santa Maria dei Miracoli, cathedral in Torcello (mosaics).
Monuments: Verrocchio's Colleoni, Rialto Bridge.

While en route to the Fundamente Nuove (via Campo Giovanni e Paolo), where we take a boat for Torcello, we might visit the small, jewel-like church of Santa Maria dei Miracoli. On the island of Torcello, in the 11th-century cathedral, the largest Byzantine mosaics are preserved. This trip will require the better part of a day. Lastly, it should be stated that a trip to the famed Lido should interest only those who enjoy bathing in the sea or gambling in the casino. The resort as such is commonplace.

A VISIT OF 4 TO 6 DAYS

Because Venice has so much to offer, a stay of four days must of necessity be a hasty one. The Accademia and all that is to be seen on the Piazza San Marco will require two days. And a day's stroll through the city will be an unforgettable experience. The fourth day could be utilized for your visiting the following edifices, using a vaporetto and starting from St. Mark's: first stop—Santa Maria della Salute; second stop—San Rezzonico Palace; third stop—San Toma, Scuola San Rocco, and Santa Maria Gloriosa dei Frari. The Ca'd'Oro stop is next, beyond the Rialto bridge, and the last stop, obliquely across from Ca'd'Oro, will bring us to the Pesaro Palace. At this point we are on the Grand Canal just midway between St. Mark's and the railroad station. All the preceding sites can be included in a day's (strenuous) tour. If two more days are added, Torcello can be seen—and a more leisurely pace established.

VENICE—FERRARA—BOLOGNA—FLORENCE OR FERRARA—RAVENNA—FLORENCE

From here on, unless traveling by car, it is best to take a sightseeing bus to Florence, a distance of about 220 miles. The route leads either via Bologna, or Ravenna, the former shorter by about 50 miles. However, interest in the Ravenna mosaics should decide which route we choose. The fastest connection to Florence is by plane or train, but it is also the most unreasonable, because riding in trains one remains isolated from the countryside—aside from by-passing Ravenna and Bologna, worthy of one's attention.

List of Sites in Ravenna: San Vitale and the mausoleum of Galla Placidia, Sant' Apollinare Nuovo, Sant' Apollinare in Classe.

List of Sites in Bologna: San Petronio church, San Francisco church, the Fountain of Neptune —and a walk through the center of the city.

FLORENCE (5 TO 7 DAYS)

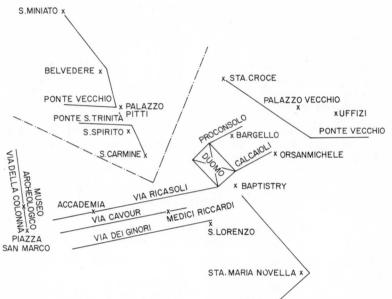

In spite of the enormous accumulation of art treasures and the large number of palaces, galleries, and churches, a well-organized plan can help greatly in seeing much of it in a relatively short time.

List of Sites

Collection of Paintings: Uffizi, Palazzo Pitti, Museo dell' Accademia, Medici-Riccardi Palace (Benozzo Gozzoli murals), San Marco Convent, Santa Maria Novella Church (14th- and 15th-century frescoes), Church of the Carmine (Masaccio frescoes), Belvedere (the Medici Fortress, fragments of 14th- to 15th-century frescoes, gathered from all over the country).

Collection of Sculptures: Bargello, Museo Archeologico (Etruscan), Museo dell' Accademia (Michelangelo), San Lorenzo Chapel (Michelangelo), Or-San-Michele, Museo dell' Opera del' Duomo (sculpture).

Churches: Duomo (Santa Maria del Fiore), Campanile (the Giotto tower), Baptistry, San Lorenzo, Santo Spirito, Santa Maria Novella, Santa Croce, with the Bardi and the Pazzi Chapels, San Miniato al Monte.

Palaces: Vecchio, Strozzi, Ruccelai, Medici-Riccardi, Pitti.

Bridges: Ponte Vecchio, Ponte Santa Trinità.

All the foregoing are important, but considering the element of time (if a five-day visit including a side trip to Pisa is planned) it will be necessary to limit the program, for example, to the following: Uffizi, Bargello, Pitti Palace,

299

Palazzo Vecchio, Duomo, Medici-Riccardi Palace, the San Lorenzo Chapel and Or-San-Michele. All these, located in the most interesting area of the city, are near one another and do not require the services of a guide (see map). If the traveler has two more days at his disposal the list can be widened to include Opera del' Duomo, San Marco Convent, Santa Maria Novella, Boboli Gardens, San Spirito, Church of the Carmine, and finally, the Belvedere and San Miniato. The two last are not within comfortable walking distance and will require transportation by taxi or bus.

FLORENCE—PISA

Pisa serves as an airport for Florence and can be reached from that city by bus or train in a little over one hour. After a visit to Florence, it stands to reason one limits himself in Pisa to the Cathedral Group alone. However one travels it is advisable to take a taxi to the site which is some distance from the center of the city.

FLORENCE—SAN GIMIGNANO—SIENA—VITERBO—ROME
or
FLORENCE—AREZZO—PERUGIA—ASSISI—ORVIETO—ROME

One can go from Florence to Rome by two alternate routes frequented by tourist buses, each requiring one day. On the first, only Siena is a "must," whereas on the second, all of the places mentioned possess great artistic significance. The most practical arrangement, however, is to travel one route south and take the other on the return trip from Rome.

Traveling by car permits a zigzag route to take in all these points in two days, in the following sequence: Florence-San Gimignano-Siena-Arezzo - Perugia-Assisi-Orvieto-Viterbo-Rome—a distance of less than 300 miles.

List of Sites

San Gimignano: Towers.
Arezzo: Church of San Francesco (frescoes by Piero della Francesca).
Siena: Duomo and Museo dell' Opera del' Duomo (statuary and paintings), Palazzo Pubblico.
Perugia: Palazzo Communale, Fontana Maggiore (by Giovanni Pisano and Arnolfo di Cambio).
Assisi: Church of San Francesco (frescoes by Giotto, Cimabue, and others).
Orvieto: Duomo (frescoes by Luca Signorelli) and adjoining museum of sculptures.
Viterbo: Vista of the ancient town.

ROME (4-8 DAYS)

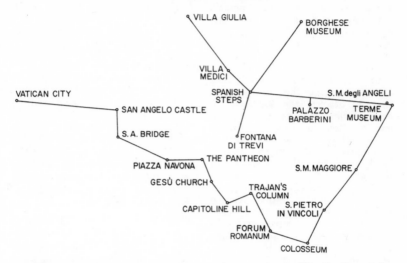

VILLA GIULIA

BORGHESE MUSEUM

VILLA MEDICI

VATICAN CITY

SPANISH STEPS

S.M.degli ANGELI

SAN ANGELO CASTLE

PALAZZO BARBERINI

TERME MUSEUM

S.A. BRIDGE

FONTANA DI TREVI

THE PANTHEON

PIAZZA NAVONA

S.M.MAGGIORE

GESÙ CHURCH

TRAJAN'S COLUMN

CAPITOLINE HILL

S.PIETRO IN VINCOLI

FORUM ROMANUM

COLOSSEUM

When the traveler is obliged to limit himself to the shorter stay, the program might proceed as follows: guided bus tour of the city, including the Roman remains (first day); one day for St. Peter's, the Sistine Chapel, and the Pinacoteca; and another day to tour city sights not previously seen; and finally, the Museo Terme. In eight days the visitor would be able to place the city vistas in perspective because he could take the time to travel by trolley (an excellent means of transportation in Rome—one route, confined to the city proper, makes the round trip in the inner circle, the so-called *circulare interno;* the second moves outside the Aurelian wall, **circulare destro,** always returning to the point where it began). Next he could visit the four remaining museums —Borghese, Palazzo Barberini, Villa Giulia, Museo Capitolino— the Fontana di Trevi, and perhaps

take a trip to Tivoli (by sight-seeing bus). At this point it becomes clear that Rome has still not been sufficiently "surveyed," for the churches, fountains, palaces, and catacombs remain unseen. Because of this complexity it is imperative to classify the material so as to give the traveler a better idea of how to plan his stay.

Paintings: Vatican's Pinacoteca, Museo Borghese, Palazzo Barberini.

Sculptures: Vatican Museum, Museo Terme, Museo Capitolino, Villa Giulia (Etruscan), San Pietro in Vincoli (Michelangelo's Moses).

Roman Remains are strewn all over the city, but we shall limit ourselves to the Forum Romanum and the Pantheon, for these are the most important ones.

Because there are sites of interest all over the city and hence not easy to reach in a limited time, it seems practical to organ-

301

ize our tours according to the location of the sites. Unlike smaller cities such as Florence, for example, Rome does not permit extensive sight-seeing in the course of a leisurely stroll.

After visiting the Vatican, we will concentrate on Roman remains, palaces, fountains, churches, and the piazzas—in that order. Starting the survey from the site nearest the Vatican, we shall circle the city (see map) to end our tour at the Fontana di Trevi, which can be reached in a 20-minute walk from the Piazza Barberini or the Piazza di Spagna.

Group 1. Vatican, Castel Sant' Angelo, and the Sant' Angelo Bridge. Not far, on the Piazza Navona, are the Church of Santa Agnese in Agone and Bernini's Fontana dei Fiumi and Fontana del Moro.

Group 2. Pantheon, Santa Maria Sopra Minerva, Il Gesù church, Trajan's Column, Campidoglio (Capitoline Hill), Santa Maria in Aracoeli, Santi Nome di Maria.

Group 3. Forum Romanum (adjoining the Campidoglio), Temple of Saturn, Arch of Septimius Severus, Arch of Titus, Arch and Basilica of Constantine, Santi Maria e Luca, Colosseum.

Group 4. San Pietro in Vincoli, Santa Maria Maggiore, Museo Terme, Palazzo Barberini, Piazza Barberini, Santa Maria degli Angeli.

Group 5. Piazza di Spagna, Spanish Steps, Trinità dei Monti, Villa Medici, Villa Giulia, Museo Borghese, Fontana di Trevi.

Outside the city, Tivoli (25 miles) and Via Appia can be visited in guided tours, each requiring half a day.

The enumerated sequence considers continuity of the tour. However, this continuity need not be maintained. We may as well start with Group 5, omit this or that site as time permits and our mood of the moment dictates.

An afterthought: After indicating a number of characteristic Roman churches, the question arises whether, having visited the Vatican, it is necessary to see the others. Paradoxical as it may appear, should one have become acquainted with the ecclesiastic architecture of other towns in Italy, Spain, or Austria, it may be sensible to omit this aspect in Rome, where there is so much else of interest.

NAPLES AND ENVIRONS (4 DAYS)

Naples can be reached from Rome by air in one hour or by train in four. The rather unspectacular landscape does not invite a trip by motor. The city itself, aside from its art collections, is full of interest, and its environs are incomparable. The following sites in Naples proper are important and all of them, with the exception of the Capodimonte Museum, are within walking distance; thus there is no need for taking a guided tour.

Starting from the Piazza Carità (which intersects the main thoroughfare, Via Roma), the following points can be reached on a leisurely walking tour: Piazza di Gesù and the Gesù Nuovo church; back to Via Roma and Piazza Dante; then along Via Tribunale to San Paolo Maggiore and the Duomo (see map). This part of the city we may call "midtown."

From the "downtown" section, which centers on the Piazza Plebiscita with the Palazzo Reale, we may proceed to the adjoining Piazza Trento Trieste (at the foot of Via Roma), with the Teatro San Carlo, and hence on Via Acton along the waterfront to Piazza Municipio (facing the main dock, Molo Angioino), with its medieval fortress, Castelnuovo.

Turning right on Piazza Bellini from Piazza Dante and hence over Via Constantinopoli, we reach the National Museum (Piazza del Museo) in 20 minutes. We are now "uptown." The Capodimonte Museum, however, is out of town, and to reach it one will have to take a taxi or a trolley.

List of Sites

Museums: Museo Nazionale (sculptures, Pompeian relics), Museo Nazionale Capodimonte (paintings).

Churches: Duomo, San Paolo Maggiore, Gesù Nuovo.

Edifices: Palazzo Reale, Castelnuovo.

A bus trip to the top of Mount Vesuvius is also recommended.

THE ENVIRONS OF NAPLES
NAPLES—POMPEII—AMALFI—RAVELLO—POSITANO—SORRENTO—NAPLES

This round trip can be made in one day by regularly run, well-guided excursion buses. The tour can also be traveled easily by car, and a guide will be required only in Pompeii, where there is always one in attendance at the entrance to the site. The visit to Pompeii will take one hour; the next stop (midday) should be made in Amalfi. Half an hour each should be given Ravello and Positano, and one hour to Sorrento, the point of embarkation for Capri. Should you plan a visit to Capri, I would recommend staying overnight in Sorrento. As I mentioned on another occasion, this guide is not concerned with hotel accommodations, but where spectacular views are the motive for our visit, what lies in front of our hotel windows is not immaterial. In Sorrento the Bristol offers the most interesting view of the coastal panorama.

SICILY (3-8 DAYS)

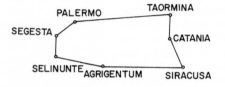

From Naples (or Rome) the flight to Catania or Palermo takes one or two hours, depending on the route. There are also overnight connections by boat from Naples to Palermo, and the train will take the traveler over the straits of Messina (cars are loaded on ferries), whence one can proceed either toward Taormina or Palermo, depending on his objective.

It is best to tour Sicily by bus, unless one prefers a train or private car. For scheduled trips one should consult the timetables of the Europabus, which offers several tours. One extending over five days (exclusive of the stay in Palermo) covers the following points: Segesta, Castelvetrano, Selinunte, Agrigento (first day); Syracuse (second day); Catania (third day); Taormina, Monte Etna, and return to Palermo (fourth and fifth days). At Taormina, a place of unique attraction, it is advisable to leave the tour and stay a few days. For the return trip to the mainland, the airport at Catania can be reached from Taormina by car or bus in less than two hours. The trip by train around the island is also very worth-while.

When taking a seven-day round trip by Europabus from Palermo, Messina, Tindari, and Cefalù with its famous cathedral will be added to the above itinerary.

PALERMO

To sense the particular charm of this remarkable city, I would recommend taking a horse-drawn cab from the center to the National Museum which is located at the waterfront slum section, and then continue to where the boulevards Via Roma and Corso Vittorio Emanuele cross. One should also take a walk along Via Roma (from Via Cavour) to Corso Vittorio Emanuele, and then up to the cathedral. Most of Palermo's great edifices are located a few blocks beyond the crossing of these boulevards and alongside the Corso.

A conducted city tour is not essential, as most points of interest are within walking distance. The abbey in Monreale just outside Palermo can be reached by taxi (or bus) in 20 minutes.

As in all large cities it is practical to organize sightseeing to avoid repeatedly covering the

304

same terrain. Hence, when we start with the National Museum and then proceed along Via Roma to Corso Vittorio Emanuele and up the Corso to the Piazza Quattro Conti di Città, we shall find, in addition to the Baroque palaces adjoining it, the church of San Giuseppe, the Martorana and Piazza e Fontana Pretoria nearby. Farther up the Corso are the Piazza Bologna and the cathedral, beyond them Palazzo Normanni, and further west, San Giovanni degli Eremiti. All are within less than two miles of one another. Only the Galleria Nazionale della Sicilia lies in the opposite direction and cannot be comfortably reached on foot (see map).

List of Sites

Museums: Galleria Nazionale della Sicilia (in the Palazzo Abbatellis, Via Alloro (paintings and sculpture), Museo Archeologico (Via Bara, sculpture).

Edifices and Churches: Quattro Conti di Città (group of Baroque palaces), San Giuseppe (church), San Cataldo Chapel, San Giovanni degli Eremiti (church), Duomo (cathedral), Palazzo Normanni with the Palatine Chapel, La Martorana (church), Monreale (abbey and cloister).

List of Sites in the Country

Around the island, starting from Palermo and proceeding west Segesta, Selinunte, Agrigento, Syracuse, Catania, Taormina, Messina, Cefalù.

GREECE (6 TO 14 DAYS)

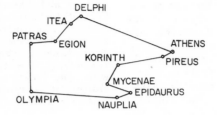

A flight of two hours brings us from Rome to Athens. If one has six days at his disposal, in addition to three days in Athens, he can visit the most important sites of antique remains—Delphi and Olympia. Two days more would add Mycenae, Epidaurus, and Nauplia. For the Aegean Islands, four more days will be needed. The sea voyage would touch on Delos, Mykonos, Santorini, Crete, and Rhodes.

Three days in Athens seems like a short time, but in this modern, faceless city our attention will be limited to antiquities and museums, of which there are three: The National Archeological Museum, the Byzantine Museum, and the one on top of the Acropolis. Of the Greek remains, the Acropolis is our first concern; other relics can be viewed in passing. Daphni is 20 minutes by taxi from the center of Athens. Here, fragments of 11th-century mosaics are preserved in a small Byzantine church which in itself is not of great interest. Those who are acquainted with the mosaics in Ravenna or Sicily will be less impressed with the modest remains in this church.

The experienced traveler who has learned to concentrate on essentials and avoid the fatigue of overconscientiousness, may omit from his program the site of the Agora, the Theater of Dionysus and the Olympieum (15 grand Corinthian columns). After the Acropolis and the National Museum everything else appears anticlimactic.

Greece is a country where, except for Athens, guided tours are indicated. The language barriers are such that one could hardly expect to receive advice or directions from a native; even in Athens, should one direct a taxi driver to go to the National Museum, he is likely to respond with a blank stare. Nor do the Greek names of most of the cities resemble the English equivalent. However, the roads are well marked, uncluttered by traffic, and in good condition.

There are two- and four-day overland tours from Athens. The two-day tours include Delphi and Olympia, the most important sites of Greek remains. The first (100 miles north from Athens) is also interesting with regard to landscape.

FROM DELPHI TO OLYMPIA

A short motor ride leads from Delphi to the Isthmus and the port of Itea. From here a ferryboat carries passengers and cars to the Peloponnesian shore in three hours' time. Since the afternoon ferry arrives too late for a visit to the site, it is more convenient to put up for the night in the city of Patras, a short distance from the Aegion (the landing point on the Peloponnesus), and double back to Olympia the next day. The return trip to Athens (a distance of 240 miles), much of it along the Isthmus, is quite scenic—except for the drab architecture. The crossing from the Peloponnesus to Attica is over the Isthmus of Corinth. When passing through that city of one-time splendor, luxury, and abundant life, one should remember: Nothing of that is left but the romantic name, the customary reassembled ruins, and a local museum. In fact nothing was left of ancient Corinth after Lucius Mummius, the Roman general, razed the city to the ground in 146 B.C. Present-day Corinth is prosaic in the extreme and without any esthetic significance.

Should the traveler wish to visit Mycenae, he will have to take a four-day trip that includes Daphni, Corinth, Mycenae, Epidaurus, Nauplia, Olympia, Patras, Aegion, Itea, and returns to Athens via Delphi. As for Greek art in its native surroundings— the purpose of our travel—a visit to sites other than Olympia and Delphi will be disappointing. But there is the Greek landscape and the nostalgia of the past, all of which may invite the traveler to undertake a sentimental journey. As I mentioned, travel by self-driven car is no hardship, however the road from Corinth to Athens is constantly clogged with heavy traffic.

THE ISLANDS

A tour of Greece would be incomplete without visiting the principal islands—and I am referring to those easiest to reach from Athens by fast and comfortable ships, sailing regularly every week. A four-day tour would include Delos, Mykonos, Santorini, Crete, and Rhodes, the most interesting of the Aegean islands, rich in antique remains and of great natural beauty.

List of Sites

Athens: Acropolis, Agora, Stoa of Attalus, Theseion, Theater of Dionysus, Horlogium, Olympieum. **The Museums:** National Archeological Museum (Patission and Tositsa Streets, sculptures), Acropolis Museum, Byzantine Museum (22 Queen Sofia Avenue, icons, architectural ornaments).

The Country

Daphni: Byzantine church.
Delphi: Museum.
Olympia: Museum, site of the Games.
Mycenae: The Lion Gate, fortress, Beehive tombs.
Epidaurus: Theater, museum.

(For travel in Scandinavia see Section IX.)